Federal Tax Reform:
Myths and Realities

FEDERAL TAX REFORM: MYTHS AND REALITIES

Michael J. Boskin, *Editor*
Robert J. Barro
George F. Break
Jerry R. Green
Laurence J. Kotlikoff
Mordecai Kurz
Peter Mieszkowski
John B. Shoven
Paul J. Taubman
John Whalley

Institute for Contemporary Studies
San Francisco, California

3-25-80

Copies of this book may be purchased from the Institute for $5.95. All inquiries, book orders, and catalog requests should be addressed to the Institute for Contemporary Studies, Suite 811, 260 California Street, San Francisco, California 94111—(415) 398–3010.

Library of Congress Catalog Number 78–61661

ISBN 0–917616–32–4

CONTENTS

vi

CONTRIBUTORS

ROBERT J. BARRO
John Munro Professor of Economics, University of Rochester

MICHAEL J. BOSKIN
Professor of Economics, Stanford University

GEORGE F. BREAK
Professor of Economics, University of California, Berkeley

JERRY R. GREEN
Professor of Economics, Harvard University

LAURENCE J. KOTLIKOFF
Post-doctoral Fellow, Department of Economics, UCLA

MORDECAI KURZ
Professor of Economics, Stanford University

PETER MIESZKOWSKI
Professor of Economics, University of Houston

JOHN B. SHOVEN
Associate Professor of Economics, Stanford University

PAUL J. TAUBMAN
Professor of Economics, University of Pennsylvania

JOHN WHALLEY
Professor of Economics, University of Western Ontario

PREFACE

Tax reform has become the dominant issue of public policy following President Carter's proposals in the spring of 1978 and the growing tax revolt, especially evident in the overwhelming passage of the Jarvis-Gann property tax limitation initiative in California.

Tax reform means different things to different people. Congress is inundated with proposals for reform—from the president's program, to the Steiger bill to reduce the capital gains tax, to the Roth-Kemp proposal for major reduction in individual income taxes. All of these proposals have important implications for individual equity, and particularly for their impact on the overall economy.

Few proposals for reform examine basic issues. Most accept the value of a tax system such as the present one, which attempts to tax income, including savings; but that basic commitment is the cause of many problems in both equity and efficiency. Economists are coming to question the wisdom of including savings in the tax base, particularly at a time of growing capital shortage and increasing concerns about economic growth. New ideas are emerging in the economics profession, but they are only just beginning to exert their rightful influence in policy discussions.

To encourage the circulation of these ideas, and of the research which has encouraged them, the Institute asked Stanford economist Michael J. Boskin to assemble a group of economists to examine the major issues raised by President Carter's tax proposals and to recommend alternatives. It will be obvious from the result that much thinking remains to be done in order to enact constructive tax reform.

This book on federal issues is part of a larger Institute program on tax issues and public finance, one element of which is the Institute's recently founded bimonthly journal on state and local government problems in these areas.

We trust this book will contribute to the national debate on tax reform.

H. Monroe Browne
President,
Institute for Contemporary Studies

San Francisco, California
September 1978

1

MICHAEL J. BOSKIN

Introduction: Taxation and the Role of Government in the Economy

Taxation and reasons for government economic activity: public goods. Third-party effects (externalities). Resource allocation and income distribution. Economic stability (unemployment, inflation). The disadvantages of government intervention— waste and inefficiency. The growth of government spending. Revenue devices. Taxation and its economic effects. Efficiency, equity—horizontal and vertical. Tax reform possibilities.

The large and growing role of government in economic activity is perhaps the most important feature of the advanced economies of North America, Western Europe, and Japan. We notice this in the large difference between our gross earnings and our net take-home pay; the sales taxes we pay when we purchase commodities; the social security benefits received by the elderly; the welfare payments received by mothers with dependent children; the expenditures on national defense; the large proportion of the labor force employed by government; and the partial support of schools, housing, hospitals, and a myriad other activities by federal, state, and local governments.

Taxes play a number of important roles in our economy. The financing of government expenditures is by far the most important. The attempt to redistribute income to encourage or discourage specific activities and to stabilize the overall economy are other, though more controversial, goals of taxation. In an economy where the government sought neither to provide certain goods and services nor to redistribute income nor to stabilize economic fluctuations, there would be little need for taxation. It is the pursuit of these goals by the government that creates the need for taxation. Since governments in all of the advanced economies actively pursue these goals, taxes amount to a substantial fraction of national income.

It was not always so. In the early part of this century, total government expenditures at the federal, state, and local levels amounted to well under 10 percent of all economic activity. Before turning to a more detailed discussion of the historical trends in public sector growth, it is worthwhile to examine in more detail the main reasons for government economic activity and hence, the rationale for taxation.

MAJOR REASONS FOR GOVERNMENT ECONOMIC ACTIVITY

In the advanced mixed capitalist economies of North America, Western Europe, and Japan, most decisions are left to firms and individuals, and it is presumed that such decisions are, in general, correct, and do not require government intervention. The vast majority of the population believes that it is undesirable for the government to attempt to run every factory and farm, to assign each person a location and job, or to tell each consumer how to spend his or her income. Ever since Adam Smith's historical *The Wealth of Nations,* economists have argued that competition leads individuals and firms, in the pursuit of their own private interests, as if by the famous "invisible hand," to the maximization of social welfare.

The conditions under which a predominantly free enterprise economy produces socially desirable results are somewhat restrictive, and are not always satisfied in the real world. For example, some goods and services cannot be produced by large numbers of private entrepreneurs. It may be the case, as with some utilities, that in order to achieve the minimum average cost of production a very large scale of activity is necessary; this creates what economists call a natural monopoly. In the United States, as in most other advanced economies, such natural monopolies are regulated— for example, by utilities commissions. In certain other cases, monopolies or near monopolies may develop in certain product or factor markets, and government may intervene to attempt to improve or increase the competitive nature of these markets. In the case of both natural monopolies and monopolies due to other reasons besides declining average costs of production, governments generally do not rely on taxes to alleviate the problem in resource allocation. They rely instead on regulation, or on laws which create penalties for noncompetitive behavior—in the United States, for example, the Sherman and Clayton acts.

Even in a mostly competitive economy, however, there are two basic resource allocation problems which may require government intervention. The first of these economists call external economies and diseconomies, or third-party effects. There are many cases where the behavior of an individual or a firm directly affects the opportunities available to other individuals or firms. There is very good reason to believe that the actions of individuals and firms are primarily motivated by the direct effects upon themselves. Thus, their decisions may sometimes benefit or harm others as a byproduct. An example of growing importance is environmental pollution. When each of us drives an automobile, we may be primarily concerned with getting to work or school; each of us adds only a small amount of pollutants to the atmosphere. Unfortunately, when a million people do this simultaneously in, say, Los Angeles, the result is dirty—even dangerous—air. Citizens with respiratory ailments are warned to stay indoors; schools shut down their physical education programs, etc. Clearly, the drivers of these automobiles have imposed a genuine cost, or external diseconomy, on the remaining population. Or consider the case of a river with an industrial plant upstream and a swimming and fishing resort downstream. As the industrial plant discharges its wastes into the river, fish die, the river is fouled, and the resort owners, swimmers, and fishermen are all harmed.

In some cases, private incentives will induce the parties involved in the external economy or diseconomy to make mergers or side payments to ameliorate the externality. However, when there are many individuals or firms involved, it is very costly and difficult to coordinate their activities in a socially desirable manner. When this is the case, governments increasingly have stepped in to help "internalize" the externality to the general social benefit. There are many methods for doing so. Rules, regulation, prohibition, fines, taxes, and subsidies are common attempts to remedy these problems.

Before proceeding any further, it is important to note that while private competitive markets may not insure a desirable allocation of resources in such circumstances, it is not certain that direct government intervention will automatically insure a better resource allocation, greater efficiency, and a lower level of the external diseconomy than would be the case with the competitive private market. There is a case for government intervention only where its benefits exceed its costs. It would be foolish, for example, for society to spend half its national income regulating and policing the reduction of air pollution. We should not forget that government interventions, whether by taxes, subsidies, rules, or regulations, are carried out by fallible individuals who have their own personal and bureaucratic incentives. We may sometimes merely substitute government failure for market failure.

The second major problem in resource allocation which private competitive markets cannot easily solve concerns goods whose provision to one person is possible only with simultaneous provision to many. As an example, while a television set can readily be sold to a single person, that is not the case for national defense or air pollution control. Such goods have the properties that the cost of adding an additional person to the group using them is essentially zero, and it is impossible to restrict access to their use. If we cleaned up the air in Los Angeles, *everyone* in Los Angeles would breathe cleaner air; if we provide defense for Jones, the same soldiers and aircraft will protect Smith simultaneously. Private entrepreneurs would find it very difficult to sell cleaner air, since it is impossible—or, at least, very costly—to restrict access to clean air. Economists call such commodities public or collective goods. They generally must be provided collectively, if at all, so once again government intervention in resource allocation may be necessary.

If it were possible to determine the value placed by each individual on the provision of public goods, each person could be taxed according to the benefits he or she received. Acting together, through voluntary exchange, each and every individual would be willing to pay his or her marginal valuation of the public good in taxes; a vote on such an assignment of taxes and provision of public goods would receive approximately unanimous support. Unfortunately, the inability to exclude some individuals from using the public goods creates the so-called free-rider problem: individuals, knowing they can add only an infinitesimally small quantity to the amount of the public good provided, will have an incentive to under-report their true valuation of such goods. Hence, especially at the national level, benefit taxation is extremely difficult to implement, and has largely been replaced with alternative concepts of ability to pay as the desirable basis of taxation.

But recall the proviso mentioned above, that the desirability of government intervention in such cases may be offset by improper action or bureaucratic waste, and we must certainly note that many goods provided or financed by governments are not purely public goods as just defined.

Since it is very costly to exclude potential users or consumers of the public service from its use, most public goods, or most goods provided by the government, have a price of zero; consumers are not charged directly for their use. Thus, the provision of public or collective goods must be financed by government revenue-raising, such as tax or debt finance. The direct purchase of goods and services to provide for such public goods—for example, the purchase of jet aircraft to provide for defense—must be financed by government revenues. It is important to note that collective goods are not necessarily *produced* by the government; their basic nature only requires that their provision be *financed* by the government. The government need not itself produce soldiers' uniforms, submarines, and other public goods; it may, instead, purchase such commodities from private firms, ultimately paying for them with tax revenues.

Another major reason for government economic activity concerns the distribution of economic well-being in society. The distribution of income which emerges from the free play of competitive market forces may leave a segment of society destitute, and make others extremely wealthy. While basically a matter of ethics, in recent years inequality has increasingly been a target of government intervention. The government has provided transfer payments to a growing percentage of persons and families at the lower end of the income distribution, and attempted via progressive taxes to reduce the command over resources accruing to the rich. Hence, one of the primary functions of government is to alter the distribution of income in society. Programs such as welfare and food stamps give direct aid to the poor. High rates of tax on corporate and individual income decrease the net wealth of the rich. These are examples of the direct attempt on the part of the government to redistribute income and economic well-being.

There are also many indirect effects on the distribution of income, intended or unintended, of government policies. Virtually every regulatory tax or expenditure decision on the part of the government has distributional implications.

The issue of income distribution is not exclusively ethical. Economics can make at least three important inputs in analyzing the problem. First, economic analysis can help reveal the ultimate effects of particular policies on the distribution of income and wealth. Second, economic analysis can help define which income distributions are even attainable through government intervention. Third, and extremely important, economic analysis can help identify the costs and benefits of altering the distribution of income. There are many government transfer payments to the poor, such as welfare, food stamps, and housing subsidies. These benefits clearly help the poor; however, they must be financed by taxing the nonpoor population, and these taxes may distort the incentives to work, save, and invest motivating that nonpoor population. If a program helps the poor somewhat this year, but dramatically reduces future incomes and living standards, these costs should be known and accounted for.

Different people may weigh benefits and costs differently, and some may even object on philosophical and ethical grounds to any government right to redistribute income. An extreme egalitarian might accept or even applaud a general decline in living standards so long as the poor were helped. On the other hand, a person concerned about the entire population might weight income gains to the poor more than those to the rich, but nonetheless restrict government redistribution because of adverse incentive effects. Indeed, in many countries, tax rates necessary to finance current government expenditures are quite high—often 50 percent, 70 percent, or even 90 percent. Thus, the debate rages between those favoring increased redistribution (which most recent government spending increases have encouraged) and those favoring a leveling off or reduction of tax rates to promote economic growth, which, in turn, will eventually help the poor.

Clearly, the redistributive implications of government policy generate the strongest disagreements about the appropriate role of government economic activity. As we shall see in the chapters that follow, the effect of taxes on the distribution of economic well-being is clearly an important consideration in the evaluation of tax reform proposals.

The final major reason for government economic activity is to attempt to increase economic stability and growth. Unemployment and inflation have plagued most advanced economies throughout the twentieth century. Active government intervention to promote stable growth is an historically recent role played by governments. So deeply entrenched was the notion that governments could not or should not do anything to ameliorate such problems that President Franklin D. Roosevelt raised taxes in 1933 in order to balance the budget! In the United States, since the full employment act of 1946, the federal government has assumed responsibility for helping steer the economy on a course of stable growth. In the economies of Western Europe, the governments traditionally play an even more active role in this regard. Thus, we have seen tax cuts and tax increases in order to deal with the problems of unemployment and inflation, respectively; the Federal Reserve has used monetary policy in order to attempt to curb inflation in recent years. But as with the case of providing goods and ameliorating external economies or diseconomies, it is not always possible for the government to dampen the booms and busts of the business cycle. For example, there are lags in recognizing the need for government intervention, there are administrative lags in implementing tax cuts or increases or spending cuts or increases, and there is waste and inefficiency. It is often necessary to trade off among different policy goals, such as redistributing income versus economic growth, and unintended outcomes may result whereby government's attempts to stabilize the economy actually destabilize it.

These, then, are the *potentially* legitimate economic roles of government. Following our now-familiar distinction, private markets generate an allocation of resources, a distribution of income, and a pattern of economic fluctuation and growth. Government economic activity is potentially desirable when it *may* improve performance in any of these spheres. It is, in fact, desirable only when it is *successful* in doing so. In considering justifications of government economic activity, it is important to remember that the gap between the potential and actual performance of the government is often very great.

HISTORICAL TRENDS IN PUBLIC SECTOR GROWTH

The enormous growth of government spending is one of the more remarkable features of the advanced economies of the world. Table 1 illustrates the growth of total government expenditure in current dollars, in constant 1958 dollars per person, and as a percentage of gross national product. Even a casual glance at this table reveals a startling growth rate. Just before the outbreak of World War I in 1913, the government was spending less than $100 per capita (in 1958 dollars), and this amounted to less than 8 percent of the GNP. Today, in 1958 dollars, the corresponding figures are almost $1,400 per person, and about 33 percent of GNP.

In fact, these figures actually understate the growth of government economic activity. For, in addition to these direct taxes, the government levies a large number of what might be called quasi taxes. When the government mandates certain

safety devices on automobile manufacturers, they are not recorded as the equivalent of taxes, but rather as an increase in
that component of GNP relating to automobile sales.
However—to pick one example—there is very little difference between the government's requiring installation of an air
bag costing $1,000 and its imposing a tax of $1,000 which is
then used to install the same air bag. Clearly, the growth of
such rules and regulations for both consumers and producers
has greatly increased these quasi taxes.

In any event, the total take of the public sector as a percentage of all economic activity has increased by a factor of 5
since the turn of the century. While it is instructive to
examine the growth of aggregate government expenditures at

Table 1

Growth of Government Expenditure
in the United States

	Expenditures		
	Total Government ($ billions)	Per capita (1958 dollars)	Percent of GNP
1890	0.8	45	6.5
1902	1.5	58	7.3
1913	3.2	89	7.8
1922	9.3	163	12.6
1929	10.3	143	10.0
1940	18.4	288	18.4
1950	61.0	484	21.3
1960	136.4	740	27.0
1970	311.9	1,138	31.8
1977	621.2	1,373	32.9

Source: 1890–1922: Musgrave and Musgrave 1973; 1929–1978: Economic
Report (1978).

all levels, adjusting for inflation and population growth, the aggregate data also hide a startling change in the composition of government spending by function, and dramatic changes in the level of government doing the spending.

For selected years from 1929 through 1977, Table 2 presents figures on total government spending, federal government spending, and federal government spending as a proportion of the total. As noted in the table, as late as 1929 only one dollar in four of government spending was done at the federal level. On the eve of World War II, the corresponding figure was one dollar in two, and today it exceeds two out of three dollars. While state and local government expenditures have grown very rapidly relative to GNP, as a proportion of total government spending they have declined substantially. The growth of state and local government spending, and of the tax systems and intergovernmental fiscal relations relating to state and local governments, are beyond our present concern. This book focuses on federal taxes and expenditures, and especially on issues relevant to federal tax reform.

Table 2

Changing Composition of Government Spending by Level of Government

	Total	Federal	Federal as Percent of Total
1929	10.3	2.6	25.2
1940	18.4	10.0	54.4
1950	61.0	40.8	66.9
1960	136.4	93.1	68.3
1970	311.9	204.2	65.5
1977	621.2	423.5	68.2

Source: Economic Report (1978).

In examining the composition of federal spending, it is instructive to note the relationship between government spending for goods and services (mostly public or quasi-public goods), and government spending on transfer payments. In 1952, transfer payments amounted to only $8.5 billion, compared to the almost $50 billion spent on direct purchases of goods and services. Since then transfers increased markedly as a proportion of total spending, and by the early 1970s, for the first time in U.S. history, the federal government was spending more on transfer payments than on direct purchases of goods and services.

In brief summary, then, total government expenditures have risen very rapidly over the last several decades. During that period, the total composition of government expenditures has shifted toward centralization at the federal level, and in recent times a dramatic rise has occurred in the proportion of total federal spending embodied in transfer payments as opposed to direct purchases of goods and services.

Table 3

Changing Composition of Federal Expenditures, Selected Years 1952–1978 ($ billions)[a]

	Purchases of Goods and Services	Transfer Payments to Persons	Transfers as % of Transfers plus Purchases
1952	47.2	8.5	15.3
1960	52.9	20.6	28.0
1965	64.6	28.4	30.5
1970	97.0	55.0	36.2
1975	117.9	131.1	52.7
1978[b]	158.4	180.7	53.3

Source: Economic Report (1978).

[a]Grants-in-aid to state and local governments, net interest payments, and subsidies, less current surplus of government enterprises excluded.

[b]Estimated.

As noted above, the major purposes for which the government raises tax revenue are to provide for public or quasi-public goods, and to support income-maintenance, or transfer, programs. The vehicles used to raise these revenues have changed markedly over time. Focusing just on federal revenues, we note that personal taxes—primarily, the individual income tax—have been the most important revenue devices throughout the post-World War II period. Corporate income taxes and indirect business taxes have also been important revenue devices. The most noticeable development, however, has been the enormous growth of social insurance taxes in the last two and a half decades. As recently as the 1950s and 1960s, social insurance taxes accounted for a very small percentage of total government revenue. Today they are the second largest, and by far the most rapidly growing, source of government revenue. Indeed, as noted by Kotlikoff (Chapter 6), social insurance taxes are scheduled to increase dramatically throughout the 1980s, and this scheduled increase has raised a roar of indignation from the general public.

In addition to raising revenues by taxes, governments have several other alternatives open to them. For example, they can sell some of the output of their enterprises to firms and individuals; e.g., electricity produced at a government electricity plant can be sold to factories. The government may also issue debt. Barro (Chapter 9) notes that issuing debt, as opposed to collecting taxes currently, is equivalent to postponing the taxes to some future date, and one can think of government debt issue as carrying with it a corresponding future tax liability.

ECONOMIC EFFECTS OF TAXES

Any tax has essentially two major avenues of economic effects. First, taxes, by transfering economic resources from private individuals and firms to government, reduce the after-tax or net income available to the private sector to spend or save. Correspondingly, they increase the revenues available to the government sector to spend or invest. Second, and in many cases more important, taxes change the relative prices of different commodities and different factors of production. For example, income taxes or payroll taxes drive a wedge between the gross wage rate paid to workers and the net, or take-home, pay of the worker. A worker earning $5.00 an hour, and working a normal work year of 2,000 hours, would have annual earnings of $10,000. If this person was in a 20 percent tax bracket, his after-tax wage rate per hour would not be $5.00, but $4.00. This reduction in the net wage rate itself has two effects on the work and labor supply decisions of individuals. First, it makes work in the market less remunerative. By so doing, it reduces the incentive to work, and this incentive may be reflected in a lower labor

Table 4

Changing Pattern of Federal Revenue Sources, Selected Years 1952–1978 ($ billions)

| | Taxes | | | |
	Personal[a]	Corporate Profits	Indirect Business	Social Insurance
1952	28.8	19.4	9.7	7.3
1960	42.5	22.3	13.2	16.7
1965	51.4	27.1	16.9	24.5
1970	93.6	33.0	19.2	49.2
1975	127.3	42.1	22.1	92.1
1978	185.5	63.1	28.5	133.7

Source: Economic Report (1978).

[a]Mostly income tax.

force participation rate, or in fewer hours of work and less work effort. Second, by reducing the after-tax income of the individual, it may make work more necessary, thereby creating an incentive to work more in order to recoup the original loss in income.

A large number of studies have been conducted to ascertain the effect of taxes on labor supply. It is beyond our scope here to evaluate each of these studies, but some are discussed in the chapters that follow. As a rough approximation, it appears that the labor supply of husbands between the ages of 25 and 55 is rather unresponsive to changes in the net wage rate, but that the labor supply of wives, elderly workers, and teenagers, often called secondary workers, is quite sensitive to such tax-induced net wage reductions. Therefore, high rates of income or payroll tax have the undesirable effect of driving potential workers out of the labor force and inducing them either to work at home or consume more leisure.

A second major effect of taxes concerns the consumption/ saving and investment choices. Under an income tax, saving is taxed twice; since income equals expenditures plus saving, saving is included in the base of the tax. When the saving subsequently earns a return—for example, in the form of interest—that return is taxed again. Suppose you put $1,000 into a savings account earning 6 percent per year; the gross return, ignoring taxes on your saving, is 6 percent. However, you pay taxes on this interest; if your marginal tax rate is approximately one-third, the 6 percent is reduced to 4 percent after taxes. Substantial evidence now exists that saving does respond quite substantially to changes in the after-tax rate of return on capital. Our heavy taxes on income from capital, such as the taxes on capital income embodied in the personal income tax and directly in the corporate income tax, substantially reduce the net rate of return to capital and hence private saving, the future size of the capital stock, future labor productivity, wages, and income. These issues will be discussed in more detail by Taubman (Chapter 5) and Mieszkowski (Chapter 2).

Taxes may also affect economic stability and growth. Many economists believe that in the midst of a very deep recession or depression a tax cut can stimulate economic activity, increase employment, and generate an increase in income. Correspondingly, some economists believe that tax increases in the face of a large inflation can help curtail that inflation. Recently, much doubt has been cast on these propositions. While it is not our purpose to review that literature here, in brief summary the argument goes that only unanticipated changes in fiscal or monetary policy will have much impact on the course of the real economy.

When taxes distort relative prices or relative factor returns, as noted above, they induce people to alter their economic activity—for example, to work less or to save less. These distortions cause an *extra* cost to be borne by society for raising taxes. Economists label this extra cost the deadweight loss of the tax. To demonstrate, when the government raises virtually $200 billion by income taxes, the true cost to society of raising that $200 billion may be much more than $200 billion, because in doing so, we have distorted the incentives of the population to work and to save. A variety of studies have attempted to measure the deadweight loss involved in different tax distortions. Most of these studies conclude that the deadweight loss is not trivial, amounting in some cases to many billions of dollars. Once again, the deadweight loss of taxes will be discussed in specific contexts in the chapters which follow. For our purposes, it is only important to note that when considering the costs of running the public sector, of providing government expenditures and transfer payments, these extra, or deadweight, losses must be added to the dollar amount raised by the government. Further, government expenditures are only desirable when, at the margin, the valuation of the government expenditures by households exceeds the total costs, at the margin, of providing the services—the total costs consisting of both the actual taxes raised and the deadweight losses incurred.

It is a fundamental tenet of economic analysis that, as more and more of a good is consumed, its extra, or incremental, value declines. The value of a small amount of food, for example, is enormous; it helps us avoid starvation. Eventually, as we consume increasing amounts of food, the value of this additional food starts to decline and may even become negative. In the case under consideration, it is reasonable to assume that as the ratio of public to private economic activity increases, the extra value of public goods declines relative to the extra value of private goods and services.

CRITERIA FOR EVALUATING TAXES

The analysis and facts presented above suggest several criteria upon which to judge the desirability of a tax system. The first goal of a tax system is to raise enough revenue to provide the desired amount of public goods and revenues for income redistribution. Public goods have the characteristic that adding an extra consumer to enjoy their use and benefits does not reduce the amount of the good available to other consumers. Hence, for public goods, we must add the marginal valuation of *all* consumers of the public good in order to obtain a measure of the marginal social benefit of the good. This must be compared to its marginal cost, inclusive of the deadweight loss involved in financing the public good.

To raise revenue efficiently, we want to minimize distortions of the major economic decisions, such as the consumption/saving choice, investment and risk-taking choices, labor supply and human capital investment choices, and the like. The only tax which has no distorting effect at all is a so-called lump sum tax, which is levied independently of the activity of any economic agent. Unfortunately, such taxes are impracticable and generally would be considered capricious. Therefore, since we must distort some choices, the task is to find the desirable combination of distortions that is "second best." For example, an income tax distorts both the work/leisure choice and the consumption/saving choice; excise taxes on different commodities distort the pattern of consumption across those commodities. Each of these distortions will be discussed in some detail in the chapters to follow. For our purpose, we merely note that the deadweight loss involved in raising a given tax revenue will be minimized if we place higher tax rates on goods which have the least elastic demands (i.e., for which demand is relatively independent of price), and factors of production—labor and capital—which have the least elastic supplies. That is, we wish to tax most heavily those goods and factors which will respond only slightly, if at all, to the imposition of taxes, and we want to avoid high tax rates on goods and services, or factors of production, whose demand or supply, respectively, are very responsive to taxation. Thus, the first criterion for determining a desirable tax system is that it be *efficient*.

In addition to the economists' notion of efficiency as minimizing the distortions created by the tax system, our tax system should also impose as small an administrative and compliance burden as possible. We do not desire a tax system which is extremely difficult to administer, extremely costly for taxpayers to comprehend and comply with. In short, we should avoid a system that requires a substantial use of resources in order to collect the revenue.

The next important criterion for determining a desirable tax system, again in combination with a desirable pattern of expenditures, is equity. Equity means different things to different people. Some argue quite forcefully for so-called horizontal equity, the equal treatment of equals—which in general has been interpreted to mean that persons with the same income or some other measure of command over resources should pay the same tax rate. In reality, of course, the items we observe to measure ability to pay, whether income, consumption, wealth, or the consumption of specific commodities, are *ex post* outcomes. They are not, that is, *ex ante* possibilities. If we have two people who are perfectly identical—suppose, for example, they are twins—and one undertakes a risky investment and the other undertakes a safe investment, *ex post* they are likely to have very different incomes, even though the difference is due to the fact that one was willing to take the risk of a very high payoff with a low probability, while the other twin was not willing to do so. As a rough approximation, horizontal equity commands much popular appeal, and it is the usual notion of equity employed by lawyers and politicians in discussing tax situations. We often hear of a comparison between Smith and Jones, who otherwise sound equal, but somehow Smith winds up paying much more in taxes than does Jones. Once again, this is sometimes due to voluntary choices made by Smith and Jones, who may have started from equal *ex ante* opportunities.

A second and much more controversial notion of equity is socalled vertical equity, the progressivity or regressivity of the tax system. Most persons find it reasonable and desirable to suggest that the rich should pay more in taxes than the poor. Some will also suggest that they should pay a higher proportion of their income or wealth or consumption in taxes than do the poor. But there is very little consensus on the desirable degree of progressivity. Our current tax system embodies in the personal income tax a nominally progressive tax system. However, as noted in Taubman's chapter, there are many exemptions, deductions, and exclusions which render the effective tax rates very different from the nominal ones. Further, the more progressive the tax system, the higher the marginal tax rate at the top becomes, and the greater are the disincentives to work, save, and invest. That is, progressivity, or increased vertical equity or equality, conflicts to a large extent with efficiency. In the last few years, there has been developed a substantial literature on trading off the twin goals of efficiency and vertical equity in the tax system. While in its pure form this question goes all the way back to the nineteenth-century English classical economists, such as

John Stuart Mill and Francis Edgeworth, in recent years the rigorous analysis of this problem has pointed out the substantial conflict between increased progressivity in the tax system and efficiency in the form of eliminating deadweight losses. This will be discussed again below, but let us take a simple example.

Suppose we made tax rates extremely high for the upper-middle and upper income classes. Further suppose that they substantially reduced their labor supplies, savings, and investments. It might then be the case that tax rates became so high that our tax revenues actually declined, leaving us less revenues to provide public goods and to redistribute via transfer programs to poor people. The lesson to be learned is quite simple. The efficiency problems of factor supply—whether labor supply, human investment, savings, or regular investment—may put a strong brake on the optimal degree of progressivity of the tax system. Further, the more progressive the tax system and the higher the tax rate, the more incentive there is to try and accrue income or wealth in nontax forms. This has been a major reason why the tax base in the United States has been continuously eroded. As discussed by Kurz (Chapter 7), and in the chapters by Taubman and Mieszkowski, there is much to be said for a simpler tax system which, perhaps, has a credit and a flat rate, or a few tax rates rather than many, with a broader tax base than currently exists.

Finally, we note the third criterion for determining a desirable tax system: its effects on economic stability and growth. Our progressive tax system has built into it a system of so-called automatic stabilizers. As income goes up, for example, people are pushed into ever higher tax brackets, which thereby act as a brake on the growth of income. Conversely, as income falls—as in a recession—disposable income, income after taxes, falls by less than total income, because taxes fall more than proportionately. Many fiscal experts feel that this is an extremely desirable feature of a tax system, especially when combined with the difficulty of implementing discretionary fiscal policy due to lags and imperfect formation.

However, a major problem exists, because our tax system is not indexed for inflation. While some would applaud the fact that taxes will rise more than proportionally when nominal incomes increase due to inflation, thereby perhaps slowing the demand pressure on inflation, there is an insidious side effect of this phenomenon: the extra revenue generated provides politicians with an easy short-run vehicle for financing their pet projects. Instead of having decisions about the size and desirability of the public sector and different public projects made on the basis of real benefits and costs, the inflation component of the tax revenue is a cushion to politicians for spending purposes. Only by continual tax rate reductions—which politicians parade as actual tax reductions when in reality they are only partial compensations for the automatic tax increases that result from inflation—can government spending be checked at all. The question of indexing the tax system and of automatic stabilizers are discussed in the chapters by Taubman and Shoven (Chapter 8).

With this discussion of the U.S. tax system and general analysis of criteria for determining government economic activity and a desirable tax system in mind, let us turn to a discussion of alternative concepts of tax reform.

THREE CONCEPTS OF TAX REFORM

Few issues stir as much controversy as does tax reform. Virtually everyone is for tax reform, but there are almost as many definitions of tax reform as there are supporters of it. Three major types of tax reform appear in popular discussion.

First, tax reform can mean a balanced reduction in taxes and government expenditures. This can mean reductions in the size of the public sector or, in a growing economy, a reduction in the growth rate of government expenditures and taxes—which would reduce the relative size of the public sector in the course of economic growth. This is the sense in which former President Ford discussed tax reform in the last election campaign. It would not be unreasonable to argue that a substantial impetus behind the recent tax revolt—as evidenced by the passage of Proposition 13 in California and the enormous outcy against the 1977 social security tax increases—comes from a feeling that government has gotten too large and too expensive. Indeed, many would argue that government—perhaps, especially, the federal government— is trying to do things now that it cannot do very well, and, in the course of doing so, a substantial fraction of the total resources spent is wasted. Many economists would also argue that leaving a larger share of total economic activity in the private sector would promote competition, efficiency, and stable economic growth.

A second definition of tax reform revolves around changing specific features of various taxes, such as dividend relief, or partial integration of corporate and personal income taxes, or changes in the investment tax credit. President Carter usually uses the term in this sense; i.e., he has stressed limitations on deductions for business lunches, reform of the tax treatment of U.S. investment overseas, and changing a variety of other structural features of current taxes.

Third, tax reform can mean changing the composition of a given tax revenue among different tax bases. Some social security programs could be shifted from payroll tax to general revenue finance, or we could begin to eliminate savings from the tax base—that is, switch from income to expenditure as the base of our personal tax system.

The major battlegrounds surrounding tax reform will likely consist of the following types of proposals: first are a variety of tax policies to stimulate badly needed capital formation in the United States. The best method for doing so would be to switch from our current income tax to a consumption or expenditure tax. Partial proposals include tax-free roll-over of reinvested capital gains, reduction of capital gains tax rates, and general tax rate reductions.

A second major battleground of tax reform likely to come to the fore in the years immediately ahead is the possibility of indexing the tax system for inflation. As noted in the chapter by Shoven, there is little justification for continuing a tax system based on nominal, as opposed to inflation-adjusted, values. A dollar in 1978 bears no more relation to a dollar spent in 1965 to purchase an asset than it does to foreign currencies, yet we are one of the few advanced economies which have not attempted at least partially to index their tax system for inflation. This not only results in a variety of inequities, but, as noted above, it offers the politician the gravy train of a greater than proportional increase in tax revenues to spend on favorite programs. In the extreme, if we did not have occasional tax cuts to partially offset this inflationary revenue gain, government economic activity would essentially drive out all private economic activity as the inflation continued.

A third major potential battleground of tax reformers concerns the appropriateness of a separate corporate income tax. President Carter originally proposed, but quickly withdrew, a partial integration of the corporate and personal income taxes. In the chapter by Break (Chapter 3), many of these proposals are discussed and analyzed. For our purposes, let us note that a separate corporate income tax makes very little sense. The income accruing to corporations ultimately accrues to shareholders, and should be so attributed. Currently, tax-exempt organizations, widows with very little income, and blue-collar workers whose pensions are invested in corporate securities, all pay very high corporate income tax rates on their share of corporate earnings. These rates would be much lower if the corporate tax were integrated with the personal income tax and their share of corporate income attributed back to them. Worse yet, the corporate income tax probably. causes a substantial distortion of economic activity between the corporate and noncorporate form of doing business.

Another major battleground is likely to be the tax treatment of our exports and imports. I do not mean only our tariff policies, although these themselves are important. In the last two decades we have several times witnessed proposals for a value added tax of the type used extensively in the Common Market countries of Western Europe. It was suggested in the 1950s as a substitute for the corporate income tax, and in the early 1970s as a substitute for property taxes. It is often the first new tax mentioned when extra sources of revenue are sought.

A final major battleground concerns welfare reform, and the possibility of the implementation of a negative income tax or some form of guaranteed annual income. Discussed in some detail in the chapter by Kurz, the negative income tax, while intuitively and initially very appealing, runs into some very basic difficulties, the most important of which is the impracticability of transferring a sufficient amount of money or resources to the very poor without also transferring a substantial amount of funds to the nonpoor.

Short of such major tax reforms as a negative income tax, inflation adjustments, substituting a value added tax for the corporate income tax, integration of the corporate and personal income taxes, substituting an expenditure tax for the personal income tax, and the like, there are a variety of partial reform proposals of the type mentioned above as structural changes in existing taxes. As discussed by Taubman, many features of the individual income tax might well be changed. These include the unit and time period of account, the level of exemptions and deductions, and the treatment of a variety of sources of income. Another example would be partial integration of the corporate and personal income taxes, such as the dividend relief originally proposed by President Carter. Included are several structural reforms in social security taxes, such as changes in the rates and base, and changes in the unit of account.

Our tax system has evolved historically through a series of compromises and reforms which have attempted, on the one hand, to achieve some level of efficiency and equity while raising a given revenue and, on the other, have reflected important political forces embodied in special interest groups. But the underlying economic forces which determine the desirability of specific features of our tax laws have changed markedly through time. Who would have predicted many years ago that we would have such a different demographic structure in the United States? It is simply no longer the case that most families have only one worker, a married male, a wife who works solely at home, and children who do not work. We have many more single people, whether never married, divorced, or widowed, than we have had at any time in our history. The age structure of our population is changing rapidly, due to the post–World War II baby boom and the subsequent baby bust of the 1970s. We have had an inflation for the last ten years which has driven prices up to an unprecedented level in the United States. We have an increasingly complex system of international trade which can be strongly affected by taxes, and, by analogy, we have an increasingly complex system of intergovernmental fiscal relations, tax liabilities, and responsibilities for expenditure programs at different levels of government.

Each of these changes in the economy, and many more, put innumerable pressures on our tax system to change in a direction that increases its equity and efficiency. It would be surprising indeed if these pressures did not manifest themselves in substantial tax reform in the years ahead.

2

PETER MIESZKOWSKI

The Choice of Tax Base: Consumption versus Income Taxation

Consumption as a measure of wealth. Dealing with gifts and inheritances. The deadweight loss of taxation. The tax on interest, and savings elasticity. Administration of the consumption tax. v. that of the income tax. Inflation and inequities. Rate differentials and structural problems. Transition, exemptions, corporate taxes, and international considerations.

INTRODUCTION

Income is traditionally viewed as the best or most appropriate measure of a household's ability or capacity to pay taxes. If measured in a comprehensive manner, income is a flow ap-

proximation to a person's wealth and can be used to approximate vertical equity (unequal treatment of equals) and horizontal equity (equal treatment of equally situated taxpayers).
Also, a broadly based income tax is capable of being differ-
entiated according to differing circumstances of a taxpaying
unit.

Consumption or expenditure is the only serious alternative
to the measurement of the means of capacity to pay tax under
a direct, progressive, tax system imposed at the household
level. As is well known, a number of distinguished
economists, from John Stuart Mill through Alfred Marshall
and Irving Fisher, believed that the taxation of income from
saving is inequitable. Nicholas Kaldor (1955) wrote a classic
book advocating the adoption of the expenditure tax, and
more recently the work of Andrews (1974) has rekindled
interest in a consumption-based system among academic
economists and lawyers.

Significantly, two major public reports, the U.S. Treasury's *Blueprints for Basic Tax Reform* (1977) and the Institute for Fiscal Studies' *The Structure and Reform of Direct
Taxation* (Meade Report 1978), have concluded, in essence,
that a consumption-based direct system of taxation is feasible
and desirable, not only with reference to the existing tax systems in the U.S. and Britain, but also more desirable than the
introduction of a comprehensive income tax.

In this chapter I shall review the arguments that favor a
consumption-based system relative to an income tax, and discuss how a progressive expenditure tax might be implemented. My principle conclusions are quite consistent with
other recent works which advocate the consumption tax on
the basis of equity and efficiency considerations. In particular, the efficiency (welfare) gains of adopting such a system
may be on the order of $40 to $50 billion a year. Also, contrary to earlier discussions, I conclude that an expenditure tax
is *not* more difficult to administer than an income tax and
may, in fact, be much simpler and more feasible to implement than a comprehensive income tax that makes provisions

for inflation indexing and is integrated with a corporate profits tax.

CONSUMPTION V. INCOME AS A TAX BASE: EQUITY, EFFICIENCY, AND ADMINISTRATIVE CONSIDERATIONS

There are a number of equity arguments in favor of using consumption as the basis of taxation. Thomas Hobbes, the philosopher, argued that the people should be taxed on the basis of what they take out of the common pool (consumption) rather than what they put in (savings, capital accumulation). Although this argument is not very precise, it conveys the view that thrift should be rewarded, and that all society benefits from a larger capital stock. Mill, Fisher, and others have argued against income taxation, on the equity ground that such a tax represents double taxation of savings. Some of the arguments presented degenerate into semantics, such as whether savings should be counted as income. The essence of the double-taxation argument is: if a person's primary endowment consists of wage income and this is taxed under an income tax, a tax on profit income generated on savings from after-tax wage income would represent a double tax. Whatever the merits of this argument, it does not carry much weight in current discussions as an equity consideration.

Kaldor's (1955) principal argument in favor of consumption taxation is that this tax base is a more accurate measure, proxy, or reflection of a household spending power or permanent wealth. For example, according to Kaldor, a person with $10,000 of wage income is not equally situated with a person with $10,000 of income from a bond. Also, persons with the same amounts of wealth will have different income, depending on their attitudes towards risk-taking and varying yields on different types of assets. Many types of income — inheritances, royalties, capital gains — are sporadic, uncertain, and maybe real or nominal due to inflation. In short, according to the Kaldorian argument, income measured as a flow is a highly imperfect measure of a person's permanent spending power or ability to pay taxes.

Consumption, on the other hand, will be closely related to the permanent, real wealth position of an individual. Capital gains, to the extent they are spent on consumption, are certainly not fictitious. Similarly, according to Kaldor, what better way of assessing the spending power inherent in disposable wealth than by measuring this power as exercised in personal consumption.

The argument that consumption is related to a person's basic endowment can also be made with reference to a simplified life-cycle model of savings and consumption. Suppose that a person enters the labor force at age 21 with a certain endowment of skills and training. For simplicity, assume that the person earns a constant wage throughout his life, and that he can invest and borrow at a constant rate of interest. In this situation, it is meaningful to define a person's endowment, or basic wealth, as the present value or discounted stream of future wage payments. If the person receives neither gifts nor inheritances throughout his life and does not plan to leave bequests, then the present value of the person's consumption must be equal to the present value of the person's wage, income, or endowment. In this simple situation, a consumption tax is equivalent, in present value terms, to a wage or endowment tax.

From a life-cycle perspective, it seems more equitable to tax consumption rather than income. For, if income is taxed, persons with the same endowments, as defined above, will pay different tax liabilities over their lifetimes. The person with a high rate of time preference will save relatively little, and will pay little or no tax on interest income. On the other hand, the person who defers present consumption, and saves for the possibility of larger amounts of future consumption, will pay more tax on interest income. In short, two persons with the same basic command over resources (wage income) will pay different taxes, depending on the intertemporal disposal or utilization of their endowments. This fact represents an equity argument in favor of consumption-based taxation.

The introduction of gifts and inheritances does not change the argument if these additions to endowment are consumed. But inheritances imply bequests, and this violates the assumption that all income is consumed over a person's lifetime. To exempt bequests from taxation would violate the principle that individuals with the same endowment should pay the same tax over their lifetimes.

One way of dealing with bequests would be to treat any estate as simply another form of consumption, and to tax bequests under an expenditure tax at the time of death. Alternatively, bequests could be taxed under an inheritance tax. I wish to emphasize that the taxation of bequests as consumption of the deceased, especially for bequests that are unplanned, do not constitute wealth taxes, but merely fulfill the requirement that a particular household be taxed on the basis of lifetime endowment. Note also that a tax on bequests goes a long way in meeting the objection that some very wealthy individuals with considerable spending power will not pay much tax because they save a great deal. The example of the miser, or an individual with a very high average propensity to spend, is often presented to discredit the expenditure tax as being inequitable. Yet, on a life-cycle basis, the miser who consumes virtually nothing, and the individual who consumes all of his wage income as soon as it is received, pay the same tax calculated on a present value basis, *as long as the miser's estate is taxed* as consumption at the time of death. The miser accumulates wealth at a very rapid rate and will pay a large tax at the time of death.

The additional tax on accumulated wealth just offsets the tax of deferring payment of the tax. In fact, in the extreme situation where the miser saves all of his income, a proportional income tax is equivalent to a proportional consumption tax that is also imposed on the miser's estate.

A life-cycle model with no—or highly uncertain—random bequest motive probably characterizes the overwhelming majority of taxpaying units. But such a model is not representative of some very wealthy households where large amounts of wealth are passed on from generation to generation; where the income from the wealth is used to finance the consumption and net saving of the present generation, and is then passed on to the next generation for preservation. This type of situation, which we can label the family with an indefinite life, is quite different from the life-cycle model, where the family is redefined for tax purposes every generation.

Even if families with very large amounts of inherited wealth were empirically important and owned a large portion of the nation's capital stock, an expenditure tax might be more equitable than an income tax. In a situation where a very large part of a person's endowment is capital that is either inherited or accumulated as a result of brilliant or lucky investment, a wealth tax appears as the most equitable form of taxation. However, if wealth cannot be taxed directly, then Kaldor's (1955) arguments, that consumption is a better approximation of spending power than is income, apply. If a family fortune is depleted through consumption by a particular generation, higher taxes would result under an expenditure tax than under an income tax. Alternatively, if a fortune is passed on to each generation intact and the income is used for consumption, the income from capital represents the family's income; the arguments developed earlier, when wages were the only source of a family's endowment, apply.

The main argument against the expenditure tax made by the advocates of the income tax is that wealthy households with low propensities to consume, or persons who have accumulated large amounts of wealth, will pay relatively small tax under an expenditure tax than under a comprehensive income tax. This, to many, seems inequitable, especially as large amounts of wealth carry security and economic power in addition to consumption spending power. There is a conflict of views on the relative merits of an expenditure and an income tax when households are consuming from accumulated wealth or are accumulating wealth rapidly. However, if it were concluded that the income tax is the more appropriate basis of taxation for wealthy households, it does not follow that an income tax should be the basis of taxation for the population as a whole.

An income tax, or tax on profit income, is an imperfect policy instrument if one of the objectives of tax policy is to insure that wealthy capitalists pay their fair share of taxes. A more appropriate, more selective policy is a wealth tax that would apply only to top wealth holders under general wealth exemption. Alternatively, a tax on profit income could be used, providing that substantial exemptions are applied. Similarly, if the objective of policy is to moderate the concentration of economic power through intergenerational transfers of wealth, inheritance taxes would be the appropriate policy instrument.

It is not clear, at least to this writer, whether on balance a simple expenditure taxation, with provision taxation of intergenerational wealth transfers either as consumption at death or as inheritance, is not a more equitable tax than a comprehensive income tax. In addition, it is more equitable to tailor the tax structure to account for different types of wealth holders. As the life-cycle model of savings applies to the overwhelming majority of savers, an expenditure-based levy should be the key element in an equitable tax system.

The argument that most, if not all, taxpaying units should be exempt from taxes on profit or interest income is greatly strengthened by efficiency considerations. All taxes distort economic choice and impose a burden on taxpayers that is larger than the resources that are released by taxes for public use. The excess burden, or deadweight loss of taxation, results from the violation of the basic principle of economic efficiency that the marginal evaluation placed by consumers on a commodity should be equal to the marginal cost of producing the commodity. In the context of intertemporal consumption choice, where savings are used to reallocate wage income over a person's life, the "commodities" are consumption at different points in time. The price of a unit of consumption at time t_1 (tomorrow) in terms of unit of consumption (today) depends on the interest rate or marginal productivity of capital. If the interest rate, i, is 10 percent, I must give up $1/(1 + i)$ units of consumption to obtain an additional unit of consumption in the next period. In the absence of taxes, welfare maximizing households will make their savings and consumption decisions so that the relative value of a unit of consumption at different time periods will be equal to the relative prices of consumption at different points in time.

If a tax on interest is imposed, the consumer will use the after-tax return on capital in determining savings decisions; i.e., for a two-period situation, when the before-tax interest rate is 10 percent and the tax on interest is 50 percent, a consumer will allocate his endowment so that, at the margin, a dollar of consumption today will be equivalent to (worth) $1.05 of consumption in the next period. But such an equilibrium is distorted, as in production a dollar of deferred consumption (savings) is worth $1.10, not $1.05, the value placed on future consumption by the consumer.

In contrast to an income tax, a consumption-based system is neutral with respect to intertemporal consumption choice. The price of future consumption is not changed by an expenditure tax.

The magnitude of the distortion or deadweight loss depends on the elasticity of demand for the commodity that is subject to tax. An income tax on interest income increases the price of future consumption in terms of present consumption, and decreases the demand for future consumption. If the demand for future consumption is highly inelastic (elastic), then the cost of the tax distortion will be small (large). Traditionally, the elasticity of demand for future consumption has been presumed to be small, because past studies of savings concluded that savings (expenditures of present consumption on future consumption) are interest-rate inelastic. Recently, Martin Feldstein (1978) has shown that this conclusion on the interest rate inelasticity is fallacious. His basic point can be illustrated by analogy to the demand for a commodity such as apples. When the demand for apples is moderately elastic with respect to price changes, it does follow that total expenditures on apples will increase if the price of apples falls, since expenditure is a multiple of price times quantity. So if the price elasticity of demand for apples is less than one, total expenditure on apples will fall. By analogy, when total savings fall as the result of an increase in the interest rate, this does not mean that the demand for future consumption is insensitive to the rate of interest. Savings are equivalent to total expenditures on a commodity. They are a multiple of a quantity (future consumption) times a price—the price of future consumption in terms of present consumption. The basic conclusion of Feldstein's reinterpretation of effects of taxes on interest income is that the distortionary cost of this tax may be quite substantial, even though the elasticity of savings with respect to the rate of interest is positive and small, or even negative. Of course, if savings are positively related to the rate of interest, and this elasticity is large, the excess burden associated with an interest income tax will be larger than when savings are not related to the interest rate.

Recent work by Michael Boskin (1978) indicated that the savings elasticity with respect to the rate of interest is about +0.4. This estimate allows Boskin to estimate the true economic burden (inclusive of the excess burden of the tax) of taxes collected on profit income to be $1.30 per dollar, an excess burden of 30 percent. For the level of income and corporate taxes collected in 1976, the absolute excess burden may be as high as $60 billion a year. As put by Boskin (1978:20), "If viewed another way, if we abolished taxes on income from capital this year, by the end of the decade, welfare would have increased by close to $200 billion, or twice the current annual yield of the individual income tax."

This estimate is very substantial, but it reflects the large distortionary effect introduced by the corporate profits tax.

Consequently, all of the $60 billion of excess burden cannot be attributed to the personal income tax. A theoretical estimate of the welfare loss associated with the substitution of a proportional expenditure tax of 33 percent for a proportional income tax of 25 percent is derived by Robert Hall (1968). He finds in a growth model that the tax substitution increases steady consumption by about 10 percent of tax collections, which is one-third of the 30 percent Boskin estimate. This is probably a lower bound of the excess burden associated with the taxation of profit income, as the mean or typical tax on profit income would be higher than the 25 percent assumed by Hall. So if an intermediate value of 15 percent of tax collections is used, the excess burden associated with the individual income tax relative to an expenditure tax system would be $30 billion. Although this is one-half of the Boskin estimate for the *combined* effects of the individual income tax and the corporate tax, it remains a very large number and represents a very strong argument in favor of the adoption of an expenditure tax.

A traditional argument against the expenditure tax, as found in the writings of Musgrave and Musgrave (1973) and Joseph Pechman (1971), is that such a tax would be very difficult to administer. This view is widespread, because there has been virtually no practical experience with a consumption-based system, and the administrative details of such a system have not been explored until quite recently. I shall argue in the section on implementations that there are no serious administrative problems to the introduction of an expenditure tax.

In fact, it probably is much easier to administer an expenditure tax than a fully comprehensive income tax. As is well known, most of the administrative and the statutory complications of the existing system are related to the taxation of capital income. The two main difficulties which are peculiar to the income tax are the estimation of true economic depreciation and the taxation of capital gains. These two problems are greatly compounded by inflation, such as the inflationary period of the last ten years or so. For equity and efficiency reasons, all taxes should be levied on a *real* rather than a nominal basis. This implies that depreciation allowances, all capital gains and losses, should be properly indexed to account for inflation. Otherwise, serious inequities will arise. For example, take a simple case where a person buys an asset for $100 and the price level doubles over a certain time interval, so that the asset is worth $200 in nominal terms. The investor's command over real resources hasn't changed, but without indexation, a positive capital gains tax will be imposed. Also, inflation introduced very significant redistributions of wealth between creditors and debtors which are only partially moderated by changes in interest rates. Under an ideal income tax, all debts as well as assets would be indexed. In principle, this indexation is feasible, as demonstrated by recent work (Aaron 1976; U.S. Treasury 1977).

But indexation would significantly complicate the administration of the income tax and the accounting rules associated with such a system. In fact, one of the main arguments in favor of an expenditure tax under the persistence of inflation is the unlikely prospect that wide-scale indexation will be introduced under the income tax and, without indexation, the taxation of profit income and real capital gains is highly imperfect, if not arbitrary.

Under an expenditure tax where profits are not taxed, depreciation rules and other provisions related to capital account would disappear. Although inflation requires rate structure indexation under an expenditure tax, *as under an income tax,* problems of defining consumption in an inflationary situation are less severe than under an income tax. If all consumption was on consumer perishables, the real burden of a proportional expenditure tax would be independent of the rate of inflation. If consumption is initially $10,000, and wages and prices doubled, consumption will also double to $20,000 and, except for rate progressivity, the real burden of a consumption tax would remain unchanged as a result of inflation.

ISSUES AND PROBLEMS WHICH ARE
COMMON TO THE INCOME TAX
AND THE EXPENDITURE TAX

In the previous section, a number of arguments were developed in favor of a consumption-based system. But in analyzing the relative strengths and weaknesses of consumption- and income-based systems, it is important to identify the issues and problems that are common to both tax systems so as to isolate the main differences between them.

One common feature is that both tax systems distort the choice between work and leisure. It is theoretically possible that, even though an income tax distorts both work choice and savings decisions, it is superior to a consumption-based system from an efficiency standpoint if the savings distortion somehow offsets or moderates the work-effort distortion. But, at present, there is no theoretical or empirical support for this possibility, so it seems appropriate to adopt an agnostic position on relative merits of income versus consumption with respect to work-effort effects.

A problem in making such a comparison is that tax rates will be different, as income is a more comprehensive tax base. The U.S. Treasury (1977) presents tables where gross consumption is estimated to be about 90 percent of comprehensive income, except for the highest income classes who consume just over 80 percent of comprehensive income. So if income tax rates are some 10 to 20 percent lower than consumption rates, the distortionary effects at the margin on work-effort will be smaller for an income tax.

As comprehensive income is a broader tax base than comprehensive consumption, average tax rates at each income bracket will be higher for a consumption tax. This fact bears on a number of issues such as whether the incentive to produce in the household (participate) in nonmarket activities will be greater under an expenditure tax, as will be problems of underreporting (fraud), the incentive to receive income in kind, and so forth. It is convenient to initially deal with these issues under the special assumption that all income is consumed. With this assumption, a 50 percent tax on income is equivalent to a 100 percent tax on consumption. A 33 percent income tax is equivalent to a 50 percent consumption tax, and so on. The general relationship between tax rates for an all-consumption economy is

$$(1 - t_y) = 1/(1 + t_c)$$

where t_y and t_c are income and consumption tax rates, respectively. When tax rates are equivalent in this special sense, i.e., they yield the same revenues, the income tax and the expenditure tax are, not surprisingly, fully equivalent. The incentive to produce various items in the home (the nontaxation of household production) will be the same for both tax systems. The incentive to evade taxes will also be the same. If I win $1,000 in a lottery and report it under a 50 percent income tax, I gain $500 of consumption. If the receipts are not reported under an expenditure tax of 100 percent, the gain in consumption is the same. The same sort of equivalence applies to income in kind. A company car that is provided to the employee at a cost of $2,000 is equivalent to $4,000 of income ($t_y = .50$), and under a consumption tax of 100 percent, $4,000 will buy $2,000 worth of consumption.

These equivalences depend on the assumption of no savings and identical tax revenues. Once savings are introduced, the expenditure tax rate must increase on an average to rates above the equivalent levels. For example, if a person earns $10,000 and initially pays a tax rate of 50 percent, and then saves one-half of disposable income, then the rate of consumption tax necessary to raise $50 is 200 percent, not the equivalent rate of 100 percent, and so the various incentives to avoid payment of taxes will be greater under a consumption tax when compared with a fully comprehensive income tax. In practice, the magnitude of the difference will be small, as gross consumption by the Treasury appears to be 90 percent of comprehensive income. In making rate comparisons, it is important to bear in mind that equivalent tax rates, as defined above, will always be higher under an expenditure tax. The U.S. Treasury (1977) compares a comprehensive income tax with a top bracket rate of 38 percent, and an expenditure tax with a top rate of 40 percent. This 40 percent rate is equivalent to an income tax rate of 29 percent when the income gained through marginal adjustments is fully consumed.

Apart from rate differentials that arise primarily from differences in tax base comprehensiveness, the imputation problems related to leisure (in addition to home production) are the same under income and consumption taxation. So are various possible imputation problems for goods and services provided by the public sector.

The structural problems related to personal exemption, joint filing, and related questions of the taxation of the family are qualitatively the same under both types of broadly based tax systems. The arguments in favor of and against preferential tax treatment for secondary workers on work incentive grounds are the same, and the methods of implementing preferential treatment, such as exempting some fraction of the secondary worker's income (receipts) from taxation, are the same on both systems.

The justification of—and issues related to—the limitation of deductions, such as charitable donations and state and local taxes, are also very similar under income and consumption taxation. Under the income tax there is no convenient justification for the deduction of mortgage interest, since no imputation is made for the implicit rent earned on owner-occupied homes. The treatment of owner-occupied homes under the expenditure tax is analyzed in the next section. It turns out to be simpler to administer the taxation of housing consumption under a comprehensive consumption taxation than to tax the implicit net income earned on owner-occupied housing. But housing is a merit good and, under a consumption tax, there would be strong pressure to give preferential treatment to housing, expenditures on education, and health care. It is possible that an expenditure tax system will quickly become less than fully comprehensive or neutral.

I conclude, in this section on similarities between income- and consumption-based systems, that the choice should not depend on secondary issues such as the structural details of broadly based tax systems and deductions, exemptions, and matters of fraud, and related problems of income in kind. The income and consumption systems are sufficiently similar in these details that they can be ignored, and proper attention can be placed on the fundamental matters of efficiency and equity.

IMPLEMENTATION AND ADMINISTRATIVE ASPECTS OF AN EXPENDITURE TAX SYSTEM[1]

It was first recognized by Irving Fisher that the flow of annual consumption and savings can be calculated by means of current cash flow information without a complicated tallying of every consumption expenditure. The general nature of this calculation consists of two basic steps. The first is to calculate all cash receipts over the tax period (year). In these receipts, the taxpayer would report wages and salaries, interest and dividends, net receipts of personal business enterprises, proceeds from the sale of all assets (except consumer durables), stocks, bonds, real capital, land, and all retirement income, social security, company pension, and so forth.

In order to calculate or to arrive at consumption, the taxpayer will be allowed to deduct purchases of all income-earning assets; real capital, stocks, bonds, savings accounts (net change in value), checking accounts, cash (other than petty cash), land, and inventories; all costs of acquiring income, whether wage or capital; various deductions currently allowed under the income tax, such as charitable deductions, and so forth.

In essence, the consumption or expenditure case would be arrived at by adding together all receipts, and deducting from this figure the current (annual) purchases of all income-producing assets where all items are calculated on the basis of current cash flow information. No information on balance sheets (stocks) is required.

While the basic Fisher cash flow approach to calculating current consumption is reasonably straightforward, there are several conceptual issues associated with the tax treatment of consumer durables and the purchase of assets, financial and otherwise. One main issue is that there are two alternative ways, *more or less equivalent,* of treating saving and dissaving under a cash flow tax.

One approach would be to allow a deduction for savings, and include all receipts from the savings in the calculation of expenditures in subsequent years. The second possibility would be to tax savings as they are made (not allow a deduction for savings), and then to exempt future consumption made possible by receipts produced from the savings.

For expositional convenience, we shall begin with a restrictive special case. Consider a situation in which the tax system consists of a single proportional tax rate, where there is one asset, and where all individuals can borrow and lend at the same rate of interest.

Then, in order to exempt savings from taxation, the ordinary or standard way of dealing with savings would be to allow a taxpayer a deduction for purchases of capital assets. So, if a taxpayer's receipts are $10,000 and he buys $1,000 of capital assets, his tax (consumption) base will be $9,000.

On the other hand, if the taxpayer sells the capital asset, he must report the receipts from the transaction as current receipts. In the more general case where there are several assets, sales and purchases of different assets would tend to cancel out, yielding the level of net saving or dissaving.

The alternative way of dealing with savings is to allow the taxpayer to prepay tax on savings that will ultimately be consumed, not by allowing a deduction when an income-earning asset is purchased, but by exempting consumption financed by receipts from this account (asset) when it occurs. This tax treatment we shall refer to as the *equivalent approach,* in contrast with the *standard or ordinary approach.*

It is a straightforward matter to see that for a proportional tax schedule the present value of taxes under both schemes are the same. Consider $1.00 of savings under the standard approach. No tax is paid when the asset is purchased and interest accumulates at a rate of r percent a year. When the accumulated wealth is sold t years hence and the proceeds are consumed, a tax equal to

$$1(1+r)^t(t_e)$$

is levied on the 1 .te, which is exactly equal to the tax that would have been paid if the asset had not been deductible from current receipts. So, without rate progressivity, the taxpayer would be indifferent between paying tax on the purchase of an asset, or paying tax on the sale of the asset plus accumulated interest (consumption) in the future. Another way of seeing through this equivalence is to note that if the tax is paid at the time of purchase, the government can invest the tax proceeds at the same rate, r, and end up with the same amount of real resources it collects on the larger tax base in the future when the assets are sold for consumption.

The same general equivalence applies in the case of loans. Under the standard or ordinary approach, loan proceeds would be included in current receipts and the repayments of interest and principal would be deductible. On the alternative or equivalent approach, the taxpayer would not include the proceeds of the loan in receipts, but would not be allowed to deduct interest and principal repayments. When the loan was made for investment purposes, there would be no tax consequences associated with the equivalent approach.

The equivalence between the two alternative ways of treating loans is of special interest for the treatment of consumer-durable loans. Before discussing the equivalence in this context, we consider two equivalent ways of dealing with consumer durables.

One way of taxing durables is to impute annual rental value to the asset. The alternative is to tax the asset when it is purchased. For example, when a person buys a durable costing $500, a tax of 50 percent would increase the cost to $750. The two approaches are equivalent, as the capital values of the services the purchaser expects to gain from the assets is equal to their cost. The nominal tax collected is larger for the rental approach, but since the payment is postponed by spreading out tax liabilities over the life of the asset, the tax liabilities in terms of present value will be the same under both the rent imputation method and the approach where the tax is levied on the purchase price of the consumer durable.

While the two approaches to the taxation of consumer durables are equivalent in present value of tax receipts, strong practical considerations point to using the full inclusion of durables in the tax base at the time of purchase. This strategy avoids the necessity of determining the rental value of consumer durables and measuring depreciation. Also, taxpayers would not have to keep complicated records.

When loans are made for consumption purposes, they can be treated either by the standard approach, where the proceeds are included in current receipts and the interest and repayments of principal are deducted, or by the equivalent treatment, where loan proceeds are exempted from receipts and deductions are not allowed for interest and repayment of principal. Although the two approaches are equivalent for a proportional rate structure, there are practical reasons for adopting one approach to loans, the equivalent or alternative way. First, record-keeping and other problems of taxpayer's compliance would be simplified, with only one tax treatment for loans. When loans are made to finance consumer-durable purchases, the taxation of amortization and interest will approximate the value of services derived from the durable.

Another advantage of the exemption of loan proceeds, and the taxation of interest and repayments of principal, relates to a consideration we have abstracted from up to this point: namely, progressivity of the rate structure and its implications for averaging. For example, if a household purchases a $50,000 house, its tax liability would go up very substantially because of the magnitude of the purchase and because of rate progressivity. If the household borrows to pay for the house and the proceeds are not taxed, the household would not face a current liquidity problem of having to pay a very substantial tax, and as it would be taxed on the mortgage payments, an automatic averaging or smoothing of its tax liability would occur.

Under the expenditure tax, the services of owner-occupied housing can be taxed according to the approach outlined above. One of the stumbling points of taxing the net income of these services under a comprehensive income tax is that this income would have to be approximated by imputation. No imputation is required under the expenditure tax, though an averaging provision would have to be made for persons who buy homes largely with equity and who would not have the automatic advantage of averaging available to households whose houses are mortgaged. One averaging device is to set up a fictitious mortgage account that would allow the homes purchased with equity to be taxed as if they had been mortgaged.

We noted in the previous section that problems of inflation are much less significant under an expenditure tax than under a comprehensive income tax. Equity issues related to inflation come up in relation to housing and other durables. For example, when inflation is unanticipated, and a family buys a home for $50,000 in 1975 and another family buys the same house in 1978 for $75,000, the second family will pay 50 percent more consumption tax, though both families are consuming the same level of housing services. Of course, under the current income tax, the capital gains on an owner-occupied house, when reinvested in housing, are not taxed, even when they are realized.

Equity considerations dictate that the cost basis of a house be changed during inflationary situations, just as it should be under a fully comprehensive income tax when rent is imputed. But this change would destroy the administrative simplicity of the tax treatment of housing under an expenditure tax, and such a practice would run into serious political opposition. As housing is a very important item of consumption, the advantage of the expenditure tax with respect to inflation should not be overstated, and if inflation adjustments were made on housing for equity consideration, the administrative complexity would be similar to those that would exist under a comprehensive income tax.[2]

We recommended, on the grounds of administrative and compliance simplicity, that households be limited to the equivalent type loans for tax purposes. Business would treat loans according to the standard approach. Of course, persons who own their own businesses could manipulate accounts so as to have the option of both types of loans.

Considerations of averaging suggest that the saver be given the option of buying some assets on the equivalent, or tax-prepaid, basis. For example, if a household can anticipate large expenditures on college education some years hence, it seems fair to allow the taxpayer to prepay taxes on these expenditures; otherwise, the lumpy nature of the expenditure and the progressivity of the tax structure would result in very large tax liabilities.

There are administrative and equity reasons for limiting the use of tax-prepaid assets. If an investor is given the option of designating an asset as a standard or equivalent (tax-prepaid), not only will every asset have to be ''tagged,'' but there would be a strong tendency to tax-prepay on sure investments, and to end up with low consumption tax liabilities from investments that prove to be very profitable.[3]

The calculation of current consumption on the basis of cash flow information involves certain items as pension receipts and insurance benefits. Two apparently very different tax treatments of items are possible and are equivalent to each other. These two treatments correspond to the standard and equivalent treatments of saving discussed above. Either the premiums could be deductible and the receipts taxable, or the premiums would not be tax deductible and the receipts would be taxable. So the choice of approach for certain items depends on averaging considerations and on social attitudes, rather than on considerations of equity.

For example, for fire insurance on homes, the premiums might not be deducted and the proceeds are excluded from receipts. The rationale for this treatment is that the insurance protects assets which generate consumption services and should be taxed as current receipts. Alternatively, premiums would be deducted and the proceeds would be included in receipts.

Similarly, the premiums on life insurance could be taxed as current consumption and the life insurance policy is treated as a tax-prepaid asset. On the standard asset approach to life insurance, the premiums would be deducted and the proceeds would be included in current receipts. For averaging considerations, the tax-prepaid approach is preferred for both life insurance and medical insurance.

For various types of social insurance—unemployment compensation, social security, and private pensions—contributions would be exempt (deducted) from income, while the receipts from such funds would be included in taxpayers' receipts. The advantage of this approach is that if contributions to these funds do not match benefits, the employee is not regarded as having received the taxes paid as income.

PROBLEMS IN ADOPTING AN
EXPENDITURE TAX

The case for expenditure tax relative to income tax is quite strong when there is a ''clean slate,'' and when one of the two tax systems is to be introduced. But at present most developed countries utilize income taxes, albeit noncomprehensive, and this may work against the adoption of an expenditure tax.

The most complicated technical and administrative problems associated with the introduction of such a tax are problems of transition or phase-in. One of the problems is associated with consumer durables. Persons would have a strong incentive to buy furniture, cars, and houses just before the introduction of the tax. There is really no satisfactory way of dealing with this problem, short of imposing a tax on the existing stock of durables. One possibility is to ignore them, and to require that the receipts from the sale of durables purchased before the effective date is included in taxable income, while the receipts from the sale of durables purchased after the effective date are exempt.

The more fundamental problem of transition is how to deal with persons who have made investments with after-tax income, and who expect to consume the proceeds free from tax. One approach to solving this problem is to provide some exemption from consumption out of wealth as a function of the wealth and age of the individual. Alternatively, during a transition period of ten years or so, two tax systems would exist side by side, and households would be given a choice of filing under one of these.

A somewhat more restricted form of transition would be to introduce the expenditure tax for most of the population, but to allow taxpayers the option of having some of the wealth taxed under the income tax.

Another, more partial, adoption of the expenditure tax would be Andrews's (1974) proposal of introducing an expenditure tax along with a very high exemption level so the tax would apply only to a small, wealthy segment of the population. During this experimental stage, administrative and statutory details could be developed and would lead to the adoption of a full-blown expenditure tax with a five- or ten-year transition, where some wealth would be taxed under an income tax. A more partial, gradual approach towards phasing in the expenditure tax would be to make certain limited reforms within the existing income tax. One of these would be to extend the income tax exemption of various contributions to private and social insurance and retirement systems, to gradually extend the practice of taxing receipts. Other reforms that would facilitate the eventual adoption of an expenditure tax would be to tax the net income earned on owner-occupied housing, and to integrate the corporate tax with the personal income tax.

The elimination of the separate corporate tax (which, as noted by Break in Chapter 3, may be desirable even under income taxation) is quite fundamental to the success of an expenditure tax proposal. If the tax were retained, a significant tax on savings would remain, as would the misallocation of capital between the corporate and noncorporate sector. Also, the incentive to finance with debt would be increased. One point favoring the adoption of the expenditure tax, rather than integrating the personal and corporate taxes under a comprehensive income tax, is administrative simplicity. There is no necessity under an expenditure tax of crediting or imputing to stockholders taxes or credits provided the corporation. The administrative complications of the pass-through to stockholders that would be required under an integration are quite forbidding.

The elimination of the corporate tax under an expenditure tax would present certain complications. Among these is the taxation of international transaction. At present, major industrial countries impose corporate taxes, and international tax treaties provide for the crediting of these taxes. International tax treaties would have to be renegotiated, and it is possible that significant international reallocations of capital would

occur as the result of the major change in tax systems. Although we cannot go into detail here, it needs to be emphasized that the introduction of an expenditure tax in the
U.S. may have wide implications on international investment
and on international relations in general. This fact may inhibit
the introduction of an expenditure tax, because of the disrup-
tion that the proposals may have on the export and import
neutrality of capital, and on harmonious international relations in general.

The general problems that international tax considerations
bring out is that an expenditure tax system has to be integrated into an international economic system, and supplemental taxes will have to be imposed on international capital
transactions.

Other tax supplements that have already been discussed are
inheritance taxes, or "consumption" taxes at time of death,
and wealth taxes imposed on the very wealthy. In fact, most
serious proponents of the expenditure tax take it for granted
that wealth taxes would buttress an expenditure tax system.
One reason for the need of a supplemental wealth tax or a
partial capital gains tax is valuable consumer durables owned
by the very wealthy. The treatment of these assets as tax-
prepaid assets (consumer durables) means that very large capital gains on art treasures and furniture will not be taxed. One
solution is to require that the assets be treated as standard or
ordinary assets. The problem with this approach would be
that the taxpayer would not be taxed on the services derived
from the durable. A compromise might be to impose a consumption tax on the purchase price of the asset, and then to
require the inclusion of receipts (net of the purchase price)
derived from the sales of durables above some minimum
amount. The danger with these rules and the other supplements and exceptions is that a rather complex system would
evolve that would be substantially more complicated than the
pure expenditure tax. The deviations from the ideal, as well
as various tax preferences that would inevitably creep into a
consumption-based tax, undermine the adoption of such a
system.

In light of the difficulties and complexities of moving to a pure expenditure tax system, it may be more appropriate and realistic to adopt a number of interim or partial steps towards a consumption-based system which would be more general than Andrews's (1974) proposal to introduce this tax for high-income households. A partial adoption of the consumption tax principal would involve strengthening the current provision of the income tax that exempts from tax the accrual of capital gains, the increase in private pension reserves, and that permits, subject to certain limitations, the deduction from current taxable income of employers' and employees' contributions to pension funds.

Provisions that might and should be considered are the elimination of the deduction restrictions of savings in private pension funds, and allowing *all* households the option of investing in savings accounts that could be used as deductions under the income tax. Financial institutions would issue special accounts, and savings in these accounts would be deducted from taxable income; current interest would be nontaxable. All withdrawals from such accounts would be taxed as current income. Another more major innovation would be to exempt employees' contributions to social security from taxation, and to gradually move to a system where social security benefits would be included in taxable income.

If provisions that exempted taxation of savings under the current income tax were strengthened, as a means of gaining the acceptance of a consumption-based system and moderating the distortionary effects of taxes on capital income, care should be taken to couple these provisions with changes that would maintain an acceptable degree of progressivity in the burden of the income tax. Private pension rights and benefits, and private savings, are highly concentrated in the top half of the income distribution, and the effect of exempting current savings in qualified tax-exempt accounts without offsetting changes in rate structure would shift the current income tax burden towards moderate- and low-income groups.

CONCLUDING REMARKS

Recent research, most notably the work of Andrews (1974),
the U.S. Treasury's *Blueprints for Tax Reform* (1977), and
the Meade Report (Institute for Fiscal Studies 1978), has
greatly extended our understanding of both the basic equity
and efficiency considerations favoring a consumption-based
system, and the technical issues involved in implementing
such a tax system have advanced significantly. My own appraisal of this literature is that, contrary to early discussion,
an expenditure tax is not more difficult to administer than an
income tax and, in fact, may be simpler and more feasible to
implement than a comprehensive income tax that makes provision for inflation indexation and integration with the corporate tax. This is not to say that there are no problems in moving to an expenditure tax—among them problems of transition, inflation associated with consumer durables, the need of
supplemental taxes on wealthy individuals, and coordination
problems with other countries.

The critics of the expenditure tax will make much of these
problems, and will use them to support the status quo or to
move towards more equitable comprehensive income tax.
One of the attractions of an expenditure tax is that so little
progress has been made in moving towards a fairer income
tax system. But if no consensus develops regarding what direction tax reform should take, the existing system will tend
to persist. What is needed is the development of a common
set of specific objectives that would be acceptable to the advocates of the income and the expenditure tax systems. The
basic problem in finding agreement is that there is, of course,
a fundamental difference in the attitudes of the two schools
regarding the taxation of profit income. One of the points of
this chapter is that taxation of profit income or wealth is a
misdirected policy for the vast majority of taxpayers whose
savings behavior approximates the life-cycle model and for
whom bequests and inheritance are relatively modest, but this

leaves open the question of how the wealthy, who continue to control a very large share of the nation's wealth, should be taxed.

3

GEORGE F. BREAK

Corporate Tax Integration: Radical Revisionism or Common Sense?

Mythology of the corporate image. Inequities in the corporate tax system. Banks or corporations—comparative savings benefits. Corporate reinvestment of retained profits. Tax reform. "Dividends only" integration. International repercussions of corporate tax integration.

Perhaps no issue in public policy illustrates more clearly people's preference for clinging to simplistic images at the

expense of their own best interests than does that of the corporation income tax. Paradoxically, the public's refusal to
take an interest in the complex interactions of the economic
system tends to turn the vision of the corporate world as a
depersonalized monster into something of a self-fulfilling
prophecy. If ignorance of economics were not so comfortable
a condition, that remote and hostile "military-industrial complex" might well be transformed from threatening beast into
household companion and servant. A mere change in the tax
system could reduce the incentives for corporate enterprise to
serve its own self-interests, as though separate from those of
its shareholders, and make it perform more effectively as the
average person's employer, provider of goods, and custodian
of invested savings. Unfortunately, such intellectual revolu-
tions are hard to accomplish.

The first difficult step in this educational process is an
exercise in objectivity, requiring people to see the corporate
world without the mark of Cain upon it. Only then can the
manner in which corporations are taxed become a topic of
rational debate. Since some 25 million individuals in the
United States are holders of corporate stock, the potential
constituency for a revision of the corporation income tax is,
in fact, large. If they were joined by the millions of other
investors of savings who hold bonds, certificates of deposit,
or passbook savings accounts, all of them having an important stake in the matter, a veritable tidal wave of votes could
be rallied to the cause. What would be needed, however,
would be a willingness, not only to depart from conventional
mythology, but also to venture into the arcane area of
economic reasoning.

Like medicine with a bitter, or at least unfamiliar, taste,
the initial stages of the revisionist thinking essential to an
understanding of the corporate tax issue are likely to deter the
fainthearted. Even the language used by economists in discussing the subject utilizes an emotionally charged vocabu-
lary. The very problems with the present system are defined
in terms that touch sensitive areas and stir up quite irrelevant

value judgments—words like "equity," "economic efficiency," and "economic growth." Suggestions for reform are no freer of emotional overtones, since the prescription approved by most tax experts has the unfortunate label of "corporate tax integration."

CORPORATE TAX DISTRIBUTION

One does not have to accept fully the message of the familiar television commercial portraying Mr. and Mrs. Average American of modest means as the real owners of the giant sponsoring corporation in order to appreciate the fact that such enterprises are indeed important sources of investment income for millions of people. Nor is it difficult to perceive that there is something questionable about a system which taxes corporate profits at the source and then makes the same profits, if distributed as dividends, taxable again as personal income to the shareholders. The problems created by this double taxation not only violate the principle of equity, but cause serious and far-reaching distortions of our economic system. An even worse effect, perhaps, is the separation created by the tax between the interests of the corporation itself and the interests of its stockholders.

The equity questions involved are of two kinds. A vast array of hard-to-pin-down horizontal inequities is inherent in the duplication of taxes on some, and not other, income, as the following discussion will show. Far easier to identify and quantify, however, is the problem of vertical equity among shareholders. Here the evidence shows the burden pattern of the double tax to be markedly regressive. Although the $100 dividend exclusion allowed under the personal income tax mitigates the effect slightly for people with very little corporate source income, the corporation tax may impose an extra tax burden of 48 percent on the corporate income of shareholders at the lowest income levels, while actually undertaxing by as much as 20 percent high income shareholders investing in companies that pay few dividends. These inequities result from the fact that the corporate tax rate of 48 percent (the nominal rate for most corporations) is applied to all investors, regardless of income or tax bracket. Since dividends are taxed again under the individual income tax, everyone is overtaxed on dividend income, but the excess burdens are highest on those with the lowest incomes, and lowest on those with the highest incomes.

The tax impact on individuals is complicated by the fact that not all corporate profits are paid out as dividends. Those profits that are retained by the enterprises are reinvested and generate, on the average, a dollar of capital gains for every dollar retained per share. For investors who hold their shares more than a year, these capital gains are taxed only when sold, and then at half the rates applicable to other kinds of income. This means a substantial reduction in the effective tax rate for investors who take their profits in the form of capital gains, and who otherwise would be subject to rates as high as 70 percent. To be sure, investors with large amounts of capital gains are subject to "minimum tax" and may also lose some tax privileges on their wage and salary income, with the result that the effective rate on their capital gains could be as high as 50 percent for those in the 70 percent bracket, instead of just 35 percent. Nevertheless, for many investors in the top bracket, retained corporate earnings that are taxed at 48 percent, and then generate capital gains that may become taxable only much later at a rate as low as 35 percent, represent a substantial tax bargain. This impact is to be contrasted with that on investors with too little income to pay personal tax, but whose share of corporate source profits bears the full corporate rate, whether retained or distributed.

This sorry picture of a sharply regressive incidence pattern is only part of the story, however. So far we have been dealing only with how the "excess" burdens of the corporate tax are distributed among shareholders. When the discussion is broadened to include comparisons with taxpayers whose income is derived from other sources, the picture becomes far more complicated. For the impact of the corporation income tax rate (nominally 48 percent for large corporations, but reduced to as little as 20 percent for very small ones) is greatly moderated for many enterprises by the presence of a number of tax incentives. These, and particularly the most important of them—accelerated depreciation and the investment tax credit—have sufficient impact to lower the effective rate for most corporations below the normal rate, and in some cases to less than 20 percent. The average effective rate is about 38 percent.

The consequences of this uneven incidence reach far beyond the corporate shareholders whose investments are directly affected. Because different types of investments compete actively with one another for savings dollars, a high tax rate on corporations diverts capital from that sector, forcing it into the noncorporate sector, where it raises the level of output and reduces both consumer prices and the rate of return of business owners. Prices and before-tax rates of return in the corporate sector rise, and the process continues until average net-of-tax rates of return are the same everywhere, and lower than they would have been in the absence of the corporation tax. This means that, to a considerable extent, the corporation income tax places its burdens on owners of all kinds of property, not just corporate shares. It also means that consumers are not necessarily made worse off by the tax, as is commonly assumed. Those with strong tastes for corporate products are indeed worse off because of the higher prices prevailing in that sector, but those with strong tastes for noncorporate output, particularly for food and housing, are better off, because prices for these items are lower than they otherwise would be. Of course, these consumer burdens are readily perceived, while the benefits are largely hidden. Seen or unseen, these changes in consumer prices have neither logic nor equity to recommend them.

A final set of corporate tax burdens remains on certain groups of corporate shareholders, particularly those with holdings in companies earning surplus profits. Even here, the stock market will adjust to the tax by lowering the prices of those shares until they yield a net-of-tax rate of return equal to that obtainable elsewhere on investments of comparable risk. This means that owners of those companies at the time the tax was first imposed (or increased) bear the entire burden of the tax, present and future. New buyers of the stock, in contrast, bear no burden from those past tax increases, because they can earn the same yield on their investments as they could have earned had there been no corporate tax. These tax capitalization effects, as they are called, would work in the opposite direction if the corporate tax were either reduced or integrated with the individual income tax.

ECONOMIC DISTORTIONS

Both present and future generations are affected in important ways by the different economic distortions created by a separate corporation income tax. One matter of great significance is the extent of the shift of resources into noncorporate enterprise resulting from the tax penalty on investment in corporate output. Assuming an average effective corporate tax rate of about 33.33 percent, and a rate of return on noncorporate investment of 8 percent, one can see that a corporate investment with comparable risks would have to return 12 percent before tax in order to be worth undertaking. This provides a strong incentive to put resources to inferior 8 percent uses rather than to superior 9 to 12 percent ones. From society's point of view, this is wasteful of productive potential, since less than the optimum amount of output is generated. The tax burden on capital, moreover, induces corporations to use less capital per unit of labor input (i.e., per unit of productive output), with the result that the available capital is inefficiently employed. Estimating the extent of this loss of output is an extremely difficult task, but Martin Feldstein and

Daniel Frisch (1977) have quantified it at $4 to $6 billion per year at 1976 levels of income. The costs in terms of both employment and productivity are major. These costs extend, furthermore, into the future, since a reduction in the rate of return on a family's savings means that they will have less to spend when they want to put those savings to use.

There is no accurate way to measure the economic effects of reduced rates of return on savings, but theoretical analysis clearly indicates that they are large. Let us suppose that a family is faced with a choice between spending $100 on current consumption or investing the same amount in a share of stock, a bond, or a savings account. Assume further that the economy is functioning efficiently, and that a reasonably safe investment could be found to yield 10 percent. By opting for the investment instead of the current purchase, the family could look forward to having $110 at the end of a year. Any reduction in the rate of return, however, such as that caused by the corporation tax, would make the investment choice less attractive and could well tip the scale in the direction of current consumption; at the least, it would provide them with a smaller nestegg for the future. Feldstein and Frisch (1977) have estimated this loss of consumer welfare at around $7 billion for 1976, and Michael Boskin (1978) argues that it could easily be much larger.

A tax on equity (i.e., stockowning) capital has the further distorting effect of biasing the manner in which corporations finance their growth and development. The tax provides a strong incentive for them to issue debt (bonds) rather than new stock, since bond interest is deductible for income tax purposes, while dividends are not. This induced increase in the debt/equity capital ratio carries with it some less-than-desirable effects. One is the increased risk of bankruptcy under adverse economic circumstances, since bonds are obligations to outsiders, while stock dividends are shared profits among corporate owners. Since debt is an encumbrance, furthermore, the risks involved tend to discourage investors from buying stock in high-debt enterprises, and also to discourage corporate managers from new and uncertain ventures.

Perhaps even more damaging to the general economy is the strong incentive provided by the tax for corporations to retain their earnings instead of paying them out as dividends. Since retained earnings are subject only to the corporate tax and not to the personal income tax, they can be invested for the stockholders on a dollar-for-dollar basis. In contrast, dividends paid to the stockholders are diminished by the personal income tax before they can be either spent on consumption or reinvested. Feldstein and Frisch (1977) have estimated that the present tax costs all shareholders an average of $0.32 on each dollar, so that retaining a dollar of earnings costs them only $0.68 of foregone spending. (This estimate is based on a 40 percent marginal tax rate on the 81 percent of dividends paid to taxable shareholders.) The obvious course of action for corporate managers, therefore, is to retain as large a portion of the profits as possible, knowing that shareholder pressure will not be strongly opposed, since the reinvested dollars are bargains. These "cheap" dollars make for large amounts of new investment funds dammed up in the hands of corporations, where they may well be invested at lower rates of return than they might be if distributed to investment-wise stockholders. The greatly reduced incentive for the corporation to put the money to efficient use is shown by the fact that the retained earnings have to yield only 6.8 percent in order to equal in value a 10 percent investment by the individual stockholder. The loss to society from such far-from-optimum utilization of resources is very great.

This clear inducement to retain earnings, whether or not they can be reinvested efficiently, results in what economists are fond of calling "the survival of the fattest, not the fittest." There is evidence that mature corporations earn a lower average rate of return than young enterprises, yet the former have plenty of "captive" retained profits to finance expansion, while the latter have to raise new funds on the security markets. If there were no tax barrier to the distribution of corporate earnings, mature companies would pay higher dividends, and young companies could raise new equity capital on better terms because shareholders would have more money to invest. This should shift capital funds into superior uses, and help maintain the independence of new businesses. Under the present system, many young companies, starved for capital, are bought up by mature companies from their ample supply of retained earnings.

Congressional leaders who would like to mount a campaign to reform the corporation tax have suggested that a principal reason for the lack of interest in change is that corporate managers prefer things the way they are. It is to their interest that substantial amounts of retained earnings are at their disposal, and that there is little pressure from stockholders to increase dividend pay-outs. Stockholders who could invest—or otherwise spend—their profits more productively are clearly losers.

PROPOSED TAX REFORM

Given the many ill effects of the corporation income tax, the question to consider is how the method of taxing corporate enterprise could be improved. Since the troubling distortions and sources of inequity come from treating corporate source income as though it were a separate and different thing, unrelated to the other kinds of income that individuals receive, the answer clearly must lie in finding a rational and systematic way to fit the corporate tax into the tax family, and particularly to coordinate it with the individual income tax.

The proposals for such "corporate tax integration" take a variety of forms, differing according to the ambition of the reformer. For many academic economists, trained to find out how to get the most output from society's increasingly scarce resources and not to worry unduly about administrative

niceties, full integration is the only answer. This would involve taxing all corporate source income currently and fully
on the same basis as any other kind of income. To do this for
distributed earnings would not be difficult. All dividends
should be taxed, once in the hands of the shareholder recipients. Retained profits are more troublesome, in part because
of the close relation between reinvested corporate profits and
the prices of the shares of common stock of the companies
involved. If wisely reinvested, profits will increase share
prices by at least the amount of the funds plowed back in.

Retained corporate profits, then, could be fully taxed in
either of two ways. One would be to have no corporation
income tax at all, to tax dividends fully under the individual
income tax by removing the present $100/$200 dividend exclusion, and to reach retained profits by taxing all capital gains
and losses on corporate shares annually as they accrue. This
would require a major change in the current tax treatment of
that kind of personal income. Shareholders would have to
value their holdings of common stock at the end of each year
and pay tax at full rates on any net gain that had accrued,
regardless of whether they sold the shares or not (net losses
would be fully deductible against other taxable income).

The other way to tax retained profits fully would be to
allocate them proportionately each year to all common stockholders, who would then include these amounts in their taxable income for that year, To prevent any later taxation of the
same income, shareholders would increase the cost basis of
their stock by the amount of the allocated corporate profits. If
their shares then rose in value by the exact amount of the
retained profits, they could receive the income in cash, tax
free, by selling the shares and realizing the capital gains
thereon. Of course, paying tax on corporate profits that have
been kept by the company and not distributed to shareholders
would put many of them under a liquidity squeeze. This
could be avoided, however, by having corporations withhold
income taxes at the top bracket rate that is applied to individual incomes. No one would then be underwithheld on corpo-

rate source income, and no one could owe any additional tax on profits allocated to them for tax purposes. Most taxpayers, indeed, would be able to use part of the withheld corporate tax to reduce their other tax liabilities, or to claim a cash refund when filing their federal income tax returns.

Having retained corporate profits allocated to shareholders for tax purposes, then, would be an event to be welcomed. Under this full integration plan, the relation between the corporate withholding tax rate and the top bracket rate under the individual income tax would be of great importance. The top individual tax rate is already set at 50 percent for wages and salaries, and proposals have been made recently to reduce it to that level on other kinds of income as well. If that change is found acceptable on its own merits, it would be an easy matter to convert the present separate 48 percent corporate tax into a 50 percent withholding levy on both dividends and retained profits, and full integration by this plan would cause no one any liquidity problems.

Considering the complexities involved in dealing with the retained profits component of any full integration plan, it is easy to understand the appeal of proposals to deal only with dividends. Complete elimination of the excess tax burdens now placed on distributed corporate source income could be accomplished in two different ways. One would be to allow corporations to deduct dividends paid from their corporate income tax base, just as interest payments on debt are now treated. Alternatively, the portion of the present corporation tax now paid on earnings marked for distribution could be converted into a withholding levy fully creditable by shareholders against tax liabilities payable on dividends or other income. Under this plan, dividends would be treated in exactly the same way that wages and salaries have been for years. A shareholder would receive each year a statement showing both the amount of dividends actually received (now shown on corporation information returns) and the amount of tax withheld on them. The sum of these two amounts, frequently called the grossed-up dividend, would be added to the shareholder's other taxable income, the total tax liability computed, and the withheld corporation tax deducted as a credit. The result would be complete elimination of any excess tax burdens on corporate source income distributed to shareholders. If the revenue losses expected from such a tax reform were viewed as excessive, partial relief could be provided to any desired extent. Corporations could be allowed to deduct only a specified portion of dividends paid from their income tax base, or retained and distributed earnings could be subjected to two different tax rates—the so-called split-rate system. Alternatively, the withholding tax credit allowed to shareholders could be set at some fraction of the total tax paid by corporations on distributed earnings.

INTEGRATION EFFECTS ON MANAGEMENT AND STOCKHOLDERS

It is interesting to speculate on the different effects on dividend payouts that the two alternative methods of "dividends only" integration might have. The answer is by no means clear, because it depends on the extent to which corporate managers pursue their own interests rather than those of the stockholders. For many managers, retained earnings are an important source of power and prestige, and they can be expected to conserve them to the greatest extent possible. Dividend integration, on the other hand, would remove the present tax penalty on distributing, rather than retaining, corporate profits, and this change would induce all managements highly sensitive to stockholder interests to raise their payout policies.

There is, finally, the question of whether the initial allocation of the tax benefits—to shareholders or to managers— matters at all. In theory, it should not; in practice, it may. With a dividend deduction, corporations would immediately be provided with increased funds, which could then be allocated between higher dividends and greater retained profits. With a shareholder withholding tax credit plan, the increased funds would go initially to the shareholders. Management might then react to the increased affluence of their stockholders by reducing dividend payouts, or at least by slowing future rates of increase. Or, as some believe to be more likely, shareholders might pressure management to increase dividends substantially because of the tax advantages provided by any dividend integration plan. Should this happen to a significant extent, a "dividends only" plan of partial integration might turn into one of virtually full integration without the complexities of dealing with retained earnings.

Corporate tax integration would raise questions about the tax treatment of several important groups of people. The easiest to deal with would be those individuals and families with too little income to owe any federal income taxes. They would participate automatically in any shareholder benefits that a dividend-deduction method of integration generated, but that would not be the case under a shareholder-credit method. The solution would be to make the corporate tax credit rebatable to anyone with insufficient federal tax liabilities to absorb it fully. Tax equity would thereby be greatly improved at little additional administrative cost.

Similar, but considerably more costly, questions arise over the treatment of tax-exempt organizations. Charities, churches, hospitals, and pension funds now own corporate shares, and hence bear whatever direct corporate tax burdens fall on shareholders. They are, in short, not fully tax exempt at all. In principle, they should receive exactly the same tax benefits as any other stockholder from corporate tax integration. The problem is that this would greatly increase the Treasury's revenue losses from integration. In their 1976 study, for example, George Break and Joseph Pechman placed the revenue loss from full integration at $19.4 billion if its benefits were extended to tax-exempt institutions, but at only $6.9 billion if they were not. Tax burden reallocations of such dimensions are not likely to be contemplated lightly.

Reexamination of the claims to tax-exempt status of different kinds of philanthropic and charitable institutions would be in order. Attention could also be given to the circumstances under which it would be appropriate to place a federal tax on the investment income of philanthropic entities. Both of these policy issues may well be worthy of congressional study, but their introduction into the tax reform picture would clearly complicate the drawing up of any corporate tax integration plan.

INTERNATIONAL CONSEQUENCES
OF INTEGRATION

Even more complicated would be the treatment of international flows of corporate source income. How should U.S. shareholders of foreign corporations and foreign shareholders of U.S. corporations be treated, and what effects would different solutions have on private investment and economic growth both here and abroad? The basic dilemma here is that corporate tax integration is derived from a residence-basis tax philosophy under which the residents of each country are taxed on their total incomes, regardless of origin. Separate corporate tax systems, in contrast, reflect an origin-basis tax philosophy under which productive activity is taxed wherever it occurs, regardless of the location of the owners of the producing units or their consumers. Since origin-based elements are now strongly entrenched in national tax systems, and since many countries would lose if these elements were replaced with residence-basis ones, it is not to be expected that the path to full worldwide corporate tax integration will be smooth, if, indeed, it is passable at all.

This being the case, both the tax planner and the interested observer must try to discover a sensible path through the dense thicket of second-best solutions. Only a few of the sharpest thorns can be noted here. One is the automatic extension of integration benefits to foreign shareholders that would result from adoption of either the capital gains or the dividend-deduction methods. A major attraction of the shareholder-credit method is the freedom it gives enacting countries to decide explicitly what to do about foreign shareholders. One strategy for the United States, if integration by the shareholder-credit method were adopted here, would be to offer to extend credit privileges to the foreign shareholders of any country that extended similar privileges to our investors in their corporations. How attractive such a proposal might be is debatable, particularly since the U.S. has about ten times as much money invested abroad as foreigners have invested here.

Interesting to note in this connection is the draft directive on corporate tax integration issued by the Commission of the European Economic Community (EEC) in 1975. Reacting to the dividend relief policies adopted by France, West Germany, and the United Kingdom, and concerned about the effects of uncoordinated corporate tax integration plans on the operation of the European Common Market, the EEC commission proposed that each member country grant its own shareholders full credit privileges on any dividends received from corporations operating in any other member country. Taken by itself, this proposal has the unattractive feature of requesting each country to give its residents credit for corporate taxes paid to some other country. The EEC Commission therefore combined it with the proposal that countries of origin transfer to countries of residence the budgetary equivalent of all creditable foreign corporation taxes. By this means, the taxation of dividends would be placed on a full residence basis, while the taxation of retained profits remained on an origin basis.

TAX SHELTERS AND INTEGRATION

Corporate tax integration, then, is both a live issue and a developing policy in the world at large, and the United States must formulate its own plans accordingly. Whatever we do, there are likely to be important changing effects on the international flow of income and investment funds. A country that grants its resident shareholders tax credit privileges on domestic investment only, for example, will reduce the relative attractiveness of investment abroad. A country that extends tax credit privileges to foreign owners of its domestic corporations will stimulate foreign investment in those businesses, particularly if other countries adhere to their separate corporate tax systems or fail to grant reciprocal privileges under their integration plans. There are complexities here, to be sure, but most experts do not regard them as constituting important arguments either for or against adopting corporate tax integration in the United States.

More important is the question of how existing corporation tax preferences and incentives, such as accelerated tax depreciation and the investment tax credit, would be treated under integration. The effectiveness of these, and perhaps their very reason for existing, depends critically on the existence of a separate corporation tax. Certainly, to minimize the Treasury's revenue losses under integration they should be eliminated, and yet this could threaten the whole program by maximizing the opposition of business interests to it. A less radical policy would be to retain existing investment incentives in whatever form would minimize the costs of administering an integrated corporate tax system and, over time, to reassess their desirability as the effects of integration on national saving, investment, and growth became clear.

Tax reformers, however, tend to be appalled by the thought of retaining these tax shelters under integration. To give all shareholders a 48 percent tax credit appears to be highly inequitable, when some corporations pay a much lower effective tax rate because of the tax preferences to which they have access. Moreover, the tax preferences might lose most of their effectiveness in the process. One solution would be to eliminate tax preferences on distributed corporate income, but keep them on retained profits. No simple way of doing this has been, or is likely to be, devised, and care would be required to avoid any undesirable tax effects on corporate decisions to pay dividends or retain profits. A simpler solution would be to convert existing tax incentives into expenditure subsidies. Paid at stated rates on all business purchases of qualified investment assets, these would lower the price of capital assets and thereby stimulate investment. Such a policy makes good economic sense, because corporate managers could be expected to react to its benefits, regardless of whether they were motivated mainly by their own interests or by those of their shareholders. The plan may lack political appeal, because its costs are more visible than those of tax subsidies, but, if this is so, the case for investment incentives must have less to recommend it than is generally assumed.

CONCLUSION

It would be a mistake to believe that corporate tax integration or any other tax reform would miraculously generate a new economic golden age. Not even the most avid proponents of integration would wish to see it oversold as a panacea for capital shortages and sluggish economic growth. What it offers, however, is a start toward greater rationality in a tax system which has a vital impact on the general economic health of the nation.

Among its certain virtues would be a lessening of the obvious distortions and inequities which the selective tax duplication of the present corporation income tax inflicts on the economy. What it might promise beyond that depends largely on the kind of taxes chosen to replace the revenue which would be sacrificed by integration. The big, hard problems of how to stimulate investment and pick up the rate of economic growth might or might not be significantly relieved. Without doubt, integration would remove a major cause of some of the serious resource misuses from which we currently suffer. Whether that improvement would lead to further advances in productivity would depend on future tax policies and on how people reacted to the tax shifts.

A major issue of central importance is the change that corporate tax integration would induce in managerial decisions to distribute more corporate profits in the form of dividends. More generous payouts would have two effects—one, of increasing the income, and therefore the potential investment funds, of stockholders; the other, of decreasing the supply of corporate savings. Simultaneously with these shifts would come increased rates of return to savers and investors generally as a result of the elimination of the double tax. What all this would mean in terms of the total supply of savings is a matter of spirited current debate among economists. The standard article of faith in the profession is that increasing the rate of return on savings will not significantly affect the volume of investment. This concept has recently been sharply challenged by Michael Boskin (1978), however. His empirical analyses of people's saving behavior, after adjusting for taxes and inflation, indicate definite positive responses to increased rates of return. If these findings are correct, corporate tax integration could provide an important stimulus to the economy's growth rate.

A factor of some significance in this picture would be the redistribution of disposable income among families with different saving propensities. Since corporate shares are highly concentrated in the hands of the highest income groups, who also tend to be the largest savers, the reduction of the tax burden on corporate source income could certainly be expected to stimulate additional personal savings among the wealthy. Whether this tendency would be counteracted by other tax measures would become an important question, particularly if expected additions from this group were essential to maintaining or increasing the total volume of savings.

While corporate tax integration is only part of a composite picture, therefore, it could be an important first step toward improvement of the outlook for saving, investment, and economic growth. Certainly it could not be harmful, and it might be decidedly helpful. Its economic feasibility is, unfortunately, not matched by its political appeal. In that area, prejudices on the part of the public, inertia on the part of stockholders, and latent opposition on the part of corporate management, stand in ironic alliance as the major obstacles in its path.

4

JERRY R. GREEN

The Taxation of Capital Gains

The nature of capital gains. The "lock-in" effect. Lowering the capital gains tax and changing portfolio composition. Tax rates and the sales/dividend ratio. Savings, individual and corporate. Efficiency aspects of tax rates. Venture capital and taxation. Capital gains taxes and inflation.

Capital gains, defined as changes in the monetary value of assets, are a form of income and are therefore subject to taxation. Because of their different nature, they receive special treatment in our tax code. Up to 1969, they were taxed at a maximum rate of 25 percent. Since then, tax reforms have raised the statutory maximum rate to 35 percent, and further provisions related to the "maximum" and "minimum" taxes can make the effective rate as high as 49.1 percent for some taxpayers. Recent discussions of tax reform, both in public forums and among economists, have directed much attention toward this issue. This is due partially to the complexity of the form of taxation and to its impact on the process of capital accumulation. But the considerable vigor with which the debate has been carried out primarily reflects the fact that capital gains are concentrated among the wealthy. They appear to be a natural target for redistributive efforts, apparently devoid of the adverse incentive effects of high labor income tax rates.

One of the basic lessons of economic theory teaches us that it is best to concentrate taxes on items in fixed quantity. Capital gains, viewed at any moment in time, are independent of any individual's actions. The only decisions concern whether or not to sell the asset and subject the gains to taxation. Apparently, from an economic standpoint, the real allocation of productive resources would be unaffected.

As we shall see, however, the study of resource utilization cannot be limited to the momentary viewpoint. Capital gains taxation, along with the taxation of ordinary interest income, may have severe effects upon savings and investment. Both the magnitude of aggregate savings and the form in which it is embodied will be sensitive to the tax rules. These issues are particularly important at a time when the question of a long-run "capital shortage" is ever-present. Other aspects of our current tax system, analyzed in this volume, also have important implications for this problem.

Perhaps the most widely discussed aspect of capital gains taxation is the "lock-in" effect. This means that an investor who has experienced a capital gain has an incentive not to realize this gain through a sale. Although other, superior, investment opportunities may be present, he cannot take advantage of them without subjecting himself to taxation. The fear of inefficiency is, therefore, two-fold. First, the lock-in effect causes a departure from the individual's optimal portfolios and a consequent misallocation of risks. Second, the fact that funds may be locked in may prevent some socially worthwhile new ventures from being able to raise the necessary capital. These are not misallocations between accumulation and consumption, but rather are inefficiencies within the investment process itself.

Finally, as mentioned above, the nature of capital gains income has required that it be taxed at realization rather than continually, on an accrual basis. This creates several complicating factors that make the analysis of the equity and efficiency implications of capital gains taxation difficult. Capital gains are taxed at lower rates than ordinary income. The fact that the tax may not be paid until a much later date makes the effective rate of taxation even lower. On the other hand, inflation causes nominal asset values to grow faster than real values. (Recent experience shows that nominal values may even grow while real values decline.) Since the full nominal gain on an asset is subject to the capital gains tax, the effective rate of taxation may actually be much higher than the statutory rate, even when one accounts for the benefits of deferral. Modest increases in the rate of inflation can cause drastic shifts in the effective tax rate. In inflationary times, therefore, there should be little surprise that the method of capital gains taxation arises as a serious public issue.

This chapter will try to analyze each of these controversial aspects of capital gains taxation—the static and dynamic efficiency of resource allocation, the allocation of risks and willingness to undertake them, and the effective rate of taxation in the presence of inflation. It will bring to bear such facts as exist, and will point toward the types of evidence and analyses necessary before these questions can be definitely resolved.

EFFICIENCY ASPECTS OF CAPITAL GAINS TAXATION

Apart from redistribution, the dual purposes of any tax structure are to raise revenue and to improve the pattern of resource allocation. When one considers financial assets and their role in the allocation of risk-bearing, as well as alternative uses of productive resources, the many facets of this problem become apparent. This section outlines some of the ways in which the allocation of society's resources is affected by the provisions of the capital gains tax.

Static Efficiency and Revenues

Capital gains are a reflection of past economic activity. If the taxing authority could recognize gains independent of realization, capital gains could be taxed without altering any economic incentives in the short run. However, because revaluation of assets is too costly to be undertaken on an annual basis, taxes can be avoided until the gains are realized.[1] Even in the short run, the allocation of resources is affected by the endogeneity of this decision.

Lock-in effects are not, however, limited to the short run. Indeed, the longer an investor has locked himself into an asset, the stronger is the incentive to continue to hold it. To evaluate the efficiency and revenue aspects of lock-in effects, we need to dissect the decision to sell an asset at any point in time from the individual's point of view. Once we have a theory of individual behavior, we can compute investors' sensitivity to the rules of capital gains taxation, and the effects of their actions on the economic environment in the longer run.

Consider an individual who owns a variety of financial assets at some moment in time. It is probably not a bad approximation to assume that he knows the market value of each of these assets, and how much of a gain (or loss) has accrued to them since the date they were acquired. He should also know his tax status and, in particular, the rate of taxation that would apply to the gains it realized. Another important factor is his tax status in future years. Someone who knows that his capital gains rate is unusually low is more likely to sell than is another taxpayer, with the same rate, who believes it to be constant. Finally, the individual is assumed to have beliefs about the future returns on his assets and their relationship to the rest of his income.[2]

With this arsenal of data and conjectures in hand, the individual must decide which of his assets, if any, to sell. Obviously, this is a complicated problem, and few individuals actually attempt a fully systematic comparison of alternative courses of action. Nevertheless, it is clear that a lower capital gains tax encourages switching within a portfolio. Selling to finance consumption is influenced positively in the short run, but negatively through the perception of permanently lower tax rates and therefore higher yields.

The estimation of the effect of capital gains taxation on stock selling is a difficult task for the economist. Data describing the complete asset position of households, including accrued gains, is not available. In any one year, only the tax rate applicable for that reporting period is calculable, and even this is tricky. The possibilities for realizing gains primarily in years when marginal rates are low cannot be ascertained from this type of data.

To my knowledge, the only systematic attempt toward a quantitative study of this problem is the recently completed paper by Feldstein, Slemrod, and Yitzhaki (1978), referred to below as FSY. Their information is derived from a sample of tax returns in 1973 on which capital gains information is specified in detail. Their technique is to compute a marginal tax on capital gains applicable to each individual, and to use this rate, together with other aspects of the tax return, to predict the quantity sold and the gain realized.

Let us consider sales first. The quantity of stock sold depends, first of all, on the amount of stock owned. Wealth is not reported, and therefore FSY use dividends as a proxy. If all individuals were to have the same ratio of dividends to stock ownership, this would not affect the results. However, there are two complicating factors. Wealthier individuals tend to hold stocks with lower dividends, on average. Moreover, within a wealth and income category, the ratio of dividends to the value of stock is highly variable across individuals.

Both of these factors affect the interpretation of FSY's results.[3] Wealthier individuals sell a lower percentage of the value of their stock in any given year than the less wealthy investors. They also face higher capital gains taxes, on average. Measuring their wealth by dividends tends to overstate the true ratio of sales to wealth, and therefore to understate the true depressive effect of their higher taxes on the sales/wealth ratio.

Nevertheless, their results are striking, because they find an extremely large effect of the estimated tax rate on the sales/dividend ratio. The ratio of sales to dividends is about 2. Since dividend yields average .03 per annum, the overall turnover rate must be around .06. FSY estimate that a 10 percent increase in a taxpayer's marginal capital gains rate (e.g., from .25 to .35), other things equal, will decrease the sales/dividend ratio by 6.7. This is obviously implausible. Other forces must be hidden in their methodology.

The primary candidate is the idea that those taxpayers facing high marginal tax rates in 1973 knew that they were only temporarily high, and therefore postponed any realization of capital gains. If this were the case, a change in the tax rules that was regarded as permanent would lead to a pattern of realizations substantially closer to the actual than the FSY estimate would have us believe.

A full analysis of this issue would require data that followed each taxpayer in the sample over several years. This is not available at present, nor is it likely to be in the near future. Still, even with the sample used by FSY, some evidence of the presence of this effect can be ascertained. If it is important, it should be the case, for example, that many individuals have capital gains at or just under the level of $50,000.

In 1973 the first $50,000 of capital gains was taxable at the rate of 25 percent, while anything over that amount was taxed at half the ordinary income rate which, for most such tax-

payers, is close to 35 percent. If there is a good deal of intertemporal substitution in the timing of realizations, we should
expect individuals to avoid the higher rate by smoothing out
their pattern of gains below the $50,000 ceiling. Extremely
wealthy taxpayers, on the other hand, knowing that they will
be above the $50,000 ceiling all the time, will not attempt to
avoid the high marginal rate by intertemporal substitution. By
utilizing a more complex functional form that accounts for
the overall structure of capital gains taxation, and not just the
marginal rate, it might be possible to infer the gains that
would have been realized had the rate been constant, or had
the schedule of rates been smoothly increasing in the amount
of the realization.

The FSY methodology can be used to simulate revenue
effects of capital gains taxation, but the results must be interpreted with care. The most important underlying determinant
of realizations is the distribution of unrealized gains latent in
the asset position of each investor. When FSY look at the
variation in realizations in response to lower rates, they are
implicitly varying these latent gains as well. Their predic-
tions, therefore, tend to understate the true response in the
short run because, at the date the rates are lowered, the unrealized gains of the taxpayers are a higher proportion of their
wealth than those of taxpayers who were in the same bracket
before the change. They are thus properly viewed as the
long-run effects that could be expected if there were no intertemporal substitutability of gains or of other income.

Dynamic Efficiency

The taxation of corporate profits, interest income, and capital
gains has a great impact on the rate of return to saving. At a
time when many economists have pointed toward a deficiency
of savings which curtails economic growth, and which may
be due in part to other features of the fiscal process, it is
especially important to recognize the impact of capital gains
taxation on the process of capital accumulation. The argu-

ment for a deficiency of savings, and a consequent dynamic inefficiency, is very simple. The real marginal product of capital has been estimated to be at least 10 percent. On the other hand, the net of tax real return to savings is much lower, say, 2 to 3 percent at most. Therefore, by encouraging more savings, society will reap a larger return than the amount necessary to compensate the taxpayer whose income is taken for this purpose.

There are two distinct channels through which the rate of taxation of capital gains affects this divergence between private and social returns. The first is prospective. An investor, when deciding how much to save, computes the effective yield he expects on each asset. Clearly, lower capital gains taxation would raise this yield and generate more savings.

Econometric work on the effects of interest rates on savings is an old subject, but not one which can properly be viewed as having reached a consensus. Yet, even if the response of savings to the interest rate is zero, the life-cycle theory of consumption implies that there will still be a substantial welfare impact of such distortions, because retirement consumption will be greatly depressed.[4]

Much of private savings in the United States takes the form of retained earnings of corporations, and this brings us to the second depressive effect of capital gains taxation. Though the theory of finance has not produced a consistent account of the dividends/retained earnings choice, it is generally recognized that increases in the capital gains tax encourage dividend payout at the expense of retained earnings.

Let us trace the effects of a shift of $1.00 from dividends to retained earnings carefully, from the viewpoint of a typical investor. If he has $1.00 less in dividends, he will have a tax savings equal to his marginal tax rate (say, .5 for simplicity), and his current income will be lower by $0.50. What will be the change in the value of his shares? On one hand, the market should be willing to pay $1.00 more for a firm with $1.00 of extra capital; if not, this firm could be profitably taken over, as it would represent a cheaper source of capital than direct purchase. On the other hand, we can consider the problem facing our typical investor. Call the increase in the value of the firm due to this $1.00 of extra capital ''V.'' If the investor sells his shares, he must pay the capital gains tax. His net yield, therefore, is .75V, assuming he is paying at half his marginal rate on ordinary income. In order for the investor to be indifferent between having the dividend or having the firm keep the $1.00 in retentions, .75V must be .50, or V must be .67. Apparently, if V were above .67, dividends should be reduced, and if V is below that level, they should be increased.

Thus, we have two theories of the valuation of retained earnings that are in direct conflict—and the problem remains one of the principal unresolved puzzles in the theory of finance today.[5] On either interpretation, however, the individual's pre-tax wealth increases by more than $0.50, and, net of tax, the present value of his lifetime consumption could be increased by something between $0.50 and $1.00.

Will savings be higher when the individual has $0.50 now, in his pocket, or a higher level of wealth embodied in a higher valuation of his portfolio? Although this is an empirical question, I will argue that retained earnings will be a more powerful stimulant to saving in the aggregate. The firm has already invested the $1.00 in productive capital; total savings is this $1.00, minus any induced increase in private consumption out of wealth, which is unlikely to be more than $0.20. Thus, $0.80 seems to be a safe lower bound, well above the amount that could be saved by the individual out of his dividend. We must note that this is not the whole story. The government, a forgotten figure in this scenario thus far, has $0.50 of extra revenue in the dividend case, and only a claim against a future, potential, capital gain if the earnings are retained. A full analysis would have to account for government saving, and for the behavior and indirect impact of government debt.[6]

There is a further, very important, aspect of financial markets that bears upon the value of V. There are many tax-exempt investors in the market. They are often large, and powerful enough to influence corporate financial policy. From their point of view, if V were less than one they would not be satisfied. They should insist on a higher dividend. Since these investors do hold a large portfolio of firms whose retained earnings are positive, can we conclude that V = 1? If not, what is the role of debt finance and its risks for holders of equity in the preferences of these tax-exempt investors?

Coming back to the main line of the argument, a reduction in the rate of capital gains taxation should increase private sector savings by encouraging retained earnings at the expense of dividends. If FSY are right, and the revenue loss would be small, or even converted into a revenue gain, this savings can arise with only the loss of the uncollected revenue on dividends. Thus, dynamic allocative efficiency can be greatly improved via a cut in the capital gains tax rate.

Efficiency of Portfolio Allocation

Individuals switch their holdings of securities in response to many forces. Increases in wealth, whether current or anticipated, may induce a person to invest in a riskier portfolio, even though his expectations have remained unchanged. New information, disseminated marketwide, will alter security prices, and investors will have to reallocate their portfolios as a result. If the individual regards the new information as not having been fully capitalized into market prices, speculative motives will affect his behavior.

The traditional theory of finance determines an optimal portfolio at each moment in time. But the "optimal" portfolio is never actually attainable. Transactions costs, complicated by indivisibilities or economies in round-lot trading, delays, and, especially, capital gains taxes due upon realization, may keep the agent from maintaining the desired holdings at every moment. The common feature of all of these impediments is that they imply a threshold nature of the decision to sell one asset to acquire another. The gross benefit derived by the individual must exceed a certain positive cost if a sale is to be undertaken.

The inefficiency of capital gains taxation in this regard is that it prevents some mutually beneficial exchanges of financial assets from taking place. Before condemning capital gains taxation on these grounds, however, we should carefully examine our concept of efficiency. One of the reasons that two investors may decide to trade assets is that they have different beliefs about the future returns. *Ex post,* the seller's gain will have been the buyer's loss. Thus, although economists would tend to prefer a definition of efficiency that recognizes *ex ante* valuations as indicative of the true social surplus to be obtained, the nature of financial assets is such that realizations must necessarily fall short of this mark. Is capital gains taxation useful for precluding trades that are only marginally valuable *ex ante* and counterproductive *ex post?*

Leaving such questions aside, the idea that sales are undertaken when their gross valuation exceeds the taxes and direct costs of transactions may provide a method for estimating these gross values and, indirectly, the propensity to trade when taxes will be lowered. One could look at transactions made by investors close to the time that brokerage commissions were changed, in order to measure the value of switching investments to the marginal trader.

Reaction of Markets to Changes in Capital Gains Taxation

There has been a great deal of public discussion about whether the historically low equity prices of the 1970s can be explained by the higher capital gains tax rates prevailing since 1969. In this context, the prospect of reverting to pre-1969 methods of capital gains taxation seems tempting.

Whether or not a significant effect on equity prices can be expected turns on the same question as the dividend/retained earnings choice which we examined in the context of capital formation above.[7] If the "takeover" theory of valuation is right, there will be no effect. Shares are already valued at the replacement cost of the capital stock, plus corporate goodwill. But if the "dividend" theory is right, the value of corporate stock represents the present value of extracting capital from the firm and returning it to the owners of equity. This may be substantially less than the replacement cost of the capital if this extraction process involves the payment of capital gains and interest income taxes.

From the viewpoint of an owner of shares with an unrealized gain, the tax reduction encourages sale. The proceeds of the sale will probably be reinvested in another financial asset, so the net pressure on stock prices should be zero, or slightly negative. From the viewpoint of a prospective owner, lower capital gains taxes increase the anticipated yield and drive up the willingness to pay. On the whole, the effect is clearly positive, but individual securities in which large quantities of unrealized gain are converted may actually decline in value, because of the first effect.

Another factor to be considered is that much of the activity in stock trading, and a considerable—though smaller—proportion of ownership, is in the hands of tax-exempt traders. Some of these are charitable or educational institutions, others are pensions. The presence of these types of investors will be a mitigating force. Large upward price movements that cannot be sustained in the long run will cause them to switch out of equities and into other assets. Given the tax advantages of capital gains, it is hard to see why these institutions are so heavily invested in shares with relatively low dividend yield. Unless these shares present a pattern of returns that cannot be achieved through another combination of market assets, one would expect tax-exempt institutions to specialize. Put even more strongly, one would expect some firms to find that, by offering a high dividend and little prospect of capital gain, they can attract capital from these institutions at a favorable price. Similarly, other firms should have a zero dividend, and should be owned exclusively by private, taxable, investors. Why this doesn't happen, and the implications of the mixed market we do have for predicting the effects of capital gains taxation, is a substantial problem and a topic for future research.

If higher equity prices do occur when capital gains taxation is decreased, it is still problematic as to whether they will spur new investment. Few corporations have issued new equity in recent years. Therefore, the cost of capital is not likely to be responsive to equity prices in the short run. Only in a longer-run situation, where the balance in investors' preferences between debt and equity must also be maintained, higher equity prices should spur investment.

Capital Gain Taxation and the Undertaking of Risks

Capital gains taxation makes the government a partner in the portfolio of every investor. The government shares in profits and, up to a certain point, shares in losses. Because of inflation, the government's bearing of real losses, which show up as nominal gains, is significant. It is well known that in such cases the taking of risks is encouraged. It is, therefore, surprising that high rates of capital gains taxation have been blamed for cutting off the supply of venture capital.

There are several reasons why this charge might, in fact, be correct. First, capital gains taxes increased, while other interest income taxes remained largely constant. The shift, therefore, was away from new ventures and small, non-dividend paying, corporations, due to a shift in relative taxes, although an overall increase in taxation might have reversed the effect. Second, investors in risky prospects of this type are optimists. They tend to believe that they will make more of a profit than they actually will, on average. Therefore, they believe that the government's capital gains taxation, even including loss-offset provisions, is an unfair gamble. Third, unlike a stockholder who intends to invest for a long time—long enough so that nominal gains are sure to be positive because of inflation—a venture capitalist is going to have a large, quick, loss if he is unsuccessful. This means that the loss will be nominal as well as real, and that the loss will exceed the ceiling permissible for write-offs against current income under the capital gains tax. Thus, the bias again favors the government's side of the balance sheet. For these reasons, venture capital markets and new equity issues by small corporations have come to a virtual standstill—and socially valuable new prospects are not being explored, with adverse consequences on technical progress and employment.

One may ask why, in light of the discussions above of tax-exempt investors, the valuable new ventures are not financed by them. The answer is that, as fiduciaries, they tend to be conservative investors, and many are forbidden from such investments, either by state law or by their own trustees. The venture capital market must depend upon private investors facing capital gains taxation.

CAPITAL GAINS TAXATION IN THE PRESENCE OF INFLATION

The delay in taxes until the realization of capital gains brings the effective rate below the statutory rate. However, since the tax is based on nominal capital gains, the actual real return on the asset is dramatically reduced. The same adverse effect of inflation applies as well to the taxation of interest income.

The higher capital gains tax liabilities imposed by inflation have been documented by Feldstein and Slemrod (1978). They find that over 40 percent of the actual capital gains taxes paid in 1973 would not have been due, had the cost bases been increased to reflect the changing price levels. Moreover, Feldstein and Slemrod have documented that the bias is to favor wealthier taxpayers in comparison to poorer ones, at least as far as one can tell based on realizations. The real capital gains realized by taxpayers with adjusted gross incomes of over $500,000 are more than 80 percent of their nominal gains; whereas for taxpayers whose adjusted gross incomes are less than $100,000, real capital gains realized are negative, although nominal gains are positive. Some of these differences reflect the different holding periods on assets sold across income groups. Very wealthy taxpayers realize very little of their accrued gain on assets held for longer periods of time. Their capital gains tend to reflect short-term speculative activity, and their success at this activity may be based on information superior to that available to the average investor. To some extent, it may reflect certain types of ordinary income which can be classified as capital gains for tax purposes, and therefore receive preferred treatment.

The formula under which capital gains taxes are computed causes an interesting contrast between the response of real net yields on assets subject to this tax and those subject to ordinary income taxation. Surprisingly, the capital gains tax tends to make the real net yield *less* sensitive to changes in the rate of inflation than the yield on interest-bearing assets. To my knowledge, this point has not been made previously, and some authors have even implied the contrary.

Consider an asset whose real interest cost to the borrower is 6 percent and whose nominal yield is higher, due to inflation. Let us assume, for simplicity, that the investor faces a 50 percent rate on interest income, and a 25 percent capital gains rate. At a 2 percent rate of inflation, a bond with a nominal yield of 8 percent has a net after-tax yield of 4 percent and a real yield of 2 percent. If the rate of inflation were 6 percent, so that the nominal yield rises to 12 percent, the real net yield would fall to zero ($12 \times .5 = 6$).

The case of a capital asset is markedly different. If it is held for ten years, the corresponding real net yields would be 4.3 percent per annum and 3.7 percent per annum, respectively.

CONCLUSION

The discussion above indicates that the effects of capital gains taxation take various forms. Some of these are easily foreseen, but others are uncertain, either because sufficient evidence has not been marshalled as yet, or because the underlying theoretical structure remains to be developed. There are four principal implications of capital gains taxation which have been traced out. First, like any other type of interest income tax, it might curtail private savings, and in any case it would distort the lifetime expenditure decisions of households. Second, because of the relationship between corporate retained earnings and individuals' tax liabilities, a higher capital gains tax encourages higher dividend payout rates, discouraging further the aggregate saving of the private sector. Third, capital gains taxation places a barrier toward a more flexible portfolio allocation process, although it was argued that the adverse effects of this inflexibility can easily be overstated. And finally, the fact that capital gains are based on the nominal accrued value of assets makes the effective rate of taxation much higher than the statutory rate when the rate of inflation is substantial. However, this bias affects all forms of interest income taxation, and it was shown that capital gains are somewhat less vulnerable than nominal interest income.

5

PAUL J. TAUBMAN

On Income Taxes

The ability-to-pay doctrine—horizontal and vertical equity. Tax efficiency and feasibility. Consumption tax v. income tax. Relationship between the tax base and the tax rate schedule. Deductions, exemptions, and tax credits. Human capital investment. Nonhuman capital income and private savings. Asset depreciation, capital gains, and earned income. Reforming the taxpaying unit.

In the private sector of the economy, people buy goods and services by paying appropriate prices. A consumer who wishes to maximize his utility will continue to buy more of a particular good until the extra utility he derives from the purchase of one more unit of that good, divided by its price, equals the extra utility obtained from buying one more unit of any other good divided by this other good's price.[1] In two important respects, books and other goods produced and sold by the government are like those produced in the private sector. First, an individual can decide how many items he wishes to consume, and second, the goods purchased or used by one person are not available to others. But most government expenditures on goods and services are like national defense, in that the same quantity of goods and services are provided to each person in the society, and the availability or use of the good by one person does not decrease the amount of this good available to other members in society. Economists generally label goods with these characteristics as "public."

Like a publisher, the government can sell books by establishing a price that covers costs. For such nonpublic goods, there is no need for a separate tax. The need for taxation arises either when there are public goods, or when government must intervene in the marketplace.

In theory, it is possible to determine the optimal amount of expenditures on public goods, the utility each person obtains from these goods, and thus the price he should pay towards this expenditure. But it is generally realized that to obtain the necessary information is much too expensive. Therefore, the tax system is based on different criteria. "Ability to pay" is one important criterion. Roughly, ability to pay means that equals should be treated alike, while unequals should be treated differently—two clauses which define vertical and horizontal equity. Other relevant criteria are economic efficiency, feasibility, and fulfillment of other social goals.

CRITERIA TO JUDGE TAX SYSTEMS

Ability to Pay[2]

Ability to pay is usually thought of in terms of *society's* estimate of the individual's sacrifice when he transfers resources to the government. It is generally accepted that each individual is subject to diminishing marginal utility of consumption. That is, the extra utility he obtains from each additional dollar of consumption is smaller, the greater is his level of consumption. If society ignores interpersonal differences in levels of utility, people with more resources have a greater ability to pay, and suffer a smaller sacrifice by paying more taxes. Resource availability is generally gauged by a broad-based measure such as income, consumption, or wealth. In general, it is total income, etc., that constitutes the tax base, regardless of how the taxpayer makes use of it. The tax law, however, permits some deductions from and refinements to income to better reflect the individual's ability to pay.

As noted above, the ability-to-pay doctrine consists of horizontal and vertical equity. Horizontal equity requires that individuals with the same resources pay the same tax. Vertical equity indicates how taxes should vary as resources increase. To a large extent, vertical equity is a value judgment.

Suppose one adopts the criterion that each taxpaying unit should be asked to make the same percentage sacrifice of utility (as evaluated by society). Further assume that there is diminishing marginal utility to consumption. These two assumptions alone do not allow us to determine whether tax liabilities should increase faster, slower, or at the same rate as resources—i.e., should the tax be progressive, regressive, or proportional (Musgrave 1959:98–106). The answer also depends on how quickly the marginal utility of consumption declines. Moreover, the answer to the progressivity question will differ if we use another criterion, such as each taxpaying unit should sacrifice the same amount of utility.

Economic Efficiency

Tax laws often change the effective price paid and the decisions made by consumers and businessmen.[3] Economic efficiency is generally measured by the total of the utility of the citizens in the economy. Taxes that cause different combinations of goods and services to be produced yield more or less efficient economies. Some tax laws may reduce the supply of various resources so much that not only is GNP reallocated, but it is also reduced in size. Thus, equitable allocation of tax burdens may not be good for society.

Feasibility

Feasibility is an important and many-dimensioned criterion. These dimensions include the cost of collecting taxes or enforcing rules and regulations, the size of the record-keeping burden imposed on taxpayers, and the extent of invasion of privacy. In subsequent sections we will use the equity, efficiency, feasibility, and other social goal criteria to examine a number of issues in the taxation of income.

INCOME V. CONSUMPTION TAXES

The United States government currently relies on corporate and personal *income* taxes for most of its revenue. The major alternative to an income tax is a consumption tax. The difference between the two tax systems thus is the treatment of current saving. Even in a consumption tax system, the returns on past saving are subject to tax.

Two major arguments usually advanced as to why the consumption tax is superior to an income tax are that a consumption tax is more efficient, and that it yields more equitable results.

An income tax, in effect, imposes a double tax on saving. The first tax occurs when the income is earned; the second tax occurs when the returns to saving are also taxed.[4] As shown in the note, the income tax alters the rate of return on saving which will cause people to substitute consumption for saving, at a given income level. This substitution is the source of extra inefficiency. As also shown in the note, the consumption tax does not alter the rate of return, and in this respect causes no inefficiency. While this argument cannot be faulted, it is incomplete.

In the aggregate, annual private saving in the United States is positive, and has been positive in all years that saving has been measured in the National Income Accounts.[5] When saving is positive, income exceeds consumption; to raise an equal amount of revenue, therefore, the government must impose a higher tax rate on consumption than on income. Neither the consumption nor the income tax is imposed on all activities that determine a person's utility or satisfaction level. In particular, both taxes are not imposed on nonmarket activities. Thus, the size of the tax rate affects the decision on how much time to spend at work. Higher tax rates cause people to substitute leisure and at-home production for market work. This substitution is also a source of inefficiency. Since the consumption tax causes more inefficiency in labor/ leisure choices, while the income tax causes more inefficiency in consumption/saving choices, which system causes the greater inefficiency is an empirical question.[6]

The available empirical evidence is not definitive. A recent study suggests that a 10 percent decrease in the after-tax interest rate may cause saving to decrease by 4 percent (see Boskin 1978). While this is a bigger effect of interest rate than that found in most other studies, it is not a huge effect. Moreover, the study, which is based on time series, is subject to the common criticism of all time series studies, that many other variables which might influence saving were not included in the equations. For example, the model assumes that people save largely to finance their expected retirement. During the forty years covered in the study, the age distribution and expected years of retirement have changed markedly. Yet neither the expected years of retirement nor the age distribution is incorporated in the study.

The available empirical evidence on labor supply is also inadequate in many respects. The available studies, however, suggest that the percentage change in hours worked for a 10 percent change in wages seems to be even smaller than 4 percent for prime age males, but greater than 4 percent for women and non–prime age males (Break 1979). The tax effects may not be limited to the quantity of labor. High tax rates may induce people to expend less effort on the job and to avoid positions with great burdens and responsibilities. There is little empirical evidence on this issue.

The other major reason given for advocating a consumption tax is that it yields more equitable results. For example, it is often noted that there are some individuals with very high income who take advantage of various loopholes and pay no income taxes. Similarly, some people conceal illegally obtained income, or don't report all their legally obtained income. Yet individuals in all these groups eat, drink, buy clothes, etc., and would find it more difficult to avoid a consumption tax levied as a sales tax. While a sales tax has many attractive features, it has the severe disadvantage that it is difficult to make the tax schedule anything but proportional.[7] Of course, it is possible to implement a progressive consumption tax by imposing a tax on income minus saving, but this requires a definition of both income and saving. Will income be defined differently than now? I doubt it.[8] Moreover, suppose it was desired to have as progressive a tax rate in a consumption tax as in an income tax system. If the ratio of consumption to income falls as income increases, it may be necessary to have marginal tax rates on consumption increase sharply. Kaldor (1955), for example, presents examples in which the marginal tax rate on consumption exceeds 100 percent. Such high tax rates would give people substantial incentives to substitute home production for goods worked for and bought in the marketplace. It is also worth noting that a consumption tax will fall more heavily than an income tax on young people who generally save little or are in debt.

I conclude, therefore, that on both equity and efficiency grounds a consumption tax is no better than a well-designed income tax, and probably is inferior to it (see Mieszkowski, Chapter 2, who reaches somewhat different conclusions). In the next section, we will consider the actual design of the current income tax system, and some important respects in which the system is far from ideal.

THE INTERRELATION OF TAX BASE AND THE TAX RATE SCHEDULE

Any tax system consists of a set of rules which define what is to be taxed (the tax base), and the tax rate that is to be applied to the tax base. Congress, tax lawyers, tax accountants, and lobbyists spend much time and resources in evaluating the costs and benefits associated with various definitions of the tax base and descriptions of the tax rate schedule.

With R as the tax revenue and B as the tax base, the average tax rate $(\bar{t})$ is

$$(1)\ \bar{t} = R/B$$

The marginal tax is given by the change in revenues divided by the change in the base:

$$(2)\ \Delta t = \Delta R/\Delta B$$

There is an important interconnection between the tax base and the tax rate schedule. Suppose for the moment that we assume that the same amount of tax revenues will be collected under all types of tax base and tax rate schedules. Then, from equation 1, we see that the lower the tax base, the higher the average tax rate required to raise the revenues. But many important choices made by taxpayers depend on the average—or, really, the marginal—tax rates. For example, a higher tax rate will affect labor supply, the supply of savings, and the willingness to bear risk.

Under the current law, the tax base differs greatly from the definition of income or ability to pay discussed earlier. For example, Minarik (1977) has calculated the tax base for 1977, using a "comprehensive income" definition.[9] Under his definition, the tax base would have been 27 percent higher than it was in 1977. In addition, limitations on such personal deductions and tax credits as nonbusiness interest, state and local taxes, and medical expenses would be equivalent to raising the tax base by another 25 percent.[10] Thus, a substantially lower average tax would yield the same revenue and more efficiency.[11]

In judging the appropriateness for any personal deduction, tax credit, or preferential treatment of a particular type of income, it is necessary to include the effects on the tax base and the average tax rate.

PERSONAL DEDUCTIONS, EXEMPTIONS, AND TAX CREDITS

Earlier we defined tax revenues as equal to the tax base times the average tax rate. This is a deliberately oversimplified view of the tax system. A more realistic picture is that income received is reduced by the sum of the value of personal exemptions and deductions to arrive at taxable income. The final tax liability depends upon this taxable income, the tax rate schedule, and tax credits. In this section, we will discuss the need for and the appropriateness of the deductions, exemptions, and tax credits, ending with a comparison of credits and deductions. Given space limitations, we will have to be very selective in our coverage. Fortunately, an informative and reasonably nontechnical paper by Due (1977) examines the issues in detail.

Two basic rationales are advanced for exemptions, deductions, and credits. The first is that income does not provide the best estimate of ability to pay. The second encourages individuals to undertake certain expenditures which generate social advantages that exceed private advantages.

Refining Ability to Pay

Income can be a poor measure of ability to pay for two different reasons. First, a taxpaying unit may be forced to incur large expenses which other units are not forced to incur. Examples include cost of a medical operation or a casualty loss.[12] These expenditures reduce a person's discretionary income, which should reduce the call of the state upon him.

Second, to earn his living, the employee at times must pay certain costs. For nonwage income, the law only imposes a tax on income minus the expenses incurred in generating these revenues. For example, brokers' fees are deducted from investment income. Net earnings should be the employee's tax base, as profit is the tax base for a business. Possible examples of this type of expense include the unreimbursed travel costs of a salesman, professional dues, and perhaps costs for child care incurred so that a parent can work.

There is no doubt that ability to pay is reduced by large medical bills, and by theft or destruction of a large amount of property. However, the actual provisions in the tax code do not limit deductions to large, atypical, dollar amounts. For example, a person can deduct all casualty losses in excess of $100 per episode, medical expenses in excess of 3 percent of adjusted gross income,[13] and half of medical insurance premiums up to $150. Yet most taxpayers expect to pay medical bills and to suffer some breakage and loss in property. For an average family with income in excess of $15,000, its ability to pay is not reduced significantly by a car accident that takes $250 to repair. I also don't see why up to $150 of medical insurance premiums is either large or unexpected. Thus, in this area, I would recommend that unreimbursed medical expenses and casualty losses only be deductible to the extent that their sum exceeds 7 percent of adjusted gross income.

Investments in Human Capital

It is sometimes argued that current expenditures on education and other forms of investment in human capital should be recognized as a cost of acquiring such capital. Advocates of this view also argue that these costs either be deducted from current earnings, or be depreciated and applied against future earnings. While it is true that the acquisition of human capital is similar to the acquisition of physical capital, there are some important differences that argue against the treatment suggested above. First, for education and many other types of investment in human capital, a major cost item is earnings foregone while investing. Even including summer jobs, for example, college students seldom work more than 1,200 hours a year. For full-time workers not in college, annual hours worked would exceed 2,300. At a salary of $4 per hour, the foregone earnings would be at least $4,400, which is close to the tuition of Ivy League schools.

Conceptually, these foregone earnings should be counted as both current income and as investment costs. The skills acquired in college and elsewhere have a much longer life than one year; hence, the total investment cost should be depreciated rather than expensed. The current tax treatment, in effect, allows the investor in human capital to depreciate instantaneously that part of his investment costs that constitute his foregone earnings. As argued in the section on accelerated depreciation, the government provides a tax advantage in the form of an interest-free loan if tax depreciation is more rapid than actual depreciation. Thus, the current tax law probably subsidizes investments in human capital. Yet it is doubtful if the law will ever be changed to include a tax on foregone earnings. Since college tuition generally does not cover costs, and since foregone earnings receive very favorable treatment, I don't see the need for depreciation of tuition charges or for tax credits.

The second problem with the treatment of expenditures on education as a cost of earning of living is that people go to college to acquire both work-related and nonwork-related skills and attributes.[14] Presumably, only the work-related share of the expenditures should be deducted or depreciated. But arriving at the proper allocation would be a severe problem.

Dependents

The tax code currently allows a deduction of $750 per dependent, and a tax credit of either $35 per person or 2 percent of taxable income up to $180.[15] The rationale for these provisions is that a taxpaying unit with the same money income and more mouths to feed is less able to contribute to the communal fund.

There are, however, two fundamental difficulties with the dependency deductions and credits. First, there have been periods as long as twenty years during which the value of an exemption remained constant, even though real income and prices increased substantially. Presumably, since higher prices increase the cost of feeding, clothing, and nurturing children and other family members, the rationale advanced above is suspect. Second, the theoretical argument ignores the available evidence that, to a large part, man and woman choose their family size. If two families have the same money income but a different number of children, then the two families have chosen to allocate their budgets differently. In general, it is only atypical expenditures forced on the taxpayer that reduce ability to pay. Thus, purely on ability-to-pay grounds, I don't think that there should be a deduction or tax credit for family size.[16] Of course, there may be social benefits from a larger or a smaller population, but at this time there is little evidence to suggest whether the United States population size and growth is above or below optimum.

Two other major deductions are the interest paid on home mortgage and other nonbusiness-related activities, and state and local taxes. People are not forced to incur mortgages, and they pay the interest in lieu of rent. Similarly, people are not forced to buy on credit. The major reason given for this deduction is thus the difficulty involved in separating nonbusiness and business-related income. For example, businessmen and investors sometimes mortgage their houses or obtain personal loans to acquire investment capital. These businessmen and investors, however, pay taxes on the income from such investments, and it is proper that only net income be taxed.[17]

This suggests that it would be better to input income to owner-occupied housing (based on assessed values), and let the individual deduct his interest and real estate taxes. Then the tax could be imposed on net income. This does not solve the problem of nonmortgage interest, but without mortgage interest deductions, I don't think interest would be a major itemized deduction (especially if the standard deduction is retained).

The tax deductibility of state and local taxes is also suspect on ability-to-pay grounds. All taxpayers pay such taxes, and receive benefits from state and local taxes. The current treatment, moreover, is an incentive to wealthy communities to adopt local socialism. For example, a "bus" service of chauffeured limousines for each family, paid for by local taxes, would be deductible. However, this deduction may be justified on the grounds that society does not want to impose excessive burdens on taxpayers. With the top tax bracket rate in the federal income tax at 70 percent, some individuals could face marginal tax rates close to 100 percent if there were nondeductible state and local taxes. Within a federal system, probably the only feasible way to handle this problem is to allow a deduction of those state and local taxes that exceed, say, 10 percent of adjusted gross income.

Social Benefits

The other major reason advanced for granting personal deductions and tax credits is that certain types of expenditures or activities provide benefits to society over and above the benefits received by the individual. Since individuals generally allocate their budget on the basis of the relative prices of various goods, the government can influence behavior by changing relative prices. A person in a 40 percent tax bracket who is given a charitable deduction of $1 reduces his taxes by $0.40, and the effective after-tax price of charity falls from $1 to $0.60. Provided it can be shown both that such extra social benefits occur, and that people increase purchases significantly when the effective after-tax price declines, it would make sense to be given tax credits. To make sure that there was periodic review of the facts and the amounts involved, each such credit should have a sunset provision.

Charitable contributions are currently permitted as a deduction.[18] A case can be made that various eleemosynary activities provide social benefits. In addition, the availability of many private charities, colleges, foundations, etc., allows individuals to support those activities they personally choose, and provides useful competition to similar government-controlled agencies. However, this competition and diversity is bought at the price of large fund-raising and administrative costs.[19] Also, many so-called charitable contributions have been used to increase the donors' income or consumption.[20]

Even if one decides that there are extra social benefits from private charity that are worth these costs, the question remains whether the current tax treatment increases contributions. The empirical evidence on the extra giving that occurs because of the deductibility of charitable contributions is mixed.[21]

Personally, I would be willing to continue the deductibility of charity, with two important changes. First, I would permit as a deduction only those amounts in excess of, say, 5 percent of income. Amounts less than that are not, in my opinion, affected by their deductibility or price. Second, I would treat the contribution of appreciated assets as a constructive realization of the gain, and tax this gain.[22]

In many ways, the social benefits argument for allowing deductions for charity is stronger than for most other items. Thus, I would be prepared to eliminate all deductions and credits advocated on social benefit grounds, unless compelling evidence is provided on both the existence of social benefits and on their responsiveness to price deductions.

We have been examining the rationale for various deductions and tax credits without asking whether it is better to give a deduction or a credit. I agree with Due (1977) that if the intent is to refine income to better match ability to pay, then a deduction is in order. A credit is more appropriate when there are excess social benefits, and when taxpayers at all income levels are equally responsive to price reductions.

TAXATION OF INCOME FROM NONHUMAN CAPITAL

In this section, we examine the actual treatment of returns to capital; the following section contains a corresponding analysis of the treatment of human capital and/or wage and salary income. The major provisions in the code which reduce the effective rate on capital income are: the tax-free status of state and local bonds; the postponement of taxation of capital gains until the gains are realized; the taxation of only one-half of long-term capital gains; immediate deduction of intangible costs of exploration and depletion allowances for various raw materials; accelerated depreciation; the asset depreciation range system; the investment tax credit.

Some general rationales are offered for this "boodle" of preferences.[23] One is to encourage or to reduce the discouragement of saving and investment. Another is to overcome the ravages of inflation. A third general rationale is to restore equity with some other type of capital income which was previously accorded more generous terms.

Incentives to Capital Formation

Three reasons are advanced as to why it is necessary to encourage saving and investment.[24] First, it is argued that income and other taxes have reduced economic efficiency by distorting consumption/saving choices. This argument is essentially the consumption-versus-income tax debate considered above. As the reader will recall, we concded that there is no compelling evidence that the loss in economic efficiency is greater with an income tax.

Second, it is sometimes argued that saving and investment confer certain benefits or externalities on society which are not taken into account by individual savers; hence, there will be too little saving and growth in the economy. One major social benefit is that it is easier politically to redistribute income when earnings are rising quickly, since those paying for more redistribution still have increased disposable income. While there is a superficial appeal to this argument, it can be rephrased in another, more damning way. Most wealth other than that in pension funds is held by upper-income individuals. Thus, a policy that reduces taxes on returns to capital in order to finance growth and redistribution is one which increases the burden of the middle class in paying for the redistribution. Rather than taxing the middle class, the government could impose higher taxes on the returns to capital, and make all the extra tax revenue available to a development bank to finance private investment.

Third, it is sometimes argued that the current generation saves too little, because it does not consider the needs of future generations. There is no empirical evidence on this point, but if true, Congress could just as easily provide for a development bank to encourage investment as it does tax cuts on returns from capital to encourage private saving.

As explained in more detail in the chapter by Shoven, inflation can distort the income figures and, in effect, cause the income tax to be imposed on capital. However, the above boodle of preferences is poorly designed to undo the effects of inflation. For example, the value of most of the capital income preferences don't vary with the rate of inflation, and were in the tax code even in those bygone days when the inflation rate was near zero. It would be much simpler to undo the effects of inflation through an inflation adjustment like that described by Shoven (Chapter 8).

I wholeheartedly endorse the argument that it is unfair for Congress not to give me a plum as big as the biggest one it gave anyone else. However, since Congress has not enacted a Taubman amendment to cover my personal situation, I also endorse the proposition that, rather than spreading plums around, Congress should be asked to eliminate those given to others.

Incentives to Physical Investment

At this point, let us examine some of these preferences in a bit more detail. We begin with three incentives to investing in physical investment. The investment tax credit, accelerated depreciation, and the asset depreciation range system all act to reduce the present discounted value of corporate and non-corporate income taxes.[25] The investment tax credit allows a firm to claim against its tax liability a credit currently set at 10 percent of the purchase price of qualified investments. Qualified investments include equipment, cattle, and movie films, but—as of this writing—exclude buildings; moreover, to be fully qualified, equipment must have a useful life of at least seven years.[26] The value of the investment tax credit is zero for firms not currently liable for taxes; and greatest for those with the highest marginal tax rates.[27] Thus, it is not surprising that a market has grown up where individuals in 60 percent and 70 percent tax brackets "buy" airplanes and trains and "rent" them to airlines and railroads, where renters agree to pay all the maintenance and operating expenses, and where the renters and buyers split the extra tax saving obtained by the buyer.

Accelerated depreciation is often identified with systems such as double-declining balance, in which annual depreciation deductions initially are larger than those available under a straight-line system. In these systems, assets are written off faster than straight line. Since assets may depreciate faster or slower than straight line, a more meaningful definition of accelerated depreciation is one that compares tax depreciation allowances with actual or "true" depreciation. If tax depreciation is faster than true, the investor benefits by postponing tax payments, or by having an interest-free loan. Congress introduced double-declining balance and other faster than straight-line depreciation systems in 1954, partly because of information compiled by Terborgh (1953) on the age profile of prices of eight types of equipment traded in second-hand markets. There is not a good second-hand market for most types of business equipment; hence, it usually is not possible to say if double-declining balance methods are correct or not for equipment. There is available, however, information on buildings, which suggests that these assets depreciate more slowly than straight line (see Taubman 1978).

The asset depreciation range (ADR) system is a method which, on average, allows firms to depreciate assets over a shorter period of time than the actual useful life of the asset. Shortening the tax life both speeds up depreciation and confers an interest-free loan. Under the ADR system, the tax life for an asset is based upon a survey on tax lives claimed by taxpayers. For a given asset or a given industry, a distribution of lives was calculated, from the shortest to the longest. Under ADR, the reference tax life for taxpayers is generally the life that was chosen by the firm at the 30th percentile in the distribution, i.e., a life shorter than median. However, taxpayers can choose any life within a range of plus or minus 20 percent of this reference life.[28] The ADR system operates in an unusual fashion, in that little or no benefit is given to the firms at or below the 30th percentile in the life distribution.[29] A consequence of ADR is that inefficient management who keep equipment too long receive a subsidy, and their after-tax profit performance will not differ as much from more efficient management; hence, ADR reduces the incentive to introduce new technology embodied in new equipment.

These three incentive systems are often thought of as substitutes for one another, because each tends to reduce the effective price of an investment below the market price. Yet a closer examination of the details of each system indicates substantial disparities in the treatment of various types of investments. For example, the investment tax credit does not apply to buildings, and does not apply fully to equipment with a useful life less than seven years. Under ADR, the difference between tax lives and actual lives depends in part on how compact the distribution of lives is. Moreover, for any given asset, the tax benefits of accelerated depreciation also are greatest for those whose true depreciation differs most from the tax pattern. Is there any rhyme or reason to the various differential preferences in these provisions? No.[30]

I am far from convinced by the previous arguments that it is necessary to subsidize capital. However, if Congress really thinks it necessary to subsidize physical investment, it could greatly simplify the tax code and reduce the patchwork quilt of differential preferences by giving a general investment tax credit, eliminate ADR, and set tax depreciation rates to conform as closely as possible with true depreciation.[31]

Incentives to Minerals

There are a number of provisions in the tax code whose avowed purpose is to encourage the exploration for and supply of various minerals. Two important provisions are the immediate expensing of intangible costs for exploration, drilling, and development, and the percentage depletion allowances.[32] The reader will recall that income is defined as consumption plus change in net worth. The depletion allowance is not based on the original investment cost, nor on the extent to which the stock (or reserve) of the mineral—and, thus, net worth—is reduced, but is based on a share of gross revenues. Therefore, it is often possible to have depletion allowances many times the original investment costs, and to reduce taxable income below true income. Similar comments apply to the immediate expensing provision.

The depletion rate varies by type of mineral and by size of firm. Again, there seems to be no rational economic explanation to account for the differences by mineral, though, in the *Rape of the Taxpayer,* Stern (1974) provides a political explanation.

The overall effect of the depletion provision is difficult to analyze, since the law can affect the price firms are willing to pay for leases, the recovery rate of the mineral, the total amount that can be recovered, the amount and type of exploration, and the price at which the mineral is sold.

Capital Gains[33]

Realized capital gains are defined as the difference between the selling price and the "basis" of a financial or real asset.[34] The basis is generally the original purchase price minus accumulated depreciation. The tax treatment of realized capital gains depends upon how long the seller has owned the asset. Currently, if an asset is held less than a year, the gain is short term and is taxed as ordinary income. If held longer than a year, the gain is long term and is subject to the following complicated, preferential treatment. First, the short-term losses in excess of short-term gains are subtracted from the long-term gains minus long-term losses. Then one-half of such net gains is included in the tax base, except that the taxpayer may choose to use an alternative tax under which the first $50,000 of such net gains are taxed at a rate of 25 percent. The other half of long-term capital gains is included in the income subject to the minimum tax. The amount of earned income eligible for the 50 percent maximum tax rate is reduced by excluded long-term capital gains. Finally, when a person dies there is no income tax on unrealized gains, but the person who inherits the asset also inherits the original or 31 December 1976 basis.[35]

The alternative tax was originally proposed to benefit individuals with modest amounts of gains. However, as enacted, it is of primary benefit to those in tax brackets greater than 50 percent. There seems little reason to continue this provision.

The minimum tax, and the linkage to the maximum tax on earned income, have reduced the difference in the tax rate applied to capital gains and ordinary income. However, since gains are taxed only when realized, the tax code still gives a substantial preference to capital gains. It is possible to tax accrued gains, or to treat the time between the gain and realization as a period during which the government has made a loan on which interest should be charged. In the context of a plan to integrate the corporate and personal income tax, Taubman and Shoven (1978) indicate that an accrued capital gains tax (with adjustment for inflation) is more desirable than a realized capital gains tax. The accrued version, for example, does not affect decisions to sell assets on which there is a gain, while the realized gain version discourages sales.

The particular reasons advanced for the preferred treatment of capital gains are to increase the flow of funds to new and risky businesses, and to reduce the impact of the progressive tax rate schedule on a large and irregular income component. While it may be true that new and risky funds are required to pay a premium to obtain funds, capital gain provisions are not limited to such firms, but are even applicable to Treasury Bonds bought at a discount. Much less costly ways could be found to encourage the start of new and risky businesses. Income averaging would provide appropriate relief for the second problem.

Since I see no particular efficiency and equity benefits flowing from capital gains, and since there are substantial equity, efficiency, and record-keeping costs, I would treat all accrued gains adjusted for inflation as ordinary income.

PREFERENCES FOR EARNED INCOME

Earned income consists of wages, salaries, commissions, royalties, and other payments for labor services. Several provisions in the tax code allow a person to reduce or postpone tax payments on earned income. The most important items are the maximum tax and pension plans.

The maximum tax is 50 percent of earned income.[36] The major reason given for this provision is that no more than half the hard-won toils of labor should go to the government. Returns to capital, not being produced by such toil, can be more heavily taxed. While toils of working has a nice, poetic ring, my judgment is that a single or joint file, whose earnings are such that taxable income exceeds $40,200 or $55,200, suffers as much from working as an investor who has saved. If workers should contribute no more than 50 percent, investors also should not pay more than 50 percent.

The law allows individuals to postpone paying taxes on funds contributed to qualified company pension plans, IRA accounts, and Keough Plans, and the accumulated interest thereon, until pensions are paid. The tax advantages arise because the person postpones paying taxes, and is generally in a lower tax bracket after retirement. Since the maximum contributions which are tax free are 15 percent to 20 percent of annual earnings, most individuals could shelter most of their saving from taxes. Thus, the income tax system is a consumption tax for many people.

THE ACCOUNTING PERIOD

The current tax code generally defines the tax base in terms of earnings and deductions that occur in a particular year. There are, however, two major exceptions to this rule. First, there are limits on the amount of certain deductions, capital losses, and tax credits that can be claimed in one year, though some excess deductions can be applied against some previous and future years' income. Second, taxpayers now can use a five-year averaging system, in which it is assumed that the average taxable income received during the last five years was spread evenly during those years.[37] The tax liability is equal to five times the tax due on this average income, minus taxes paid in the last four years. This averaging system was instituted because, with a progressive income tax, over time a person with a fluctuating income will pay more taxes than another person with the same average income. For example, suppose the tax system is that given in Table 1. A person who always had $15,000 taxable income would pay $2,000 a year. A person whose income fluctuated, taking on the values of $10,000, $15,000, and $20,000 once every three years, would have an average annual tax liability of $2,167. Thus, the person with fluctuating income would pay on average 8 percent more taxes, though he is not in any better position.

In judging whether or not an annual accounting period imposes a serious burden and, if it is a burden, whether five-year averaging is a satisfactory solution, it is useful to have some information about the stability of a unit's annual taxable income. There is relatively little direct evidence on this subject.[38] However, some estimates are available on the earnings, which constitute about 70 percent to 75 percent of income and are more stable than income. During a seven-year span, Lillard and Willis (1978) indicate that about 70 percent of the variance in a male's earnings represents variance across individuals, in average or ''permanent'' earnings, while the remaining 30 percent represents year-to-year variation around each individual's average. Over periods of time as long as fourteen years, the correlation of individual earnings is less than .5 (see Schiller [1977] or Taubman and Wales [1973]). This suggests that averaging is needed, and that five years is too short.

In a world where tax laws never changed and all people were always single, it would be easy to establish a workable lifetime averaging system. As Vickery showed (1939), the only information required would be total income and taxes paid in previous years and ages. The Treasury could easily maintain the data by updating last year's totals with this year's information, and could print out the information on previous income and taxes on each person's tax form. When

Table 1

Hypothetical Tax Liability

Taxable Income	Tax Brackets	Bracket Tax Rate	Total Liability
$10,000	0/$10,000	10%	$1,000
$15,000	$10,001/$15,000	20%	$2,000
$20,000	$15,001/$20,000	30%	$3,500

tax laws change, or people marry and divorce, things are more complicated. However, this problem is not insurmountable with modern computer technology. The Social Security System now maintains a record from 1951 to date of annual covered earnings and taxes paid for each person with a social security number. The Internal Revenue Service (IRS) could do the same, and could even recompute what taxes would have been in, say, 1960 with the existing tax rate structure. The IRS could also allocate the tax equally between husband and wife who file jointly to maintain separate records for each.

HOW PROGRESSIVE A RATE SCHEDULE?

The current tax rate schedule begins at 14 percent of positive taxable income, and reaches 70 percent on taxable income at about $102,000 and $203,000 for individuals and families, respectively.[39] While this conjures up an image of average tax burdens rising rapidly with income, various provisions in the income tax code cause the average federal income tax rate ($\bar{t}$ in equation 1) for groups of people to rise only gradually, and to be about constant over wide ranges (for example, see

Okner [1978]). There is, however, a wide disparity in the average tax rate paid by people with the same income level.

Is a top bracket rate of 70 percent too high or too low? In part, this is a question of what is vertical equity. As noted earlier, the answer to this equity question depends on the sacrifice criteria to be used, and how rapidly society thinks the utility of consumption decreases. But in judging the 70 percent question, it also is important to consider the efficiency and feasibility implications. Lewellyn's (1968) study clearly indicates that top corporate management spend time and invest resources to minimize their own tax burden. There is also abundant evidence to indicate that wealthy individuals buy into tax shelters to reduce their taxes. Lower tax rates would reduce the need to invest resources to minimize tax burdens, and these resources could be put to more productive uses. The high tax rates may also discourage labor supply and savings, though, as noted earlier, the empirical evidence on the size of the effects is far from definitive. It would be possible, however, to reduce the marginal tax rates while retaining the same average rate by reducing loopholes, tax preferences, and deductions. It is hard to see how such a step would have harmful effects on the economy or on society.

THE TAXPAYING UNIT

There are some difficult problems involved in deciding whose income and deductions should be combined in calculating taxable income, and whether the tax rate schedule should vary by the composition of the unit.[40] Under current law, a taxpaying unit consists of either a single individual or a married couple filing a joint return. Different tax rate schedules apply to single individuals, unmarried heads of households, and married couples filing joint returns.

To understand the difficulties and a potential way to overcome these problems, it is useful first to consider the reasons for the three different tax rate schedules. Before 1948 there was only one tax rate schedule which, like the current one, had higher rates as income increased. In the early postwar period, some wealthy families from community property states filed returns in which each spouse claimed half the income. This practice was upheld by the Supreme Court; therefore, to restore equity to married residents of noncommunity property states, Congress amended the tax law so that married couples filing jointly were subject to a new rate schedule in which the tax brackets (within which rates were constant) were twice as big as for single people. By doing so, Congress extended income-splitting to all married couples. But by thus restoring equity among all married taxpayers, Congress caused single persons with the same money income to pay higher taxes than a married couple.[41] Currently the differential is as large as $12,110.

Under an ability-to-pay approach, to justify higher taxes for the single person with the same money income, he or she must have greater discretionary income. Since two cannot live as cheaply as one, and since the extra expenditures of married couples are often on necessities such as food and clothing, the single person would have greater discretionary income.[42] On the other hand, since spouses can provide services for each other that a single person may have to buy, it is possible that a couple with the same money income as a single person has more utility or total income. Even if it is judged that a couple has more expenses, it still must be decided if the extra taxes paid by the single person should increase with the level of income. The ability-to-pay doctrine sometimes distinguishes between minimum and other needs in calculating discretionary income. The extra minimum needs of the couple could be met by a fixed dollar deduction or credit rather than by splitting income, whereby a family with income of $200,000 pays $12,110 less taxes than a single individual with the same income.[43]

In 1969 the tax code was amended so that a single person would not pay taxes in excess of 120 percent of those paid by a married couple. While this amendment reduced taxes paid by single people, and perhaps restored equity between married couples and a single person with the same taxable income, it also established the so-called "marriage tax penalty." This penalty arises when both the male and female members of a family receive an income. There are situations in which the unit's taxes will be greater if the couple is married than if they were unmarried but living together. The amount of the marriage tax penalty tends to be greatest for a couple with a large income contributed equally by each. As shown in McIntyre and Oldman (1977:230), married couples with $30 to $40 thousand in taxable income may pay 3 percent to 4 percent more in taxes than an unmarried couple with the same income.

To make matters more complicated, there is also an important efficiency difficulty. As noted earlier, the labor force participation and hours worked by women, and especially married women, is positively related to the after-tax wage rate received by women. Most men between the ages of twenty-five and fifty-four are continuously in the labor force, but now only one-half of the married women work in any year. Thus, for many women who are deciding whether to work and, if so, for how many hours, the effective tax rate on their wages begins at the top income tax rate paid by their husbands, to which must be added the social security tax rate. Thus, a married woman faces higher taxes than an unmarried woman living with someone or by herself.

We began this section by noting that one issue is to determine whose income should be combined in calculating taxable income. Implicit in our subsequent discussion is that people who pool their resources should be taxed on the pooled income. Again, this can be justified on ability-to-pay grounds, as it seems almost certainly true that there are economies of scale in the use of food, housing, television sets, etc. Such economies of scale presumably occur for both unmarried and married couples of mixed and the same sex.

Yet it is not administratively feasible to determine which unmarried couples pool resources.

The definition and treatment of the taxpaying unit involve
complicated problems of equity, efficiency, and feasibility. I
doubt that there is any practical way of resolving all the issues. It is possible to improve the situation with the following
plan:

(1) A married couple can choose to file either a joint return or
two separate returns.

(2) Joint returns will be subject to a tax rate schedule that will
have brackets (within which rates are constant) only one-half
as wide as the brackets for single persons.

(3) Married couples who file separate returns must allocate all
deductions on the basis of their adjusted gross income, except
for their own medical expenses.

(4) Married couples who file separate returns must split all
nonwage and salary income on the basis of legal ownership,
with income from jointly owned assets split in half.

Item 2 by itself will insure that married couples in community property and noncommunity property states will be
treated equally. This item will also mean that couples filing
jointly will pay the same taxes as an equally situated single
person. Items 1, 3, and 4 will insure that there is no married
tax penalty.

There are, however, some drawbacks to the proposal. Married couples who would choose to file separately presumably
would do so because their taxes are lowered. Thus, there may
be some instances in which married couples with the same
income pay different taxes. To reduce this possibility, an
extra deduction could be given to joint return filers, but I
don't recommend this, since this group will include those
couples with only one working spouse—a group which presumably has more nonmoney income. Taxes will be lowered
most for those couples both of whose members have approximately equal incomes. Thus, families will have a tendency

to transfer legal ownership of income-yielding assets to the spouse with the lower earnings. If the current high divorce rates don't check this activity, it would be possible to replace item 4 with an alternative that splits all nonwage and salary family income equally, regardless of legal ownership. The disadvantage of this alternative provision is that one cannot impose the equal splitting of nonwage income on unmarried couples. Thus, some couples will still be subject to a marriage tax penalty.

6

LAURENCE J. KOTLIKOFF

Social Security, Time for Reform[1]

Public dissatisfaction with social security laws. Initial purpose and mechanism. Regressive features of social security tax. Unfunded financing. Link between contributions and benefits. Income transfer—intergenerational and intragenerational. Eligibility, and the earnings test. Practical reforms.

The social security system is currently the object of intense public concern and academic scrutiny. This concern reflects the enormous growth in social security taxes and benefits in the last twenty years, as well as prospects for substantially higher social security taxes in the near future. Since 1960 the combined employee and employer social security tax rate has doubled from 6 percent to 12.1 percent. Over half of the nation's income recipients now pay more social security taxes than federal income taxes (Campbell 1977: xiii). During this period, the number of social security recipients has more than doubled, and benefits—including retirement, disability, and old age health insurance payments—have almost quadrupled in real terms.

In the past year, Congress has passed and the president has signed major new social security legislation requiring substantially higher social security tax contributions for many Americans, and radically changing the formula under which social security benefits will be calculated in the future. The new law represents the most important social security legislation enacted since the program was established in 1935: it spells out the nature of the social security system through the turn of the century and beyond. However, public reaction to the higher social security payroll taxes provided in the new law has led some members of Congress to propose its repeal. Thus, the future nature of the social security system is still quite undecided. The social security system stands today at a crossroads. The paths lying before it branch out according to the choice of financing and the size and structuring of benefits. Each path has different implications for economic efficiency and interpersonal equity. A prudent choice of paths requires knowledge of the purpose and history of the social security system, as well as an examination of its impact on the efficiency and equity of our economy.

This chapter will briefly discuss the rationale for the social security system, and sketch the structure and enormous historic growth of the program. An outline of the provisions of the new social security legislation will provide a background for consideration of three major social security issues, the extent of interpersonal fairness or equity within the system, the effect of social security on savings and aggregate capital accumulation, and the extent to which social security reduces labor supply. The final section of the paper suggests reforms that would increase both the equity and efficiency of the social security system.

THE ROLE OF THE SOCIAL SECURITY SYSTEM AND ITS RATIONALE

While the social security system provides disability and health insurance, engages in inter- and intragenerational income redistribution, and provides supplemental welfare payments to the aged, its main role is to force people to accumulate for their old age. It is important to keep in mind this primary function of social security—requiring people to save for their old age—when considering proposals to "reform" social security. Some proposals and, indeed, some provisions of the current legislation contravene the main purpose of social security.

Social security was initiated in 1935 in the middle of the Great Depression. The high unemployment rates of the time, and the failure of financial institutions, resulted in large numbers of indigent aged people. Social security was designed to protect future generations of the aged from the vagaries of macroeconomic fluctuations and the concommitant loss of employment by requiring savings in the form of payroll tax contributions when young; these contributions would then be returned in the form of annuitized benefits when old. While the system was not set up on a strictly individualized basis, guaranteeing a return of principle plus interest on tax contributions, the original concept and the actual system today is strongly based on the individual. The system is not now and has never been simply a tax transfer scheme in which benefits received are unrelated to past tax contributions.

Social security requires savings of individuals who might otherwise imprudently, but with full knowledge, arrive at retirement with no means of support, and it also insures indi-

viduals against the uncertain length of one's working life. An
unexpected decline in health (short of complete disability),
motivation, or stamina, the loss of relative productivity due
to unanticipated technological change, along with economic
recessions, make the exact age of retirement uncertain for
many individuals.

While much more empirical work must be done to determine conclusively the extent to which individuals "irration-
ally" undersave, and hence "need" social security to save
for them, Peter Diamond (1977) has presented some initial
evidence pointing in that direction. Diamond analyzes the
asset positions of individuals at the age of retirement, and
finds that over 35 percent accumulated substantially less
wealth than appears prudent. There is also evidence suggesting that the exact age at which one retires is highly uncertain.
I compared the 1966 expectations of retirement age of 1,787
working men aged 45 to 59 with their actual behavior and
new retirement expectations in 1973; over 52 percent of these
men either retired earlier than they expected in 1966, failed to
retire in accord with their 1966 expectations, or changed their
expected age of retirement (Kotlikoff 1977). Whether due to
myopic planning or unanticipated random events forcing
early retirement, many individuals might find themselves destitute in old age in the absence of social security.

THE STRUCTURE OF SOCIAL SECURITY TAXES

Since its inception, social security benefit payments have
been financed by a proportional payroll tax on labor earnings
up to a specified ceiling. The inaugural legislation called for a
1 percent tax contribution from both employers and
employees on earnings up to $3,000. Today the OASDHI
(Old Age Survivors, Disability and Health Insurance) tax is
6.05 percent each for both employer and employee on earn-

ings up to $17,700. Of the combined 12.1 percent payroll tax, 1.1 percent is used to finance the "HI"—Medicare—portion of social security.

There is virtually universal agreement among economists that the distinction between the employee and employer contribution has no long-run economic significance. Whether the employer mails in the social security tax check or the employee mails in the tax check, total labor costs facing the employer equal the employee's after–social security tax wage plus the combined social security tax payment. Employers take the total of labor costs into account when determining how much labor to employ. Assuming competitive conditions and fixed supplies of capital and labor, increases in either the employee's or employer's social security tax will reduce the net wage received by labor; in economic jargon, the burden or incidence of the tax will fall on labor. As will be discussed below, however, social security may alter the long-run supplies of both labor and capital in such a manner as to shift more than 100 percent of the tax onto labor; i.e., the long-run gross (before tax) wage may be reduced because of social security.

Considered in isolation, the social security payroll tax is regressive, since tax payments as a fraction of earnings fall—for levels of earnings—above the taxable ceiling. However, since the social security benefit schedule rewards low-earner contributors at the expense of high-earner contributors, the system as a whole is much more progressive.[2] Some economists favor replacing the payroll tax with more progressive general revenue financing through the federal income tax.[3] Such a procedure would undermine the individually oriented nature of the system, and have serious disincentive effects on labor supply. While the relationship between taxes paid in and benefits received has changed over time, workers paying into the system could in the past, and can today, anticipate the return of at least principal, if not interest, on their marginal tax contributions.

If the payroll tax were replaced by higher income taxes and
benefits received were not tied to taxes paid in, then payments to social security would be perceived as taxes rather
than as a form of savings. The return to marginal labor effects is already highly taxed under federal, state, and city
income taxes; under the current federal income tax, a married
male with two children, earning an annual income of
$18,000, faces a marginal federal income tax rate of about 22
percent. Marginal state income tax rates average about 2 percent. If we now add a 12.1 percent rate increase for social
security, the individual will end up paying $0.36 in taxes on
the last dollar earned. Maintaining the link between social
security taxes paid and benefits received, and the perception
of these taxes not as taxes but as a form of saving, will be
even more important in the future. The new social security
amendments call for tax rate increases up to 15.3 percent by
1990. To the extent that additional income redistribution is
politically desirable, the federal income tax rather than the
social security payroll tax is the proper vehicle.[4]

SOCIAL SECURITY BENEFITS

The Social Security Administration calculates retirement benefits on the basis of an average of monthly covered earnings
(earnings subject to taxation) over the worker's lifetime. (The
current computation uses the years after 1950, or after age 21
if later.) A primary insurance amount (PIA) is computed,
which constitutes the worker's own benefit. In addition, dependent and survivor benefits are available for spouses and
children under 18.[5] Dependent benefits equal 50 percent of
the worker's PIA for each dependent up to a maximum family benefit. The survivor benefit equals 100 percent of the
deceased spouse's PIA, and is available to the surviving
spouse and children as well. If both spouses have work his-
tories, dependent and survival benefits are available only to

the extent that they exceed the amount the worker could collect on her or his own account.

Workers may retire at age 62 or beyond and collect permanently lower benefits. For early retirement before age 65, benefits are "actuarially" reduced five-ninths of 1 percent for each month of early retirement. For recipients younger than 72, social security benefits are subject to an earnings test. In 1978 beneficiaries could earn up to $4,000 without foregoing benefits. Beyond the $4,000, the beneficiary loses one dollar of his annual PIA for every two dollars he earns. When he earns enough to exhaust his PIA, he loses all his dependent benefits as well. Beyond age 65, the social security earnings test presents individuals with a 50 percent marginal tax rate on earnings in excess of $4,000 (up to twice the annual PIA); this 50 percent tax is in addition to the regular social security tax, and federal, state, and city income taxes.[6] For some individuals, the combined marginal tax rate on the 4,001st dollar exceeds 100 percent.

HISTORICAL GROWTH OF THE SYSTEM

The 1935 Social Security Act provided compulsory coverage for all private sector (nonrailroad) employees in commerce and industry. Over the years, coverage has been extended to include the self-employed, members of the armed services, and farm workers. Today about 90 percent of jobs are covered under social security; the residual 10 percent corresponds primarily to federal, state, and local government employment.

The original 1935 legislation authorized the accumulation of a large trust fund from tax contributions. This trust fund was meant to invest tax contributions, and to distribute the principal plus interest in the form of social security benefits to past contributors upon retirement. However, the goal of fully funding social security was essentially abandoned with the

1939 amendments. These amendments provided for the payment of benefits to aged persons who had paid little or nothing into the system. In addition, the link between individual tax contributions and individual benefits received was weakened by the provision of dependent benefits. Today the system is essentially unfunded. The 1977 OASDHI trust funds of $49.4 billion were smaller than that year's $84.3 billion OASDHI expenditures; the trust funds are a minor fraction of the more than $1 trillion outstanding social security liabilities (Boskin 1977b).

The unfunded social security financing has been called "pay-as-you-go"; young workers pay into the system, and their tax payments are immediately paid out as current social security benefits. The entire scheme is quite analogous to a chain letter; the benefits that each generation of old people receive depend critically on the willingness of the corresponding young generation to continue the chain by continuing to pay in taxes. When the number of young workers is large relative to the number of retirees, and benefit levels are modest, the tax contribution required from each young worker is small. Within the past few years, however, real benefit levels have risen markedly, due in large part to the 1972 overindexation of benefits to inflation. In addition, the national fertility rate, which reached a post–World War II high of 3.7 children born per woman in 1957, has fallen dramatically; the 1976 figure was 1.8. The lower fertility rates imply that the ratio of workers to retired beneficiaries will fall from a current level of 3.2 to about 2 by the middle of the next century (Cowan 1977:7). The reality of a $3.2 billion excess of benefits over tax receipts in 1976, and the prospects for large short-run and even larger long-run deficits, prompted the 1977 legislation.

THE 1977 SOCIAL SECURITY AMENDMENTS

The new social security legislation addresses both the short-run problem of the proper indexation of benefits for inflation and the longer-run problem of a declining ratio of workers to beneficiaries. A new formula will calculate benefits on the basis of average indexed monthly earnings (AIME). The procedure automatically adjusts for inflation; in addition, the structure of replacement ratios, the ratio of real benefits to past real earnings, will remain constant over time as the economy grows. Hence, as real wages rise due to increases in the productivity of labor, real retirement benefits will rise proportionately. Inflation by itself will not affect any real variables.

To finance these high and rising benefit levels, the legislation calls for increases in the payroll tax rate from its current 12.1 percent value to 15.3 percent by 1990. The major increment in taxes will come, however, from increases in the ceiling on taxable wages. The current ceiling of $17,700 will rise to $31,800 by 1982. Thereafter, the ceiling will increase with increases in average earnings in the economy. This constitutes a very hefty tax increase for the middle class. Assuming a 7 percent inflation rate from now till 1982, $31,800 in 1982 corresponds to $24,275 in 1978 dollars. Social security taxes paid in 1978 on earnings of $24,275 are $2,141.70. Using the 1982 tax rate and ceiling, the tax liability on $24,275 is $3,252.85, representing a real tax increase of 52 percent or $1,111.15 in 1978 dollars.

Even these massive tax increases may prove quite insufficient to finance the program through the first half of the twenty-first century. A. Robertson (1978:21-36), the Chief Actuary of the Social Security Administration, projects that if the current law is maintained up to the year 2025, tax rates would have to increase by more than 8 percent to meet benefit payments. Projecting far into the future is, of course, a hazardous business; still, forecasts of a 23 percent or greater social security tax in 2025 do not augur well for a continuing social security chain letter.

The new law earns points for preserving and strengthening the link between individual contributions and benefits; the higher ceilings on taxable earnings increase the progressivity of the system; and Congress has finally figured out how to correctly adjust benefits for inflation. The new benefit formula is quite simple, and permits workers, for perhaps the first time, to calculate with some precision their expected return on tax contributions. On the other hand, the lawmakers appear unwilling to reduce benefits, or even their rate of growth, in order to mitigate the tax increases. Some leveling-off of benefits appears preferable to the massive tax increases now ordained, and may be necessary to maintain public acceptance of the program. In addition, growth in real benefits is tied to growth in real wages, rather than growth in the real tax base. While the real tax base may increase with average real wages, it need not. For example, a reduction in the labor supply of young workers would raise real wages, and thus benefits; at the same time, the tax base could fall, depending on the elasticity of labor demand. Higher benefits and a lower tax base spell only one thing, higher tax rates.

SOCIAL SECURITY—THE ISSUE OF EQUITY

The redistribution of income both within and across generations has been, and is today, a major feature of social security. The intergenerational redistribution from young to old is associated with the start-up of the system and the unfunded financing. Rather than accumulating a large trust fund, social security tax contributions were immediately paid out as benefits to elderly retirees who had spent few years paying taxes into the system. For single males retiring at age 65 in 1940, 98 percent of benefits received were unearned—i.e., exceeded the return of their tax contributions plus the market rate of interest. For a single male retiring in 1970, 68 percent of benefits were unearned. The annual size of this intergenerational transfer has been enormous, comparable in magnitude to the total of all other government public assistance programs (Parsons and Munro 1977:65-86). The intergenerational redistribution is, however, a steadily diminishing feature of the system. Current age 62 retirees were age 21 in 1937, and some have paid in taxes for forty-one years.

The intragenerational transfers are, on the other hand, an enduring feature and can, in many instances, be characterized as grossly unfair. Within a generation, the system redistributes from males to females, from blacks to whites, from working women to nonworking women, from single people to married couples, from employees to the self-employed, from nongovernment workers to government workers, and from working elderly age 65–72 to nonworking elderly age 65–72.

The male/female and black/white redistribution results from the shorter life expectancy of males relative to females and blacks relative to whites. Using current life tables, the average white male age 26 will live to age 72, while the average white female age 26 will live to age 79. For blacks, the respective figures are 67 and 75 (Census Bureau 1977*b*:66). In Table 1, I estimate the rate of return different single workers will receive on their tax contributions under the new law. The table assumes that work begins at age 26 in 1978 and retirement at age 62; earnings grow from the initial age 26 values at a 2 percent real annual growth rate. Table 1 reports the rate of return the workers would realize if she (he) enjoyed the typical life span for her (his) sex and race.

These numbers are based on assumptions which, if anything, make them uniformly somewhat high.[7] The first point to make is that even under these favorable assumptions, the historically high rates of return arising from the intergeneration transfer will not continue into the future. White single males can anticipate a 2 percent real rate of return on their social security contributions; while not strikingly high, 2 percent compares favorably with the negative real return available today on most savings accounts.

There is a 2.5 percent difference in the rate of return for a white male with initial earnings of $7,000 and a white male with initial earnings of $25,000. This reflects the overall

Table 1

Projected Rates of Return from Social Security

Annual Earnings at Age 26	Male		Female	
	White	Black	White	Black
$ 7,000	.020	−.015	.038	.030
$10,000	.015	−.021	.033	.025
$15,000	.008	−.031	.028	.019
$25,000	−.005	−.050	.017	.007

progressivity of the tax/benefit structure. The male/female and black/white differences are quite large. The dollar equivalents of these different rates of return depend on how one compares dollars receivable in the future with dollars received today, i.e., on the choice of discount rates. At a zero percent discount rate, the redistribution from black to white males age 26, earning $10,000 initially, is $36,580. In other words, the social security system can be thought of as handing the typical white male $36,580 more than the typical black male at age 26. At a 5 percent discount rate, the redistribution is $4,167, and at 10 percent, it is $477. Hence, exactly what one makes of these different rates of return depends on the choice of discount rate. Correcting these distributional anomalies by paying higher benefits to—or collecting lower taxes from—males relative to females and blacks relative to whites appears infeasible. Since the extent of the redistribution is proportional to the scale of the system, these comparisons are, therefore, very important for choosing the optimal size of social security.

The table assumes that black and white mortality is independent of income. This may be invalid; to some extent the lower black life expectancy may reflect the lower income levels of blacks. There is very little solid evidence on the relationship between mortality and income, but what evidence is available suggests that poor people do have much shorter life spans (Kitagawa and Hauser 1973; HEW 1975*a*). Until we understand more fully the relationship between income and longevity, it will be difficult to appraise the overall progressivity of the social security system. For example, if "poor" white males earning initially $7,000 have the same life expectancy as black males do on average, then the "poor" white males' rate of return of $-.015$ would lie below that of the richer ($25,000) white males of $-.005$. Differences in life expectancy by income might offset the progressive benefit schedule by enough to make the entire system regressive.

Dependent and survivor benefits still mandated under the new law can give rise to gross inequities of the following type. Consider two families, A and B. In family A, Mr. A and Mrs. A both work, and both initially earn $10,000 at age 26. In family B., Mr. B works and Mrs. B doesn't. Mr. B starts out earning $20,000 at age 26. All four spouses are the same age; the three workers all enjoy a constant 2 percent real wage growth, pay in yearly 12 percent or more of their earnings in taxes, and retire at age 62. Although the two families pay identical taxes for thirty-six years, family B received (in real 1978 dollars) $1,305 more in yearly benefits than family A, as long as all four people remain alive. If Mr. A and Mr. B die at the same time, the surviving Mrs. B will receive $3,309 more each year in benefits than the surviving Mrs. A. The story behind these numbers is the following: When the two As and the male B retire at age 62, the two As collect $7,318 each in benefits. Mr. B receives $10,627 in benefits on his own account, and $5,314 in dependent benefits for his wife. The combined benefits of the Bs, $15,941, exceed those of the As, $14,636, by $1,305. When Mr. A and Mr. B die, Mrs. A continues to receive benefits of $7,318 based on her own earnings record, while Mrs. B is eligible for the survivor's benefit, which equals 100 percent of her deceased husband's benefit, $10,627. While Mrs. A is, in theory, eligible for survivor's benefits, her survivor's benefits are reduced dollar for dollar by benefits she collects on her own account.

Not only can two families pay in identical taxes and receive different benefits under social security, but two families can pay in different amounts in taxes and receive identical benefits. Let Mr. A and Mr. B both earn $15,000, and Mrs. A earn $5,000. Upon reaching age 62, Mrs. A can collect $4,697 as a dependent, which exceeds the $4,689 she can collect on her own account. The As and the Bs will receive identical benefits, although Mrs. A has paid in 12 percent or more of her earnings each year to social security for thirty-six years! Since Mrs. A receives no additional benefits for her thousands of dollars of social security contributions, those contributions are perceived not as savings, but as taxes on her labor supply. This implicit taxation of female labor supply—or male labor supply if the female earns substantially more than the male—may be reducing the work efforts of millions of females. In 1975 there were 33.7 million husband-wife families where the husband was between the ages of 25 and 65. Of these, 17.3 million, or 51.3 percent, were families in which both husband and wife worked. The typical wife's earnings represented between one-quarter and one-third of the total family income, putting most wives in the range of the implicit social security tax bite (Munnell 1977:46-47).

Although the ranks of the self-employed include doctors, lawyers, dentists, accountants, and economic consultants, the government grants the self-employed a 4 percent (4.55 percent by 1990) lower tax rate than other covered workers. For self-employed workers with earnings above the ceiling, the tax break equals $708 in 1978. While their taxes are lower by 34 percent, the benefits the self-employed receive are calculated as if they had had no tax break.[8] The rationale for this tax break presumably arises from the employee/employer tax distinction. Since the self-employed have no employer paying in taxes for them, why should they have to pay the full tax? The answer is that the nonself-employed workers pay the full tax. The requirement that the employer pay 6.05 percent of wages to social security means that the amount he can afford to pay to his workers is 6.05 percent less than it would otherwise be. The employer/employee tax distinction is a fiction—it has no economic significance. While this point is demonstrated in every decent introductory economics course, using simple supply and demand curves, the message apparently has not yet reached the Congress. As a result, many of the richest members of our society enjoy a social security tax advantage which can be justified by neither economic logic nor social justice.

Eligibility for social security payments requires only forty quarters, ten years of covered employment. Government workers who are not covered under social security can quit their jobs at age 52, work for ten years in the private sector, and begin collecting benefits at age 62. Alternatively, they can work part-time in the private sector for forty quarters and become eligible. To the Social Security Administration, these government employees appear as poor workers, since their computed averages of indexed monthly covered earnings (AIME) are very low. These workers then become eligible for the fairly high minimum social security benefit which was designed to redistribute to lifetime low earners. Having worked just a few years under social security, and having paid in very little in taxes, past government employees can collect today the minimum annual benefit of $1,461 plus dependent benefits. The number of retired federal workers who take advantage of the system is large. Fully 43 percent of retired federal workers receive both civil service and social security benefits (Campbell 1977:133). Fortunately, the new law freezes the minimum benefit at the 1978 level; the minimum benefit thus will be a smaller source of inequity as time passes. Even so, the progressivity of the new benefit schedule with respect to tax contributions will still give government workers high rates of return on their low levels of tax contributions.

There is no compelling reason for excluding government workers from the program during their years of government employment. The fact that government workers have their own pension plans is not persuasive, since a large fraction of the private work force is covered under non–social security pensions. To the extent that social security is engaged in re-distributing from the lifetime rich to the lifetime poor, all the lifetime rich, including rich government employees, should be obliged to contribute to all the lifetime poor, which in-cludes poor government employees.[9]

Of all the problems of fairness cited above, the unequal treatment of working persons age 65 to 72 and nonworking persons in the same age span is the most visible and troubling to retired persons themselves. Prior to age 72 (age 70 after 1981, under the new law), the social security earnings test reduces or eliminates benefits for many working aged. Why should elderly people who have worked and contributed to social security for years and years receive no benefits be-tween 65 and 72 simply because they desire to continue working and contributing to the productivity of the nation? Not only do these aged workers forego benefits, but they re-ceive no return on social security taxes they continue to pay.

The earnings test was designed in the 1930s as a mechanism to help reduce the rate of unemployment—over 20 percent—existing at the time. The idea was to induce old people to retire, thus opening up jobs for young workers. Economic conditions and economic understanding of un-employment have changed considerably since the 1930s; the unemployment rate has averaged about 5 percent over the last twenty-five years, and is simply not related to the social se-curity earnings test.

The earnings test has also been justified as a means test, the notion being that people who earn more than a certain amount are well off and don't need social security. In 1978, the earnings test begins at $4,000. Individuals working forty hours for fifty-two weeks, earning the minimum wage of $2.65/hr., can hardly be called well off, yet they must forego $756 of social security benefits. If a means test is really desirable, it should be based on all income, not simply wage income, and should start at a much higher income level. Our current system takes $756 in benefits from the age 65, minimum-wage, full-time employee, while giving full benefits to retirees who have million-dollar dividend incomes.

The only sensible argument for the earnings test arises from viewing social security as a form of insurance. In the case of fire insurance, one receives payments only in the event of fire; equivalently, it is argued, one should only receive benefits after the uncertain event—namely, retirement—has occurred. While more research is needed to determine exactly how uncertain retirement is, there is an acute problem of the availability of this "retirement insurance" generating adverse incentives to retire early. The problem of adverse incentives, called moral hazard by economists, seems so severe in this case that the goal of structuring social security as a pure insurance scheme should be abandoned.

SOCIAL SECURITY AND SAVINGS

The past few years have witnessed a growing concern over an aggregate capital shortage. The debate has identified the unfunded social security system, since its introduction in 1935, as a potentially major factor in reducing the nation's savings and the capital stock. Martin Feldstein has pioneered research on the effect of social security on savings. In a provocative article, Feldstein (1974) suggested that the social security program may have reduced aggregate savings and the long-run capital stock by 38 percent. Since capital and labor are the primary factors of production in our economy, a 38 percent reduction in one of these inputs has enormous implications for the level of per capita income.

The unfunded financing of social security is central to this debate. Had the government taken tax dollars from the young, invested them in a trust fund, and returned the principal plus interest as benefit payments to the actual contributors, then social security would simply have substituted public for private savings with no effect on total savings. This, however, did not occur; instead, at the start of the program, taxes paid in were immediately paid out as benefits to elderly people who had contributed very little or nothing. This intergenerational transfer, the argument goes, leads to greater consumption by the elderly than would otherwise have been the case. The initial (start-up) generation of young people, on the other hand, treat their tax contributions as equivalent savings, since they anticipate receiving benefits when old in return for their past tax contributions. Rather than saving privately, the young feel that they are saving through social security. The substitution of public for private savings does not lead the initial generation of young to alter their consumption. Since the consumption of the initial generation of young is not affected, but the consumption of the start-up generation of old people is increased, total consumption increases and aggregate savings falls. Aggregate savings is not only reduced in the short run, in this scenario, but it is permanently lowered; under "pay-as-you-go," unfunded financing, young people are forever handing their savings (tax contributions) over to old people as benefits; the old people consume these benefits; hence, the savings of the young never get invested in the economy and never augment the capital stock.

Robert Barro (1974) has raised a major theoretical objection to this view. Barro points out that intergenerational transfers occur in the absence of social security; these transfers take the form of support by young people of their older relatives, as well as bequests and gifts from the elderly to younger cohorts. Barro suggests that the imposition by social security of a forced transfer from young to old may simply lead to an offsetting change in private, voluntary, intergenerational transfers, with no effect on any real variables. The unearned benefits received by the initial (start-up) generation of the old are handed back to the young as gifts or bequests; alternatively, benefits paid to the old reduce private voluntary transfers from the young to the old, dollar-for-dollar, resulting in no change in consumption by either young or old, and no change in aggregate savings. While the range of estimates vary, Michael Darby (1978:30) has estimated that over 70 percent of the U.S. capital stock can be attributed to savings for bequests. This fact adds considerable strength to Barro's argument.

Since 1974, much research has been conducted on the question of social security and savings. I have examined the long-run impact of unfunded social security within a model of a growing economy (Feldstein 1977; Kotlikoff 1977). The findings suggest that, at the current scale of the social security system, the maximum possible reduction of the capital stock in an economy closed to international capital flows is more on the order of 20 percent. While smaller than 38 percent, 20 percent is still quite large. However, when one takes into account the openness of the U.S. economy to the importation of capital from abroad, the theoretical reduction in the U.S. capital stock is much smaller. In an international context, capital may be imported from abroad, offsetting to some degree the reduction in capital brought about by unfunded social security.

Empirical investigations of the impact of social security on savings may be succinctly summarized by one word— inconclusive. In addition to Feldstein, three other economists (Munnell, Barro, and Darby) have examined time series data relating U.S. savings to social security variables. The estimated effect of social security on savings is quite sensitive to the choice of statistical specification. These estimates range from no impact to Feldstein's 38 percent figure, and are generally statistically insignificant. The main problem with the time series analysis is that social security variables are highly correlated with other variables that affect consumption, such as the unemployment rate. Hence, it is difficult to disentangle a separate social security effect from the data.

Studies using cross-sectional micro data have not fared much better. Here the paucity of data on earnings and tax contributions over an individual's lifetime is a constraining factor. In my own investigation of cross-sectional data (Kotlikoff 1977) I found little support for the notion that social security has reduced national saving. Large differences in lifetime wealth generated by the intergenerational transfer do not appear to influence savings. Those differences in lifetime wealth are, however, highly correlated with earnings, marital status, age structure of the family, and working status of the wife. As with the time series studies, it is not clear whether the social security effects obtained in our statistical procedures really reflect social security, or whether they are proxying for closely related variables.

To summarize, there is no hard empirical evidence that social security has reduced the nation's savings and its capital stock. One hopes that better data will become available in the near future to resolve this important issue. We should be aware, however, that any future increases in the scale of the social security system that are associated with additional intergenerational transfers may greatly reduce savings and economic growth. Some economists are so concerned about the issue of social security and savings that they have proposed using social security to increase savings; they suggest raising taxes above their current high values to accumulate a trust fund, thereby increasing aggregate savings. While greater national savings may be desirable, it is by no means clear that the social security system is the appropriate tool to achieve that result. There are alternative mechanisms, such as the investment tax credit and accelerated depreciation allowances, that can be employed to generate increased capital accumulation.

SOCIAL SECURITY AND LABOR SUPPLY

Social security was established to raise the relative income position of the aged. Despite the massive growth of the program, the relative income position of aged families with household heads age 65 and over is lower today than it was thirty years ago. Between 1947 and 1976, median nominal family income increased by a factor of 4.77 for families with heads age 65 and over. For other age groups over age 24, the increase ranged from 5.03 to 5.53 (Census Bureau 1949, 1977a). It is ironic that the social security system may, itself, be largely responsible for this relative decline in the income position of the elderly. Evidence is mounting that the social security earnings test is a major deterrent to labor supply by the aged.

Labor force participation rates of the elderly have dropped dramatically since 1940. Most of this reduction has been concentrated in the post–age 62 group whose members face the social security earnings test. In 1940 the participation rate for males age 55 was 89.5 percent; in 1976 it was 83.4 percent. For those 61 years old, the corresponding figures are 81.4 percent and 70.1 percent. While the 11.3 percent reduction for men 61 years old is impressive, for those 62 years old there is a 20.8 percentage point drop, from 79.7 percent to 58.9 percent. For men 65 years old, there is a 32.7 point reduction, from the 1940 value of 66.9 percent to the 1976 figure of 34.2 percent.[10] Certainly, rising standards of living, together with a desire for more leisure, explain part of the general trend towards early retirement; but what, besides social security, can explain the differentially greater reduction in labor supply at age 62 than at age 61? One answer is that the ages 62 and 65 may simply have become institutionalized retirement ages in our economy, and would have been critical ages with or without social security.

Using *Current Population Survey* data, Anthony Pellechio and I have generated more convincing summary evidence that the social security earnings test distorts the labor supply decision of the elderly.[11] Table 2 presents the distribution of workers aged 65 to 71 by $200 earnings brackets. In 1967 the earnings test started at $1,500. From 1968 to 1972 the figure was $1,680; it reached $2,100 in 1973, and $2,400 in 1974. Social security subtracts a dollar of benefits for every two dollars of earnings, and thus imposes a 50 percent tax rate on marginal earnings above this exempt amount.

The table clearly indicates that many aged workers adjust their labor supply to work just up to this exempt amount and no more. In 1967, with the exempt amount at $1,500, 11.5 percent of males age 65 to 71 earned between $1,400 and $1,600. In vivid contrast, only 1.9 percent earned $1,600 to $1,800. As the exempt amount increases over time, the proportion of both male and female workers in the earnings brackets just under the exempt amount increases as well. Eliminating the earnings test would unquestionably increase the incomes of many elderly, as well as generate more payroll tax revenue.

The social security earnings test significantly increases the complexity of the retirement decision. A rational decision about retirement now requires that workers fully understand the complexities of the earnings test and the provisions for actuarial reduction; they must also know the potential benefits, including dependent benefits, they forego if they continue to work. The ages and working decisions of spouses and children are essential pieces of information, since there are age requirements for dependent benefits. In addition, dependent benefits are reduced by the social security earnings test not only if the main beneficiary earns too much, but if the dependent earns too much as well. All this information is relevant, as is knowledge about the value of one's assets and one's life expectancy.

More sophisticated econometric modeling of this complex retirement choice, as well as better data, are now being employed to estimate the effect of the earnings test. Empirical analyses by Boskin (1967), Boskin and Hurd (1977), and Pellechio (1978) strongly support the story portrayed in Table 2. For example, Pellechio's results (1978:41), using 1972 data, indicate that eliminating the earnings test would lead to an additional 151 annual hours of work for workers age 65 to 72. Using the current $5.53 average hourly wage in the private nonfarm sector, 151 additional hours would translate into an additional $101 in payroll tax revenue per elderly worker (BLS 1978:37). Since there are about 2.35 million workers age 65 to 72, roughly $237 million in annual tax revenue might be generated from this source alone. About 8.8 million people age 65 to 72 do not work at all during the year.[12] While no estimates are currently available, it seems quite likely that a sizable fraction of this group would return to the labor force if the earnings test were eliminated. Many of these people may currently be unable to find part-time jobs, but would work full time if social security benefits were not subtracted. The 62 to 65 age group is another major source of additional payroll tax revenue. Despite actuarial reduction, the earnings test appears to be reducing labor supply for this group as well.

The costs of eliminating the earnings test do not appear that large. While eliminating the test starting at age 62 would mean paying benefits to many persons age 62 to 65 not currently collecting, actuarial reduction implies that, for this group, the future savings because of permanently reduced benefits would essentially offset the current cost. The real costs of eliminating the earnings test arise from paying full benefits to workers age 65 and over who currently have their benefits partially or completely eliminated by the earnings test. This group is not that large. As of June 1977, only 544,856 persons age 65 and above had benefits completely withheld (HEW 1978:83). At most, another 500,000 persons had benefits partially withheld. Increased tax revenues from the additional labor supply of the aged would offset a large proportion of these costs of eliminating the earnings test.

PROPOSALS FOR REFORM

The current structure of the social security program can easily be modified to eliminate existing inequities and labor supply disincentives. The original purpose of requiring people to accumulate for their old age should serve as a benchmark for reform proposals. For example, social security was not established to redistribute from single people to married people. It was established to insure that neither single nor married people reach old age insolvent. Since more resources are required to sustain two people than one, married couples should be required to accumulate more through social security than single people. In situations where one spouse does not work, contributions of the working spouse should either be divided and counted as separate contributions by each spouse, or additional tax contributions should be required to pay for the future survivor and dependent benefits available to the non-working spouse. This same philosophy of making people pay more if they are getting more extends to the case of married couples with children. Tax breaks to the self-employed cannot be justified and should be eliminated. Since redistribution to government workers is also not a founding principle of social security, government workers should be brought into the system as well.

These proposals would go a long way towards making social security fair, and towards strengthening the individual nature of the program. They would simultaneously eliminate the taxation of female labor supply, and reduce the perception of the social security contribution as a tax on labor effort rather than as a form of savings.

If we intend as a nation to maintain our level of per capita income in the face of enormous demographic changes, it will be necessary to reverse the trend towards early retirement. Congress has just passed a law eliminating mandatory retirement prior to age 70. The social security earnings test represents a remaining obstacle to fully utilizing the enormous talents and energies of the aged. The earnings test serves no useful purpose in our modern economy and should be eliminated.

Finally, I would suggest that some reduction in real benefit levels may be preferable to the substantial increases in social secuity taxes slated for the near future. This reform could be easily carried out by simply modifying the new benefit formula, while retaining the indexing procedure. Somewhat lower benefit levels may be the price we have to pay to insure that future generations of the young do not break the social security chain letter.

Our current system is exceedingly complex; it needs to be streamlined. Eliminating the earnings test and tightening the relationship between individual payments and individual benefits are important steps in that direction. The system should be structured so that contributors can easily understand what they have paid in and what they can expect to receive back.[13]

It is time to make the system fair. And it is time to make the system contribute to the efficient operation of our economy rather than subtract from it. It is time to return to founding principles—to reassess and to reform social security.

mate formulation in the goal of Johnson's "Great Society" to abolish poverty. It is far from clear why income redistribution has been adopted as a goal, and the views on this subject are diverse. On the extreme left, we have the view urging equalization as a basic human "right." In his book *Beyond the Welfare State,* Gunnar Myrdal (1960:38) suggests the view of the Social Democrats, according to which equalization has evolved as a social "urge" following the decline of the capitalist market economy. On the right, income redistribution has been recognized as an inevitable outcome of the democratic process through which people with large blocks of votes cannot be denied a share of the national produce.

Apart from social ideology involved in the view of poverty, the deeper fact is that we do not have a real consensus on the causes of poverty: is it a social ill, or does it result from insufficient individual will? On one side of the fence, we have those who favor the eradication of poverty on grounds of general principles of efficiency and equity. They suggest that poor people are simply the victims of a social disease, and any one of us could have been afflicted by it. Here, equalization follows from the responsibility of society towards the poor, who are the victims. The opposite extreme view, which opposes the use of public funds to eradicate poverty, finds its support in the opinion that poverty is a self-inflicted condition. It results from insufficient drive, motivation, and economic will, and for that reason the solution of the problem should not be placed in the public domain. The attitude that regards welfare recipients as "lazy," "unmotivated," or "lacking economic drive" is fairly widespread in the United States today.

The diversity of views on welfare policy is brought up here, since it is this diversity which has made the policy vulnerable, the attempts at its reform hotly debated, and thinking about it rather complex. In considering the issues, we inevitably find opposing forces at play in any of the plans which were proposed, and these same contradictory forces make it impossible to adopt a reform that would last longer than a short duration.

It will be useful to briefly review the criticism of the existing welfare system, noting the opposing critical views:

(1) *The existing welfare system has not eliminated poverty.* On one side, some argue that welfare payments are not large enough, and the opposite view is that the welfare system created its own dependent clients by providing the social haven for the lazy and unmotivated.

(2) *The eligibility rules of the welfare system are wrong.* One view suggests that the welfare system should not be categorical, and should aim to eradicate poverty wherever it is; therefore the eligibility rules should be expanded to be universal. The opposite view suggests that the welfare system has already expanded far beyond its original intent, which was stated to be a program to assist families with dependent children. It has been expanded to cover food stamps, assistance to the needy, aged, and blind (SSI), unemployed parents (WIN), and medical care (Medicare).

(3) *The system has failed in the use of discretion.* One view suggests that the system has become degrading to its recipients. The welfare stigma has created, according to this view, a stagnant population which is dependent upon the discretion of the welfare bureaucracy. The opposite view suggests that the system has not used its discretion with sufficient vigor, thus allowing a growing segment of the population to live off public resources when in fact they should have been induced to seek employment.

It is gratifying, however, to note that on some issues all sides of the debate are in agreement:

(1) The welfare system today is too expensive relative to its achievements.

(2) The system provides negative work incentives, and does not sufficiently reward those recipients who work.

(3) The system is composed of a variety of cash and in-kind assistance programs which are not well coordinated, and are too complex for both the recipients and the welfare administration.

(4) The system suffers from widespread fraud, with the natural outcome of reduced credibility and effectiveness.

One should note the overwhelming fact that in the early 1960s the total expenditures for all welfare programs totaled around $5 billion (1960 dollars), while in 1976 these expenditures exceeded $48 billion (1976 dollars), and they are projected to rise over $74 billion (1976 dollars) by 1982. This has occurred during a time when our economy has experienced a most dramatic rise in per capita income. It is clear that in absolute terms there are fewer "poor" people today than in 1960. This proposes that the rise in the welfare component of our social expenditures, coupled with the growing heat of the debate on redistributional questions, reflect the growing forces in our society which are capable of bringing about such redistributional programs. This viewpoint suggests that the rise of welfare expenditures on the one hand, and the growing criticism of the welfare system on the other, are nothing but the manifestations of an on-going social struggle of the poor for a larger share of the national output.

The idea of negative income taxation was proposed by such thinkers as Lady Rhys-Williams in the United Kingdom, Earl Rolph and Milton Friedman in the United States. The idea was followed later by people of diverse persuasions, as a reasonable compromise with many valuable attributes. The next section aims to explain why negative taxation was viewed as such, and what are the alternative views on it.

TYPES OF NEGATIVE INCOME TAX SYSTEMS

The original view of negative taxation was not motivated by egalitarian or ethical considerations, but rather by the pragmatic view that, if income redistribution has to take place, then we may as well do it as simply and effectively as we can. In this context, the idea was that if people with high income pay income taxes in proportion to their income, it is sensible to assume that at some critical income level, Y*, the positive tax should reach 0, and for incomes less than Y*, the individual should receive money from the government in proportion to his income. Hence the term *negative* income tax. The principles of such an IRS-managed system are easily summarized:

(1) The negative tax is based on income only, and is therefore noncategorical.

(2) It is universal, and applies to all families, without any eligibility provisions.

(3) It is totally nondiscretionary, and should be managed as part of the IRS rather than by social workers. The system would thus remove much of the stigma of being a recipient of public money.

(4) The system is simple and inexpensive to administer, since it does away with all in-kind benefits and translates them into a cash equivalent. It requires no decisions by social workers or welfare administrators.

(5) The system can be managed by the states or the federal government, provided an agreement is reached on the issue of allocation of cost.

Thus "negative income" taxation was proposed as an ideal system that would integrate all the redistributional programs, putting them on a cash basis, with simple operating principles which are completely symmetric to the positive tax system. To complete the description, let us introduce two terms: first, the support level, S, or the "guarantee," which is the amount of money a family would receive if it has no income at all. Second, the "negative tax rate," t, which is the rate at which the payments are reduced for every \$1 of family income. Thus, if Y is family income, the basic formula of negative taxation is

Payment = S − tY for Y less than or minus Y*

Note that we defined Y* earlier as that break-even level of income at which the payment to the family reaches zero. The break-even level is thus defined as

$$Y^* = S/t$$

For example, if $S = \$1,200$ and $t = .50$, then $Y^* = \$2,400$, and the family will receive some negative payments as long as its income is less than $2,400.

It is now important to observe that as long as the level of support, S, is not very large, for moderate values of t (between, say, 30 percent and 60 percent) the break-even level, Y^*, is not excessively high. This means that if negative income taxation is not regarded as a vehicle of total redistribution, aiming to provide poor families who have no income with an adequate standard of living, it could probably be implemented.

When negative taxation evolved as a possible substitute for the welfare system, the level of support, S, was taken more seriously as a level of income needed to support a family without any means at all. We shall now see that this view leads to a basic conflict which is at the roots of the debate on welfare reform. To see this, note that if you select a realistic support level of, say, $5,000 for a family of four with a negative tax of 50 percent, the break-even level, Y^*, is equal to $10,000. This means that if the system is *universal*, without eligibility requirement, then all families with income below $10,000 per year become receivers of public assistance rather than taxpayers. In this case, we need to completely redesign the positive tax system so as to abolish all income tax payments for income below $10,000 a year, and make positive tax payments start at that level!

On the other hand, if you want to provide an adequate support to the very poor, but at the same time phase out the system rapidly so that the break-even level is low, then you must raise the negative tax rate, t. Such an increase would cause serious work disincentives, which are politically unacceptable today.[1] It is important to keep in mind that raising the negative tax rate operates on work incentives in a way completely analogous to the effect of raising the marginal positive tax rate on the desire to work by higher-income people. In both cases, the high marginal tax simply leaves in the hand of the worker a small fraction of every dollar he earns, and thus reduces the incentive to earn this dollar. In addition to work disincentives, a high negative tax rate makes it difficult to integrate the negative with a progressive positive tax system, since at Y^*, when the family transits from the negative tax to the positive tax system, it may face a jump from a high negative tax rate to a relatively low positive tax rate. It is generally recognized that such jumps in the tax system are not desirable.

To clarify this basic dilemma, consider Table 1, which shows that if we establish the goal of providing adequate support of at least $4,000 for a family of four without any income, but also insist on an adequate work incentive so that the negative tax does not exceed 50 percent, it is clear that the range of break-even income levels will rapidly go over $10,000. This means that, with these kinds of break-even levels, a large number of families who are not poor and who currently *pay* taxes will become receivers, rather than payers, of tax money. Furthermore, in order to support this "new" population, a dramatic increase in the positive tax rates of incomes above the break-even level must take place. Since such a rise of tax rates of middle-income and higher-income families is not possible, it makes the whole idea of negative

Table 1

Break-even Incomes for Different Supports and Negative Tax Rates

Support	60%	50%	40%	30%
$2,000	$3,333	$ 4,000	$ 5,000	$ 6,666
3,000	5,000	6,000	7,500	10,000
4,000	6,666	8,000	10,000	11,333
5,000	8,333	10,000	12,500	16,666

taxation, as outlined above, simply unfeasible. But once the original, and perhaps simple, idea of negative taxation is rejected, we are confronted with a complex set of conflicting options. We shall discuss some of these now.

Should a Redistribution System be Categorical?

A categorical system attempts to specify those groups of individuals who are eligible for support, with the aim of concentrating the limited tax revenues available on specific groups of families who are judged to be in greatest need. Examples of such categories include families with dependent children, the aged, the blind and disabled, etc. Note that such categories are not defined by income, but rather by other characteristics.

One may observe that the fact is that most of our transfer systems are categorical in nature. This revealed preference of the electorate appears to contradict the earlier stated social goal of *income* equalization. Thus, our society seems to say that it is willing to support some poor people, but not all, and those who should not be supported are judged as capable of taking care of themselves. The categorical system attempts to isolate the causes of poverty, and to support those individuals who have a demonstrated cause for poverty which is declared supportable. But, in fact, the underlying motive behind such categorization is the deeper belief that we should help only those poor who cannot help themselves.

The weakness of categorical systems is that the categories themselves change as the political process proceeds. Our welfare system started with Aid to Families with Dependent Children (AFDC), a program to support the families described in its title. Later, other groups were added: the aged, the blind, the disabled, and finally, intact families with two heads where the parents are unemployed (WIN).[2] The existence of categorical assistance brings up serious questions of horizontal equity, and with them comes the political pressure of other groups demanding expansion of the coverage. Since the selection of any categories is based on arbitrary criteria, such a system invites pressure and renders itself expensive and unacceptable in the long run. In addition to this, the management of categorical systems tends to be more difficult, since it entails the establishment of eligibility criteria and the need to investigate the qualifications of each applicant.

A very strong case against any categorical system relates to its social effects. In the present welfare system, an important provision is the fact that it will not provide support to intact families with an employed head. But this means that the system provides an incentive either to the breakdown of the family, or to an abuse of the system by cohabiting adults who do not marry because of the extensive cost of losing welfare support if they did marry. It then appears that our welfare system is a natural outcome of the basic contradictions in our thinking about poverty and income redistribution: if it is the right of any individual not to be poor, then we should have a universal system which provides adequate support with minimal adverse work incentive effects. This is unfeasible. Then, as we modify our view and attempt to establish a categorical system, it is bound to lead to serious problems of horizontal equity and to have unacceptable social side effects.

Should We Have In-Kind Supports or Should It All Be Cash Assistance?

The classical view of negative taxation concentrated on cash transfers as the only vehicle to be used. This view was based on the idea that a poor household is the best judge of its own needs, and given adequate budget, it will allocate it well by itself. Yet our redistribution system contains very large segments of in-kind supports. These include food subsidies (food stamps, school lunch programs, etc.), housing subsidies, support of medical expenditures, and such. Table 2 provides information on the cost of various welfare programs in 1976. The table does not provide a complete picture of the in-kind supports, since the category "AFDC" includes such items as "work-related expenses" which are, in fact, in-kind subsidies. It is well known that such a complex structure of cash and in-kind supports cause basic distortions in the social allocation mechanism, inducing waste and inefficiency in addition to being expensive to administer.

The fact that taxpayers are willing to support specific in-kind programs and often oppose general cash assistance can be explained only in terms of a rather paternalistic social view of poverty. The implied social view is that the poor household is unable to select the proper food, shelter, medical care, and other services for its members. Thus, we—the rest of the society—must make this choice for them, and insist that if they wish to receive public assistance, they must spend it in accordance with our social preferences rather than their own private preferences. This kind of reasoning reveals one more dimension of the contradictions within our social consciousness regarding the issue of poverty.

A more sympathetic evaluation of in-kind support would present an argument suggesting that society should aim to eradicate poverty, and that, by subsidizing food, shelter, medical care, and other basic necessities, we ensure that children of poor households will receive the basics needed. The argument is that this will improve the chance of their getting out of the "culture of poverty." Moreover, by insisting on the basic needs, we increase the chance that the adults themselves will stay healthy and thus increase the probability of their becoming gainfully employed. Those holding this view would insist that the objective of the policy is not only to raise the immediate well-being of the poor, but also to try and solve the long-term poverty itself. Therefore, when a poor household elects to spend its resources on the consumption of alcohol, which will only perpetuate its state of poverty, the above two objectives conflict, and society may elect not to support this consumption.

Although appealing, in my view the main problem with this argument is that it has insufficient empirical support. It is far from clear that assistance in the form of in-kind subsidies

Table 2

Cost of Current Welfare Programs
by Level of Government, 1976
(billions of dollars)

Program	Cost to Federal Government	Cost to State and Local Government	Total Cost
AFDC	5.77	4.81	10.59
SSI	5.03	1.78	6.83
Veterans' pensions	3.05	–	3.05
Food stamps	5.68	.26	5.93
Child nutrition	1.92	.96	2.88
Housing assistance	2.25	–	2.25
Medicaid	8.31	6.33	14.64
Earned income tax credit	1.30	–	1.30
General assistance	–	1.20	1.20
Emergency assistance	.03	.03	.07

Source: Congressional Budget Office (1978:39).

help solve the poverty problem better than the equivalent cash support. Moreover, the evidence seems to suggest that, over the long run, the causes of poverty are so diverse and so complex that focusing on the in-kind supports rather than cash assistance is of very little significance. What is, perhaps, one of the most striking results of modern research is the realization that a good portion of observed poverty is transitory in nature: a household may fall into the state of poverty for a time and then get out of it, and the causes for such transitions are very complex indeed.[3] The causes for these transitions are those that determine the size of the poor population in our society, and it does not seem convincing at all that transfers in kind, compared with cash assistance, either reduce the causes of entering the state of poverty or increase the chance of getting out of it.

Should the System Be Discretionary?

Apart from the issue of determining the subpopulations to be supported and what form the assistance should take, one may now raise the question of the *level* of the support. The simplicity of negative taxation lies to a large extent in the fact that it establishes a clear formula for the benefits which depend only upon income, and leaves no room for special considerations of "need." The fact is that most of our existing welfare benefits are based on general concepts of "need," where even the notion of "poverty" and the "poverty level" are determined by some arbitrary conditions of need. Furthermore, the system allows state and local discretion to be the final determining factor in the level of assistance. Due to this discretion, it is possible, in principle, to observe large variations in the level of benefits received by welfare recipients with the same income. These variations would be due to the differences in judgment of different case workers, or supports established in different localities. Such differences within any given state have narrowed down in recent years, due to continuous pressure from outside the system. However, as Table 3 shows, extensive differences in welfare benefits exist across states. These differences are partly due to variations in the cost of living, but it is obvious that this variable is not the only one present. Important differences in political ideology and attitudes towards poverty across the country are important contributing factors to the observed variations in the level of welfare benefits in different states.

The main advantages of the discretionary system of support follow from the fact that it allows society to establish fine criteria of the specific individuals it wishes to support and the level of benefits it wishes to give different groups of recipients.

Table 3

Maximum Annual AFDC and Food Stamps Benefits
for a Family of Four, 1978
(selected states)

State	Maximum AFDC Payment	Food Stamps Benefits Based on Maximum AFDC	Total AFDC and Food Stamps
Arizona	$2,408	$1,838	$4,246
California	5,145	1,017	6,162
Connecticut	5,425	933	6,358
Kentucky	2,858	1,703	4,561
Mississippi	729	2,342	3,071
New York	6,848	506	7,354
South Carolina	1,423	2,134	3,557
Washington	5,060	1,042	6,102
Wyoming	3,284	1,575	4,859

Source: Congressional Budget Office (1978:150-51).

The opposition to the discretionary system of support will point to the dependence of the welfare recipients on the system as having had a degrading and stigma-creating effect. The discretionary system is wasteful, since it has to respond to any political pressure by expanding the coverage or by changing the level of the benefits. Moreover, if "need" were the only consideration in determining the level of benefits to different households, then a truly equitable system would have established uniform standards across the country, except for differences in cost of living. The fact is that the variations in level of benefits are much greater than would be expected, due to this factor. The large variations in level of benefits within and across states is simply the result of variations in the attitude of voters towards poverty, political ideology, economic conditions of local government, and personal biases of the welfare administrators. Therefore, in reality, a discretionary system provides a legal shelter to a program which is basically discriminatory and unfair.

How Best to Use Administrative "Work Requirement" Provisions?

The mounting evidence on the work disincentive effects of negative income taxation has caused a growing tendency to introduce work requirement provisions into welfare reform proposals. We shall review the empirical evidence on work disincentives in the next section, but wish to reconsider here one specific aspect of our earlier discussion relating to the constancy of the negative tax rate. Recall that given a limitation on the break-even point, Y^*, we had to face a trade-off between the support level, S, and the higher negative tax rate, t; this trade-off was specified by the formula

$$Y^* = S/t$$

Note, however, that instead of a constant tax rate t, we may consider a *declining* tax rate with some important consequences.

Let us examine the declining marginal tax rate function, which is defined by the following formula:

negative tax rate = $\alpha - \beta Y$

with a formula for negative *payments* specified by

negative payments = $S - (\alpha - \beta Y)Y$
for Y less than or equal to Y^*

As an example, consider the high support level of $4,800. With a constant negative tax rate of 50 percent, it will result in a break-even level of $9,600, which is clearly high. On the other hand, for the same support level of $4,800, a linearly declining tax rate with an initial tax rate parameter of $\alpha = 100\%$ and a declining parameter $\beta = 5\%$ for each $1,000 of taxable income, the resulting tax table is shown in Table 4. It is clear that in this case we provide a very high support of $4,800, but end up with a break-even point of

$8,000 and a marginal tax rate of 20 percent at that break-even point. Leaving aside, for a moment, the work incentive issue (to which we will return later), it is clear that the negative taxation system with declining tax rates has the following basic characteristics:

(1) *It allows a low break-even point,* even when the support level is high.

(2) *It is less expensive.* Since the initial tax rates are high, the scheme is cheaper than an equivalent constant tax system with the same support and break-even point. This follows from the fact that, except for zero income, the negative tax payments are smaller under the declining tax system at each income level.

Table 4

Tax Table for a Declining Tax Structure: Support of $4,800, Initial Tax of 100%, and Declining Rate of 5% per $1,000

Taxable Income	Average Negative Tax Rate	Negative Payments	Marginal Negative Tax Rate
$ 0	100%	$4,800	100%
1,000	95	3,850	90
2,000	90	3,000	80
3,000	85	2,250	70
4,000	80	1,600	60
5,000	75	1,050	50
6,000	70	600	40
7,000	65	250	30
8,000	60	0	20

(3) *It merges better with the positive tax structure,* since one can design the declining scheme so that around the break-even level it has marginal tax rates similar in magnitude to the positive tax rates in that range.

(4) *It is regressive.* Since the marginal tax rate is higher for lower incomes, this means that we have tax regressivity on the negative side. When integrated with the positive tax, the entire structure will appear surprising and perhaps unfair, in that it is progressive on the positive side and regressive on the negative side.

Turning now to the issue of work disincentives, consider the standard model of choice between leisure and income. In Figure 1, a person is confronted with a decision of choosing the number of hours of work. If he does not work at all, he has no income, and he takes L_0[4] hours of leisure. On the other hand, the less leisure the person takes (i.e., the more he works), the more income he has. The budget lines in diagrams 1a and 1b of Figure 1 summarize these options, and we wish to compare the budget lines within the two schemes under consideration. In the two diagrams of Figure 1, the bold lines represent the budget lines of an individual who can select a combination of income and leisure without a negative

Figure 1

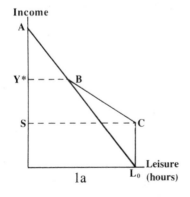

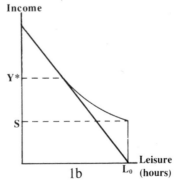

tax scheme. The diagrams are drawn for the case in which the individual has no unearned income at all.

In diagram 1a, a support level, S, is introduced, with a constant negative tax resulting in a budget set with two linear segments, AB and BC. In diagram 1b, when we introduce a declining marginal tax rate, the lower portion of the budget line becomes nonlinear with the indicated curvature.

To examine the work disincentive effects, consider first an individual who remains working a significant number of hours after the introduction of a negative taxation scheme with a constant rate. In Figure 2 we examine the behavior of this individual under a scheme of constant negative tax, with his behavior under a scheme of declining tax rates, but with the same support and break-even levels. Under the constant tax scheme, the individual works a significant number of hours $(L_0 - L_1)$, at which point the introduction of a declining tax system provides for a marginal tax rate which is lower than the rate of the constant tax regime. Due to this, the declining tax scheme causes him to decrease his leisure from L_1 to L_2, and thus to *increase* his work effort by the amount $(L_1 - L_2)$.

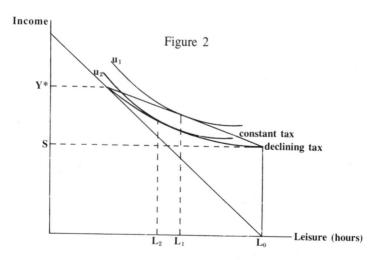

Figure 2

On the other hand, in Figure 3 we consider an individual who works a very little amount ($L_0 - L_1$) under a constant negative tax regime. After the introduction of a declining marginal negative tax scheme, the individual faces a higher tax rate and decides to quit the labor market altogether.

On the basis of the above analysis, a comparison of the declining negative tax with a constant tax scheme yields the following conclusions:

(1) The regime of declining marginal rates provides a stronger work incentive for people who work a significant number of hours, since it provides for a lower marginal tax for them.

(2) The regime of declining marginal rates causes a stronger disincentive effect for individuals who work little under a constant tax regime.

We can now complete our discussion of the optimal use of administrative "work requirement" provisions. Recent proposals regarding welfare reform believe that by significant job training, job search, and job creating programs, administrative "work requirement" provisions can result in inducing welfare recipients to seek and hold part-time or full-time employment. If this is the case, then the use of a negative taxation system with a high support, high initial tax, *and declining marginal rate* is superior to a negative tax scheme with the same support and break-even level, but with a constant tax rate. The reason for this conclusion follows from the observation that administrative methods and job programs can be used to induce recipients to work a significant number of hours. Once this is achieved, a structure with declining marginal tax rates has the great advantages of being cheaper from the budgetary cost viewpoint, providing better work incentives, and being easier to integrate with the positive tax structure.

To provide a better understanding of the work disincentive problem of negative taxation, we shall now briefly review some of the experimental evidence which has become available in recent years.

Figure 3

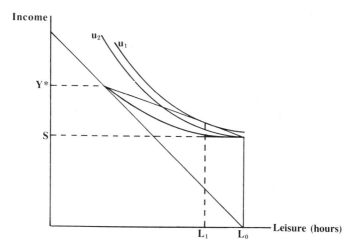

WORK INCENTIVES:
SOME EXPERIMENTAL EVIDENCE

When the introduction of negative income taxation was first contemplated in the 1960s, the most widespread reaction to the idea was the fear of a dramatic reduction of labor supply by primary wage earners. At that time, many labor economists were beginning to estimate labor supply functions, providing some preliminary measurements of the size of the substitution and income effects (see, for example, Hall [1973] and Boskin [1973]), and these estimates could have been used to indicate that the original fears were unfounded. Nevertheless, Congress decided to initiate a sequence of social experiments in which the work response would be directly measured, and thus they would provide exact quantitative measures of the work disincentive effects of alternative negative tax programs.

The first experiment in New Jersey and Pennsylvania was completed in 1973; its report was circulated in 1974 and appeared in various forms. In a summary paper, Watts and Rees (1975) reported to a Brookings conference the results of the experiment. Because of the complexity of the issue, the results are sensitive to the group under investigation and to the method of analysis. Concentrating here on the broad view only, we can state that the New Jersey–Pennsylvania report concluded that when assigned to negative income tax programs for three years, male heads exhibit no significant negative work response at all. On the other hand, married women tend to exhibit a reduction of 20 percent in the number of hours of work when they are assigned to a negative income tax program with a support level equal to the poverty level and a negative tax of 50 percent. More precisely, the report finds that when white male heads are assigned to a negative tax program with a support level equal to the poverty level and a negative tax rate of 50 percent, they reduce their weekly hours of work by 2.4 hours, or 6.3 percent. For Spanish-speaking male heads, the decrease is even greater, amounting to 7.3 hours per week. These results do not hold for black heads, who not only do not show a decrease in hours, but in some cases show *increases* in hours of work.

When considering the total hours worked by all family members combined, the report finds that, if given a negative tax program with a support equal to the poverty level and a negative tax of 50 percent, the average reduction in hours will be as follows: white families reduce hours by 8 percent; black families reduce hours by 3 percent; Spanish-speaking families reduce hours by 6 percent.

The New Jersey–Pennsylvania experimental report attempted to give the impression that the work disincentive effects of negative taxation on male heads were small and statistically insignificant. The intention was to indicate that the original concerns of Congress were to be regarded as unjustified.

It is interesting that a paper by Hall (1975), which was presented to the same Brookings conference, arrived at different conclusions. Using different statistical techniques, the author argues convincingly that although the estimated effects may be small (in absolute numbers), they are clearly statistically significant; thus the New Jersey report's claim for statistical significance of the male head's response was to be rejected at the outset. Recently, a new study by Cogan (1978), using the same New Jersey data, criticizes the way the econometric model of the New Jersey report treated the welfare option of participants, and the fact that a portion of the eligible population did not participate in the experiment. Using a different approach, Cogan (1978) finds that had the New Jersey analysis corrected for the welfare option, the results would have shown a decline of 4.22 hours per week for white male heads, which is a reduction of 11.1 percent in their hours of work. If, on the other hand, one controls for the option of not participating at all in the negative tax experiment, then Cogan (1978) finds that, *for participants,* the decline is 6.5 hours per week, which is 17.1 percent of their average initial hours.

The most comprehensive negative tax experiment has been conducted in Seattle and Denver. This experiment is almost six times larger than the experiment in New Jersey and Pennsylvania.[5] Also, the data base in Seattle-Denver is more reliable than the one assembled in the New Jersey–Pennsylvania experiment. In a recent interim report covering the first twenty-four months of the experiment, Keeley, Robins, Spiegelman, and West (1977) report that the mean effects of the experimental treatments on participants are as follows: a reduction of 5.3 percent in the hours of husbands; a reduction of 22.0 percent in the hours of wives; a reduction of 11.2 percent in the hours of single female heads.[6] All these results are statistically significant. In a separate study, Robins and West (1977) examine the same data, but attempt to take into account the fact that, due to high income or other causes, a certain fraction of the assigned population did not participate in the experiment. They estimate two separate models, and report that, correcting for participation, the decline in the hours of work of husbands ranges from 4 percent to 5 percent, for wives, from 18 percent to 22 percent, and for single female heads, from 9 percent to 11 percent.

The Seattle-Denver reports do not find significant differences in the response of the three race groups, and thus suggest a rejection of the finding in the New Jersey–Pennsylvania study with regard to the black subsample.

The total cumulative weight of all these results seems to be very clear. They suggest that if a negative tax program was introduced with a support at the poverty level and a tax rate of 50 percent, it would not cause most participants to quit their regular jobs, but it will cause significant reductions in the amount of work that people would like to do in addition to the existing work disincentives in our society. These additional reductions are such that they cannot be ignored by any welfare reform package. With regard to wives and single female heads, the results are drastic, while the additional reduction of 5 percent to 6 percent in the work effort of male heads should be viewed as a significant fraction of our national output.

NEGATIVE TAXATION AND WELFARE REFORM

One of our main conclusions in this chapter is that the prevailing attitudes in contemporary society are not conducive to the introduction of negative taxation in its originally intended form. These attitudes seem to oppose the universal, non-categorical, all-cash redistribution scheme. Moreover, since the prevailing view seeks to provide adequate support to the poor with minimal work disincentives, it is clear that a negative tax system that can achieve this implies a massive redistribution of income and a restructuring of the positive tax system. These changes, however, do not appear politically feasible, and therefore it must be concluded that a universal negative tax system for the U.S. is not a realistic possibility.

At best, we can hope to introduce a modest negative tax scheme into the tax structure, so as to achieve a small amount of redistribution via a universal, noncategorical, cash-transfer method which could replace a few other redistribution programs. Beyond that, a welfare reform which will provide adequate assistance to the poor with minimal work disincentive effects will have to be a fundamental compromise of opposing forces.

Taking a realistic view of the process, one may note that once we accept the idea of having a categorical and discretionary welfare system, it means that we are inviting ongoing political pressures to expand it or to provide more benefits to one group or another. Given the political forces at hand, any system under such pressures will develop problems; regardless how good a compromise it is at the time of its initiation, it will become a burden at a later date. This means that under the above conditions, "welfare reform" as a mechanism for redistribution must be viewed as an *ongoing* process with a continuous revision of our beliefs, social institutions, and methods of coping with the problem of poverty. With this process in mind, the employment component of the Carter administration's welfare reform proposal entitled "Program for Better Jobs and Income" (PBJI) is important. It emerged as a result of the growing desire to counter the negative work incentive effects of any welfare program by administrative tools, or by requiring recipients to return to the labor market and search for a job. The idea is interesting, but in a world of a 6 percent to 7 percent unemployment rate, a job requirement provision in a welfare reform is meaningless if the government cannot offer recipients a job. The Carter administration, therefore, proposes to create up to 1.4 million public service jobs to be available for those eligible for public assistance.

At a time of growing pressure on public budgets, with growing taxpayer revolt against public waste, the idea of using the public sector as an employment vehicle for the poor appears rather counterproductive. Two tendencies will certainly take place: if the individual taking the public service job is efficient and productive, then sooner or later he will replace an existing employee of the state or local government simply as a result of the growing budgetary pressure on these governments. If, on the other hand, the employed individual is inefficient and not productive on the job, then he will make one more contribution to further discrediting the public sector as a haven for social waste and as the sector which provides the hidden unemployment of the U.S. economy. Yet the Carter administration's proposal boldly recognizes the need to ask ourselves serious questions about the job opportunities at the lower scale of the wage distribution. It is obvious that a significant portion of the welfare problem in the United States would be alleviated if there was a greater abundance of jobs at lower wages. The creation of 1.4 million public service jobs is one way to think about it. But a broader consideration of the welfare problem will relate it to our policy with respect to the minimum wage, our attitude towards open immigration, and our willingness to engage in tax reform and other policies to encourage more investment. Our welfare policy is particularly contradicted by our minimum wage and immigration policies. Clearly, if we wanted to make jobs available for more of our poor, raising the minimum wage and allowing further immigration of poor workers will not achieve the stated goal. Thus, from an integrated policy's viewpoint, the Carter administration's proposals appear inadequate.

Deeper consideration of the ''work requirement'' component of welfare reform is not possible here. However, it should be noted that our argument above suggests that if the job component of PBJI is successful, then we should seriously reexamine the negative taxation component of the cash assistance component. The PBJI proposes to set the support at $4,200 for a family of four, with a constant tax rate of 50 percent. Our analysis here proposes that if the job component is successful, then a superior negative tax scheme should allow for a negative tax schedule with a *higher initial tax rate, but with a declining marginal tax rate,* so that at the break-even point of $8,400, the negative marginal tax rate is significantly below 50 percent.

One cannot conclude this chapter on an optimistic note, since it does not appear likely that negative taxation in its universal form will be a major tool for redistribution of income in our society. Welfare reform will, unfortunately, need to be an ongoing process of social compromises, where each compromise solves the outstanding problems for a short duration. Due to the nature of the forces at hand, it would be best to recognize that, regardless how good any reform may be, it will soon be found to be inadequate, and will thus represent the foundations of the reform to follow.

8

JOHN B. SHOVEN

Inflation and Income Taxation

The income tax—personal and corporate—and its interaction with inflation. Interest income and expense. Capital gains and accrual taxation. Depreciation allowances and inventories. The needed taxation and accounting adjustments.

INTRODUCTION

It would be difficult to name two aspects of American economic life more universally disliked than income taxation and inflation. These two evils are not independent, however, and it is their interaction which produces some of the most undesirable results and which form the topic of this chapter. The tax laws in the United States are not only inequitable and distorting, as described in the other chapters of this volume, but they are not designed to work well in a world in which the value of the basic unit of account, the dollar, is unstable and generally diminishing. This is a problem which affects both the personal income tax and the less visible and less well understood corporation income tax.

The severity of the problem of inflation's interaction with the tax laws has increased immensely in the past five to ten years, in that the pace of inflation has accelerated and become more volatile. This fact, of which the reader is undoubtedly painfully aware, is illustrated in Figure 1. Much of the price increases have caught even sophisticated investors by surprise, as is evidenced by the large losses that long-term bond purchasers have experienced in aggregate over the period. The undesirable and distortionary consequences of inflation are the greatest for just such a situation—one with rapid, volatile, and largely unexpected increases in the price level. The reason, of course, is that in such an environment individuals cannot readily protect themselves from the effects of inflation.

INFLATION AND THE PERSONAL INCOME TAX

The impact of inflation on the personal income tax can be divided into two separate issues. First, there is the problem that inflation causes people's incomes to rise, forcing them into higher marginal tax rate brackets, and reducing the real value of such features of the IRS code as the $750 personal exemption, the standard deduction, and the $100 dividend exclusion. These effects together mean that when incomes rise by 10 percent because of inflation, income taxes, in aggregate, rise not by 10 percent, but by approximately 15 percent. The real tax burden is increased through time unless tax rates are cut periodically, and special tax credits, exemptions, deductions, and exclusions are made more generous in nominal terms in order to maintain their real value. The effect can be an undesired increase in the size of government, a drag on the macroeconomic position of the economy, and added uncertainty about what future real tax burdens will be over the life of an investment.

What has actually happened since, say, 1960 is that we have experienced a series of discretionary tax "cuts." The reality of these reductions is debatable, in that we pay as taxes a higher fraction of personal income today than we did eighteen years ago. However, the inflationary effects have largely been cancelled in aggregate by periodic congressional action. Real taxes are up because real income has risen, and because society has collectively chosen to transfer control of a slightly larger fraction of total income to the federal government.

Indexing the tax code so that it automatically adjusts for inflation is both feasible and desirable. It would increase certainty about future taxes, and would perhaps allow political attention to be focused on real tax reform rather than on these artificial inflation-offsetting tax reductions. The method of accomplishing such code indexation need not be difficult; in fact, the Canadian personal income tax system is inflation-indexed in a satisfactory manner.

The personal tax code could be inflation-adjusted by multiplying the many dollar numbers in the tax computation by a factor reflecting inflation. For example, if there had been 10 percent inflation in the year, the $750 personal exemption of last year would be raised to $825. The $2,200 standard deduction for single returns would be increased to $2,420, while the $32,000 to $38,000 income range subject to the 50 percent marginal tax rate would be lifted to $35,200 to $41,800. If this procedure were followed, an individual whose income tax base rose an amount equal to the inflation rate would find his nominal taxes had also risen by that percentage. That is, real tax bills would be constant for those with stable real tax bases. Relative to the current system, taxes would be adjusted more continuously and automatically for inflation, perhaps aiding economic stability.

This aspect of inflation and personal income taxation is probably the easier one to deal with and, unfortunately, the less important matter. Not only is the tax code itself designed for a dollar of constant value, but the determination of income and taxable income is based on that faulty assumption. The point is that we not only need to modify the manner in which taxes are determined from taxable income, but we must further correct the accounting for taxable income itself.

Most of the difficulties in determining real taxable income involve capital income. One of the most widely understood aspects of inflation is that it tends to make creditors worse off and debtors better off. This is most clearly the case for an unanticipated inflation. Once a deal has been struck between borrower and lender for the future transaction of money, the future payer is clearly better off if the value of the payment is reduced by inflation, while the future recipient is made symmetrically worse off. Everyone recognizes this except the IRS's tax accounting procedures. For example, a saver receiving 8 percent interest, in a year in which prices rise 7 percent, only has a real interest income of 1 percent. Similarly, the holder of a 9.25 percent mortgage has a real cost of money of only 2.25 percent. The tax codes do not reflect these facts, but subject the full 8 percent nominal interest received to taxation, and allow the entire 9.25 percent mortgage interest to be recorded as a deductible cost. Interest recipients are penalized by this system, which can result in taxes with zero or negative real income, and interest payers are made better off. So one correction in moving towards a system which taxes real income would be to correctly account for interest income and expense.

The treatment of capital income is flawed in other ways. A particularly important—and yet often ignored—distinction is whether an asset is taxed on an accrual or a realization basis. Does an individual earn income as his investment appreciates, or only when that appreciation is realized? This is an issue with philosophical implications, although the majority of economists would argue that a person's income should be independent of consumption/investment decisions, and that an unrealized gain involves an implicit reinvestment. That is, they would assert that unrealized profits do constitute income, and that income taxation should be on an accrual basis.

The remarkable feature of current practice is that it is totally inconsistent. Some assets, both long and short term, are taxed on accrual, while others offer the advantage of permitting taxes to be postponed until realization. Examples come easily. Corporate bonds, whose primary return is interest, are taxed on accrual. The interest on savings accounts, even on long-term certificate accounts which are quite illiquid, is likewise taxed as it accrues. The interest on some U.S. government bonds (series E), however, are taxed on realization, as is the income offered on the appreciation of corporate bonds selling at discount. The dividend payment on a common stock is taxable at time of payment, even if the funds are retained by the corporation through a dividend reinvestment plan. However, the appreciation of the value of the firm due to retained earnings is not taxed until realized. Gains on investment durables such as gold, antiques, paintings, and oriental rugs are taxed on a realization basis. Likewise, the earnings of pension funds are taxed on a realization criterion.

In general, people of modest financial wealth have a large fraction of their accumulated savings in interest-bearing accounts and are taxed on an accrual basis, whereas wealthier households hold a larger proportion of their assets in categories which are taxed only at time of realization. The difference between the two systems of taxation can be enormous for assets held for a substantial period of time. As an example, consider an individual in a 50 percent marginal tax bracket. This person wishes to set aside $10,000 for retirement, which is some twenty-five years distant. Two assets are available, each of which earns 10 percent, but asset A is taxed on accrual while asset B is taxed upon realization. After payment of all taxes on both assets, how much will our individual have in twenty-five years? The answer is that asset A will yield $34,903.43, while the more favorably treated asset B nets $65,912.47, almost twice as much. These figures were calculated as if the gain experienced on asset B was subject to 50 percent taxation after twenty-five years, whereas the gain on asset A was taxed each year. Effectively, asset A compounds at 10 percent per year and is subject to a large amount of tax upon realization, whereas asset B compounds only at 5 percent per year. The difference reflects the power of compound interest rates. Actually, the difference has been understated, however. Without significant exception, the gains on assets which are taxed on a realization basis are classified as "capital gains," and taxed more lightly than other sources of income. If we compute the above examples with a 25 percent tax rate on asset B, the investor ends up with $93,869, or 270 percent as much as the saver in assets taxed on accrual. Clearly, the distinction between an accrual and realization basis can be important.

The tax laws should be made to be consistent, fair, and logical. Certainly, there are reasons to tax capital income lightly, particularly given current accounting. However, it is not at all clear why the investor in antiques should be favored relative to the savings and loan depositor. The first step that needs to be taken is correctly measuring income. The interest recipient should not be required to pay taxes on the inflation premium he receives, and the holder of stocks or physical assets should be offered a correction for inflation. We should decide whether we want to follow the philosophy of a realization-based tax system to its logical limit (a consumption or expenditure tax), or attempt to tax as many assets as possible on an accrual basis, which seems more aligned with the concept of income taxation.

Correcting capital income figures for inflation need not be terribly difficult. Let g be the percentage appreciation of an investment over the year, and let p be the inflation rate. With accrual taxation, the investor would pay tax only on $g - p$, the excess of appreciation over inflation. Some assets will probably continue to be taxed on a realization basis, and for these the original cost basis of the asset must be raised by a factor reflecting the total inflation during the holding period in order to prevent taxation of this pure inflationary gain. Once real capital income has been correctly determined, the debate on how heavily it should be taxed can be opened. For many assets and investors, full taxation of real accrued capital income would be preferable to the present favorable treatment of nominal income.

There is not the same severe problem with labor income. In a world of 10 percent inflation, if your labor income goes up 10 percent, you are penalized by the tax system only because of the code indexing problem mentioned earlier. Therefore, with respect to the personal income tax, two major changes need to be accomplished in order to alleviate its severe interactions with inflation. First, a major reform is needed in accounting for real capital income. This problem can be subdivided, with interest income/expense and capital gains requiring particular attention. Second, the IRS code needs to be indexed, with all nominal income figures growing at the rate of inflation. This will assure that those with constant real incomes pay constant real taxes. The two steps, income redefinition and code indexation, are entirely separable. Either reform could be accomplished alone, and would probably be independently desirable. However, with inflation at its current high level and seemingly accelerating, it would be desirable to have complete inflation adjustment and accounting in the U.S. federal personal income tax laws.

INFLATION AND THE CORPORATION INCOME TAX

The personal income tax system is not alone in failing to handle inflation well. The corporation income tax similarly is nonneutral with respect to the rate of price increase. Conceptually, the problem here, too, can be divided into (1) adjusting the code for inflation, and (2) accounting for real rather than nominal income. The code problem is much less severe than with the personal income tax, since corporations face a constant marginal tax rate of 48 percent after the first $50,000 of profits. For large corporations, the tax is essentially proportional. The only real impact of inflation is that it lowers the small amount of real profits exempt from the corporation surtax. In contrast, the problem of income determination with inflation is more severe for corporations than for individuals.

Textbooks frequently state that a corporation's income equals revenues less costs. Unfortunately, this computation is far from simple. Most of the difficulties in appropriately determining a corporation's income arise in allocating to this accounting period (say, a year) costs of assets and liabilities whose lifetime exceeds that length of time. The job of an accountant would be an easy one if only a firm set up business, sold all its output, and liquidated assets and cleared liabilities within the accounting period. The difficulties of determining a corporation's real profits will be divided into three categories: (1) depreciation, (2) inventories, and (3) gains and losses on financial assets and liabilities. It should be emphasized that a correct accounting of real profits is of value for several purposes other than tax base determination. These figures are useful in assessing the distribution of income, in evaluating the performance of management, and in gauging the macroeconomic position of the economy.

The inflation-related issue regarding corporate income accounting which receives the most attention is depreciation—

the current cost allowance for the effects of wear and obsolescence on the firm's capital stock. Current practices are
accurate only in an environment of absolutely no price
changes, and only to the extent that real depreciation matches
the presumptive time schedules of write-offs used by firms.
Corporations depreciate assets by some fraction of their original cost and carry them on their balance sheets at depreciated
(i.e., reduced) original cost. In a world with assets of
twenty-, thirty-, and even forty-year lives and significant
inflation, these figures bear no resemblance to those which
would give an accurate impression of the cost incurred on the
plant and equipment, or the value of these items in calculating the worth of the firm.

Ideally, one might want to value the plant and equipment
of a firm at its used market value, and depreciation over the
year would amount to the decline in this valuation. The im-
practicality and undesirability of this approach stems from the
fact that reasonable used markets exist for only a small fraction of depreciable assets. An alternative inflation-adjusted
method, referred to as "general value" depreciation, is to
carry assets on balance sheets, and to base depreciation on
original cost stated in current dollars. The accounting procedure would be straightforward. The historical cost of the asset
would be multiplied by the ratio of the present general price
level to the price level at the time of purchase. The capital
item would be listed on the balance sheet at this value multiplied by the fraction of value as yet undepreciated, whereas the
cost deduction for depreciation on the income statement
would multiply the general value depreciation base by the
fraction reflecting this year's wear, tear, and obsolescence.

Although current depreciation allowances are based on historical cost and therefore tend to be inadequate, the IRS has
steadily become more generous by allowing shorter service
lives for depreciation purposes, and by permitting more accelerated patterns of write-offs. These liberalizations have
partially offset the effects of inflation, but do so accurately

only for a particular rate of price change, for certain firms, and for particular types of assets.

Given that firms differ widely in their growth rates, that we live in a world with capital equipment of substantially differing durabilities and a widely fluctuating rate of inflation, inflation-adjusted depreciation combined with a pattern of write-offs more closely aligned with actual experience would be infinitely preferable to the present imperfectly offsetting factors—acceleration and historical cost. The current system favors particular firms and asset types to an unacceptably large degree.

Such accelerated depreciation methods as double-declining balance and sum-of-years digits open a new type of discrimination into the tax system, that between rapidly growing and more slowly growing firms. These techniques allow deductions substantially in excess of the more conservative straight-line approach during the early years in an asset's life, and are correspondingly less generous in the latter years. A growing firm benefits, because a larger percentage of its assets are new. This means that its depreciation will be higher and taxes lower on two accounts. First, it deducts from revenues a larger fraction of the historical value of its capital stock as a current cost. Second, the historical value of its capital stock is closer to market value, again because the plant and equipment are relatively newer. The advantage continues as long as the firm grows relatively rapidly, and while it will eventually disappear should such growth cease, the tax savings need never be repaid.

The author was involved in a study (Shoven and Bulow 1975) of how general value depreciation would have affected firms as a whole, and also how different individual firms would have been affected. Figure 2 illustrates that the adequacy of aggregate tax depreciation relative to a straight-line, inflation-adjusted method has been widely fluctuating. Only during World War II, when sixty-month amortization was permitted for all defense-related facilities, and during the

1962–1967 period of rapid growth, liberal acceleration, and (by today's standard) moderate inflation, was aggregate tax depreciation sufficient.

When one examines the impact by firm of inflation-adjusting depreciation allowances, the results can be best described as highly variable. Firms today differ a great deal in their accounting practices. Even the same firm may change techniques from year to year, presumably in order to smooth the bottom line net income figure. Companies are permitted—and almost universally use—different depreciation methods for their books (i.e., annual reports) and their tax returns. Typically, a firm will use straight-line original cost for its books, resulting in relatively low depreciation and high profits, while adopting an accelerated technique for tax purposes, thereby reducing taxes. In some cases a firm reports to stockholders that it is making money while its tax return indicates net losses. Switching to a universally required, general value, straight-line depreciation method would greatly improve the equity of the tax law, and would simplify both the law and any comparisons one would desire to make regarding the profitability of different firms.[1]

The second area in which inflation distorts the accounting for corporate taxable income is inventories. The problem arises in determining the cost of goods sold or used, and the value of items remaining in stock. The accounting profession and the IRS have long recognized that even small businesses would find it difficult to keep track of the cost of each specific item in inventory. They do not require that a firm's inventory accounting technique bear any relation to the company's actual inventory management practices. However, unlike the situation just discussed with depreciation, firms are required to be consistent for book and tax purposes with regard to inventory accounting.

The two most commonly used inventory techniques are first in, first out (FIFO), and last in, first out (LIFO). Under the former, FIFO, the cost of the goods sold is taken as if they were the oldest items in stock. The remaining stock is

valued as if these items were those most recently produced. This procedure may have appeal, in that it corresponds to reasonable inventory management practice. The problem, however, is that the firm reports as profit the cost and price increases which occur between production and sales, even though the item must be replaced in inventory with a higher cost unit. For example, consider a firm which has been producing radios at $40 a unit and selling them for $50, maintaining an inventory of ten items. Now, production cost jumps to $60 and selling price to $70. When this sudden price change occurred, the firm had ten units in stock which cost only $40 to produce. Is its unit profit on these items $30 ($70 less $40) or $10 ($70 less $60)? The answer is not obvious. While they cost only $40, they will require $60 to replace. The FIFO system answers $30, and thus results in much larger paper profits (and real taxes) than the LIFO system, which would answer this question with $10.

FIFO, which still is the most commonly used technique, records as taxable profit all nominal increases in value which a firm experiences on its inventoried stock. With inflation, of course, this gain may simply reflect the rising price level and not any real income for the firm. So the income statement may be distorted by FIFO inventory accounting under inflation and, more seriously, taxes may increase without any corresponding change in real income. On the other hand, an advantage of FIFO is that the balance sheet carries a fairly accurate appraisal of the value of the inventoried stock as it reflects the most recent production or acquisition costs.

LIFO is not without its drawbacks. If a firm's acquisitions or production at least matches sales or use of inventoried items (i.e., if the stock is not declining), then LIFO will record no profit on the appreciation of inventories, whether that gain reflects inflation or not. For example, if the inventoried item were gold, and its price changed from $100 to $180 while all other prices increased 20 percent, LIFO would record no income.[2] Worse than this, the balance sheet for a LIFO accounting company may bear little relationship with reality. The inventoried stock is valued at historical prices, which in some cases may be decades out of date and differ from current market prices by large orders of magnitude.

As with depreciation, accountants and the IRS should require consistent real income determination. The fact that different firms use different methods can only cloud cross-firm comparisons, as well as make the tax law inequitable (particularly since, once a choice is made, the firm is not free to alter that choice). A particular, consistent, real inventory accounting procedure has been referred to as Constant-Dollar FIFO (Shoven and Bulow 1975). It would record as profit any real or relative appreciation of a firm's inventoried stock, while not reflecting the pure inflationary gain. It also would have the advantage of being FIFO-based, and would therefore yield meaningful balance-sheet valuations.

The impact of switching to this inflation-adjusted FIFO technique was estimated in this earlier study, and it was found that recorded aggregate corporate profits would have been lower in every year since 1945, meaning that aggregate taxes would have been reduced. The results across firms were again highly variable, depending on whether they are currently a predominantly LIFO or FIFO firm. All present FIFO firms would gain in the sense that their tax bill would be lowered by the inflation adjustment applied to inventories, while some LIFO firms would be worse off if their assets experienced relative appreciation (an example being oil companies in recent years). Again, however, the advantages of being consistent, and also neutral with respect to the inflation rate, seem to be compelling.

Both inflation adjustments discussed so far—depreciation and inventories—would generally lower corporate paper profits and taxes. Two points are important to keep in mind. First, real cash flow or profits are not being affected, except that the tax bill is dependent on these procedures. Otherwise, we are simply discussing whether the numbers accountants write down on paper accurately reflect the fortunes of the firm. Second, while these two adjustments usually receive the

most attention, there are other equally important inflation adjustments which tend to go the other way—that is, to increase recorded profits and therefore taxes. It is to these we
now turn.

Both depreciation and inventories refer to the physical assets of the firm. However, if we want to correctly determine a
firm's real income, attention must be paid to its total
position—its liabilities and financial assets. Much earlier in
this chapter, we repeated the well-known truth that inflation
makes creditors worse off and debtors better off. Particularly,
we stated that interest recipients are taxed on a grossly
exaggerated statement of their real income, while interest
payers are allowed equally bloated interest deductions from
their tax base. The point here is that this analysis applies
equally well to corporations, which are, in aggregate, huge
net debtors. As of 1974, U.S. nonfinancial corporations were
net financial debtors to the extent of approximately $300 bil-
lion. With inflation running at about 10 percent that year,
these firms in total gain some $30 billion from the real "de-
preciation" of their nominal liability. That is, offsetting their
large net interest payments is the fact that their real liability is
reduced, in that it can be paid back in "smaller" dollars after
the period of inflation. This offsetting gain amounts to the
tidy sum of $30 billion.

The existence of a gain for firms because of their net
debtor position is fairly universal, although its extent varies markedly across firms because of their varying financial
structures. Some of the strongest companies in the country,
of course, have little or no debt, and so gain slightly if at all.
The gain of the company (stockholders) is, of course, exactly
matched by the loss of the holder of the bonds as an asset.
The reason that one is better off is also the reason the other
party is worse off. Both positions are affected not only because of inflation, but further, because the rise in long-term
interest rates has depressed the nominal value of its security.
The bondholder not only has an asset which today is worth
"smaller" dollars, but at current market quotations it is also

worth "fewer" dollars. By the end of 1974, the average corporate bond of maturity one year or longer was selling at only 76 percent of issue price. In total, these bonds were $81 billion below what bond purchasers had originally paid for them at time of issuance. Just as the bondholders are worse off, those who owe them the money (the firm or stockholders) are better off. The contract between the parties is a zero sum game. Corporations have gained, because they have locked in low interest rates on long-term loans and that has turned out to be a fortunate financial strategy. Over the years, the total gain that they have experienced has amounted to $81 billion, but this has accrued in an uneven pattern across firms and through time. The correction advocated here would be to carry liabilities at market value, in the same way that assets are treated, and to recognize that a change in the real value of liabilities affects income just as directly as a change in the value of inventories, for example.

If all of the changes advocated here in the accounting of real corporate income were instituted, the effect on reported income of various corporations would be both dramatic and uneven. Two of the more impressive examples in the Shoven and Bulow study (1975) were AT&T and General Motors. The real 1974 income of AT&T was estimated as $8.2 billion rather than their reported $3.2 billion, while the 1974 situation for GM was reversed, with the real figure ($410 million) being less than half that reported ($950 million). Such dramatic adjustments as these indicate the desirability, perhaps necessity, of quickly adopting consistent and inflation-corrected accounting procedures for the determination of corporate income and taxes.

CONCLUSION

Inflation is so embedded in the U.S. economy that its effects on American institutions need to be examined and considered. One of the most severe problems of an escalating price level is its effects on our federal tax system. A basic assumption of the IRS—that a dollar is a dollar regardless of the date of reference—does not accurately reflect reality. A dollar spent on a factory in 1950 is literally no more equivalent to a dollar today than is a British pound.

Given that we are dealing with a world with a dollar of diminishing value, this situation should be reflected and accommodated in the tax laws. Failing to do so creates unnecessary inequities and inefficiencies. It has been argued that two steps are necessary to correct the federal income tax systems for inflation. The first is to correct the actual code and tax computation for inflation by continuously adjusting such nominal income figures as rate-break incomes and deduction ceilings. For both the personal and corporation income tax, this is a fairly simple matter, the implementation of which should be considered immediately.

The second type of adjustment discussed—the accounting or determination of real income for corporations and households—is the more difficult, but probably the more important. Several proposals have been suggested to implement real income as a tax base and, at least for corporations, the adjustments are very large and important. None of these proposals seem so difficult that their implementation should be impeded on these grounds. It is time that the federal government, which directly or indirectly must be held accountable for inflation, adjust its major revenue sources to take its existence into account.

9

ROBERT J. BARRO

Public Debt and Taxes*

Comparative ratio of the public debt and the GNP. The chain-letter mechanism. Bonds or taxation? Capital market imperfections. Future tax liabilities. Government debt fluctuations. The national debt, private investment, and the future.

The national debt, representing the accumulation of past choices to borrow rather than levy taxes, is frequently thought to constitute a burden on future generations. This burden is sometimes viewed as operating through direct income transfers from younger to older generations, and is sometimes described through the crowding-out of private capital formation. Alternatively, it has been argued that (domes-

*This chapter was prepared while I was a National Fellow at the Hoover Institution, Stanford University. I have benefited from research support on related work by the National Science Foundation.

tically held) government bonds represent internally canceling debts and credits, and are therefore of negligible economic significance.

The first section of this chapter provides a brief examination of the historical development of national debt in the United States and the United Kingdom. In both cases, the principal increases in the ratio of debt to income are associated with wars and major economic contractions. The normal peacetime pattern, which applies also to the post–World War II period, is a declining debt/income ratio. The current ratios in both countries are not high by historical standards.

The next section discusses the effect of shifts between taxes and debt issue on perceived private wealth. The analysis centers around the so-called Ricardian theorem, that substitution of debt for taxes would not alter perceived private wealth. The sensitivity of this proposition is examined in relation to the finiteness of life, the imperfection of private capital markets, uncertainty about future tax liabilities, and some other factors. Finiteness of life would not be important if the typical individual were connected to future generations by private intergenerational transfers, either from parents to children (during life or at death) or from children to parents. The imperfection of capital markets is significant only if the government has some technical advantages over the private sector in the execution of loans—which is more likely to be important in underdeveloped countries than in developed countries such as the United States. Uncertainty about future tax liabilities has an ambiguous effect, but, overall, the Ricardian theorem stands up theoretically as a plausible first-order proposition.

The final section relates the wealth effect of debt issue to the central economic questions, which include the burden of the debt on future generations, the crowding-out of private investment, and fiscal policy. The analysis demonstrates that the validity of the Ricardian theorem rules out a public debt burden or a crowding-out effect on private investment. The theorem also insures that fiscal policy, in the sense of tax changes accompanied by compensating adjustments of the government deficit, is impotent as a device for stabilizing the economy.

SOME DATA ON PUBLIC DEBT

Table 1 provides an overview of the behavior of the national debt in the United States since 1860. Column 1 shows the par value of nominal, interest-bearing federal debt net of holdings by U.S. government agencies and trust funds and the Federal Reserve. This concept of national debt is limited to the funded portion that corresponds to interest-bearing government bonds. As discussed by Feldstein (1974), the debt definition can be widened substantially to include the anticipated expenditures payable under social security and other governmental transfer programs. However, the present chapter limits consideration to the narrow national debt concept. Column 2 expresses the quantity of debt in real terms after division by a general price index (the GNP deflator), and column 3 indicates the ratio of nominal debt to nominal gross national product. The quantity of public debt outstanding in 1860 amounted to only 1 percent of GNP.[1] During the Civil War, extensive deficit finance increased the debt/GNP ratio to about 25 percent in 1865. The long, essentially peacetime period that followed showed a steady decline of the national debt to about 2 percent of GNP in 1916. The figure rose sharply during World War I to a peak value of just under 30 percent of GNP, and then fell during the postwar period to about 14 percent in 1929. The large federal deficits and the decline in nominal income during the Great Depression increased the ratio to more than 40 percent in 1940. The ratio then increased sharply to just over 100 percent because of the vast debt issues of World War II. As in the peacetime periods following the Civil War and World War I, the debt/GNP ratio since World War II has steadily declined. However, because of the chronic inflation associated with the ''new monetary standard,''[2] the debt figures expressed as dollars do not show the steady decline that characterized the earlier postwar periods. In 1974 the ratio fell below 20 percent, but increased to 24 percent in 1976 and 1977 as a consequence of the strong economic contraction. These figures show that the current debt/GNP ratio is not high by historical standards, and is well below the values that prevailed during the 1950s.

Over the past fifty years, federal spending has increased dramatically as a percentage of GNP, rising from 3 percent in 1929 to 23 percent in 1976 (see Table 1, column 4). Since World War II, this increased federal spending has been accompanied by a steady decline in the debt/GNP ratio.

State and local government debt and spending are shown in columns 5 through 7. Here, the debt/GNP ratio (column 7) has increased from 1902 (9 percent) to 1940 (16 percent), except during World War I, when the rise in nominal GNP reduced the ratio. After a sharp decline during World War II, the ratio of state and local government debt to GNP rose gradually to its pre–World War II level, which was attained by the mid-1960s. The ratio has remained steady at that value to the present.

It is interesting to compare the U.S. experience with that of Great Britain. Figure 1, which is taken from on-going research by Dan Benjamin and Levis Kochin (1978), plots the ratio of British national debt to national income since 1801. As with the U.S. experience, there is a strong positive effect of major wars on the debt/income ratio. The extensive deficit finance of the Napoleonic Wars produced a debt/income ratio of almost 3.0 in 1821—a value almost three times the peak ratio reached in the United States in 1945. The British experience shows a long period of declining debt/income ratios from 1821 until the start of World War I. A strong increase in the ratio during the war was extended to the depressed economic period of the 1920s and early 1930s. A further

Table 1

Values of Government Debt and Expenditures in the United States for Selected Years

Year	Federal Government				State and Local Government			
	(1) B_f	(2) B_f/P	(3) B_f/Py	(4) G_f/Py	(5) B_{sl}	(6) B_{sl}/P	(7) B_{sl}/Py	(8) G_{sl}/Py
1860	0.06	0.4	.01[a]	.01[a]				
1865	2.22	8.7	.24[a]	.10[a]				
1867	2.24	8.8	.23[a]	.04[a]				
1880	1.71	9.1	.13	.02				
1902	0.93	5.6	.041	.02	2.1	12.7	.09	.05
1916	0.91	3.8	.018	.02	4.5	19.0	.09	.06[b]
1918	20.5	59.9	.26	.23	5.1	14.9	.06	
1922	21.6	67.1	.29	.04	7.9	24.5	.11	.08
1929	14.9	45.3	.14	.03	13.6	41.3	.13	.07
1940	41.5	142.6	.42	.10	16.4	56.4	.16	.08
1945	228.2	600.5	1.07	.40	13.4	35.3	.06	.04
1948	193.6	364.6	.75	.13	17.0	32.0	.07	.06
1956	198.1	314.9	.47	.17	44.5	70.7	.11	.08
1964	218.1	300.0	.34	.19	90.4	124.3	.14	.09
1974	269.9	231.9	.19	.21	211.2	181.4	.15	.11
1976	408.5	305.3	.24	.23	236.3	176.6	.14	.11

Source: Barro 1978*t*.

[a]Based on a trend value of real GNP.

[b]Value is for 1913.

Key: B_f is nominal, par value, interest-bearing federal debt in billions of dollars, net of holdings by federal agencies and trust funds and the Federal Reserve. Values since 1916 are at the end of the calendar year; earlier values are at midyear.

P is the GNP deflator (1972 = 1.0). y is real GNP (1972 dollars).

G_f is total nominal federal expenditure.

B_{sl} is the end-of-year value in billions of dollars of net nominal state and local government debt.

G_{sl} is total nominal state and local government expenditure less transfers from the federal government to the state and local sector.

sharp expansion of national debt occurred during World War II, although the peak debt/income ratio remained somewhat below that attained in 1821. Finally, as with the U.S. experience, the British debt/income ratio has steadily declined since World War II. Again, the current ratio of public debt to national income is not high by historical standards.

ECONOMIC EFFECTS OF THE DEBT/TAX CHOICE

What difference does it make for the economy if the national government finances its expenditures by debt rather than by taxation? The argument that there is no first-order difference, which dates back to Ricardo (1951:1:244-48, 4:184-89), begins by observing that public debt issue implies a stream of future interest payments and possible repayments of principal. These future payments must be financed either by future taxes (including future money creation, which is a form of taxation that works through its effect on the price level) or by additional deficits, which would further increase future interest and principal payments. The option of financing interest payments solely through new debt issue raises the possibility that taxes could be escaped through perpetual deficit finance. But this possibility depends on a chain-letter mechanism in which individuals would be willing to hold ever-expanding amounts of public debt without regard to the government's limited capacity to raise revenue for debt repayment.[3] Generally, it seems safe to ignore this "free lunch" possibility, and to assume that debt issue implies a corresponding increase in the total of taxes that must be collected. As a simplification, I also assume that the future interest payments implied by current debt issue are exactly matched in magnitude and timing by additions to future taxes. This case, in which future interest payments are not financed by additional debt issue and in which future taxes are not high enough to retire outstanding

debt, turns out to be adequate for examining the major economic effects of the debt/tax choice.

Suppose that an additional $1 million of current government expenditure is financed either by current taxes or debt. In the former case, individuals experience an additional one-time tax liability of $1 million. In the latter case, assuming the interest rate on government bonds to be 5 percent per year, government interest payments and, by assumption, tax collections are raised "forever" by $50,000 per year. (It is assumed that there are no direct administrative costs associated with public debt issue, and also that, aside from the difference in timing, the incidence of the $50,000 annual tax is identical to that of the lump-sum $1 million collection. Otherwise, an additional pure income redistribution effect would be added to the analysis. Basically, the representative taxpayer would view the choice between debt issue and taxation as equivalent to the choice between a share of the $1 million current tax and a like share of the $50,000 annual tax in perpetuity. The two options would be viewed as equivalent—producing what economists call the Ricardian equivalence theorem on the public debt (see Ricardo 1951)[4]—under the following conditions: (1) there is no possibility of escaping part of the perpetual tax liability, either by dying (which introduces an effect of finite lives) or by leaving the jurisdiction of the government; (2) everyone can borrow and lend funds at the same interest rate as the government; (3) there is no uncertainty about future tax shares, which might be induced by uncertainty about individual income or other characteristics that determine tax shares; (4) the future tax liabilities implied by public debt are accurately perceived; (5) the volume of government expenditures is independent of the method of finance; and (6) no other channels exist for effects of the choice of finance method on the prices, rates of return, and so on, faced by individuals.

Considering the length of this list, it is obvious that not all of these conditions could be exactly satisfied. In evaluating these factors it is therefore useful to distinguish between first-

and second-order effects and to weigh the likely balance of forces. I discuss, first, the various issues from the viewpoint of the effect of debt issue on how individuals evaluate their personal wealth—and second, the connection of these wealth perceptions to the burden of the public debt argument, to crowding-out of private investment, and to fiscal policy.

FINITE LIVES AND RELATED MATTERS

Suppose that interest payments and associated tax liabilities extend beyond the expected lifetime of the representative current taxpayer (as is clearly the case when the debt principal is "never" paid off). In this situation, an individual who is unconcerned with the welfare of his descendants, and who can borrow and lend at the same interest rate as the government, would be better off with a share of the $50,000 annual liability than with the like share of the single payment of $1 million. Consider an individual who expects to live twenty years, and who meets the one-time tax cost of his share of $1 million by reducing his interest-bearing assets by a like amount. Since these assets have a 5 percent yield, by assumption, annual income is reduced by the share of $50,000—the same annual cost that arises under the debt-finance option and which could have been met from the interest on the same assets, which could then have been maintained intact. Although the two finance options balance in this respect, there is a difference in the taxpayer's estate after twenty years. Under the tax option, the estate is reduced by the share of $1 million. Under the debt option, with no further tax payments required after twenty years (i.e., after death), this reduction does not apply. Anticipating this outcome, a taxpayer wishing to leave a zero (or fixed-size) estate, would therefore increase his lifetime expenditure under the debt option (financed by consuming the capital that would otherwise remain in the estate) than under the tax option.[5] Thus, finite lives imply that the representative current taxpayer would perceive himself wealthier under debt issue than under taxation.

The choice of taxation versus debt produces a wealth effect associated with finite lives, because some of the future tax liabilities needed to pay future interest are shifted to members of later generations. If the added liabilities on descendants were fully counted in wealth calculations by current taxpayers, then the present distinction between the debt and tax options would disappear. Essentially, public debt issue enables members of current generations to die in a state of insolvency by leaving a debt for their descendants. Current taxpayers are "wealthier" if they view the implied governmental shifting of income across generations as desirable. In fact, most individuals already have private opportunities for shifting income across generations that they have chosen not to exercise. Parents make voluntary contributions to children in the form of educational investments, other expenses in the home, and bequests. Children—especially before the expansion of social security— provide support for aged parents. To the extent that private, voluntary, intergenerational transfers of this sort are operative—and casual observation suggests that such transfers, in the appropriate, broadly defined, sense, are pervasive—the shift from tax to debt finance (or, analogously, the introduction of a pay-as-you-go social security scheme) would not present the representative individual with a new opportunity for extracting funds from members of other generations. Rather, the private response to debt issue or to more social security would be to shift private, voluntary transfers by an amount sufficient to restore the balance of income across generations that was previously deemed optimal. In this case, a shift from tax to debt finance would not affect the perceived wealth of a finite-lived taxpayer.[6]

A taxpayer can also escape some part of the future taxes associated with debt by leaving the jurisdiction of the government. Presumably, this option is more pertinent for state and local governments than for the national government, and is generally more important where out-migration costs are low. However, the incentive for individuals to leave an area with a large accumulated debt would arise only where the quantity of government-owned real capital was not sufficient to generate income offsetting the debt-finance costs. At a local level, therefore, debt issue will tend to be associated more with large capital projects than with financing of current expenditures. One further consideration involves the capitalization of taxes—especially property taxes—into property values. To the extent that a higher flow of anticipated future taxes is already reflected in reduced property values (and, correspondingly, in a reduced annual cost of housing, etc.), individuals would not be motivated to move out of the jurisdiction with these higher future taxes.

IMPERFECT PRIVATE CAPITAL MARKETS

The argument that debt and tax finance are equivalent depends also on the correspondence between private and governmental interest rates. Suppose, instead, that some individuals have poor collateral on private loan markets, and therefore face borrowing rates that are much higher than the government's rate, still assumed to be 5 percent. The high private borrowing rates would reflect both risk of default and administrative costs associated with the operation of loan markets. Suppose that the government reduces current taxes by $1,000 on an individual (Person A) with a high or infinite borrowing rate, and substitutes the issue of a $1,000 bond, which would be held by a different individual or firm (Person B), who regards 5 percent per year from the government as a satisfactory rate of return. I assume that the $50 per year flow of taxes to finance the interest payments on the bond are levied on Person A, so that no direct redistribution of income results. The net outcome of this debt-creation process is that Person A borrows $1,000 at a 5 percent interest rate from Person B. With his high private borrowing rate, Person A is likely to be better off, because he may be willing to pay much more than 5 percent annual interest (even for a loan on which default is "impossible") in order to shift expenditures from the future to the present. Person B is satisfied, because the 5 percent yield is guaranteed by the government, although he would not accept such a return on a direct loan to Person A. Apparently, the shift to debt finance would therefore raise the average perceived wealth of current taxpayers.

The government's debt issue functions as a successful intermediation in the credit market, because it avoids the high transaction costs of private loan market operations that are implicit in the initially high borrowing rate of Person A. There is a hidden assumption that the government is more efficient than the private market in carrying out credit market operations. The omitted costs are those entailed by the collection of the flow of future taxes (rather than the single current tax) from Person A. If this individual is a poor credit risk who requires large "supervision" costs on the private market, he is likely, despite the government's coercive taxing powers, to be a similar risk on public loans. The argument that debt issue raises perceived wealth because of imperfect private capital markets assumes that the government is more efficient, at the margin, than the private market in carrying out the loan process.[7]

A related argument is that the superior marketability (which economists call liquidity) of public debt securities allows the government to sell its bonds at lower interest rates than those applicable to private obligations. This point seems to apply with most force to "high-powered" money—which consists, in the United States, of currency and reserves of commercial banks that are members of the Federal Reserve system—where the government has some clear monopoly power. In the United States, this monopoly position does not seem to extend significantly to interest-bearing debt, since the private market seems able to generate, at similar underlying administrative costs, close substitutes for both short- and long-term government securities. Therefore, from the liquidity standpoint, it seems unlikely that shifts between taxes and interest-bearing debt would, at the margin, significantly alter perceived private sector wealth in a developed country such as the United States.

UNCERTAINTY ABOUT FUTURE TAXES

It is often argued that, since the future individual tax liabilities implicit in public debt issue are unpredictable, they would be heavily discounted in calculations of wealth positions.[8] In fact, risk-averse individuals would tend to give higher, rather than lower, weight to a given anticipated amount of future taxes when the uncertainty attached to these liabilities increases.[9] On this count, the substitution of debt issue for current taxation will tend to diminish perceived wealth.

Offsetting this conclusion, some future tax liabilities reflect movements in uncertain future individual incomes, rather than changes in other individual characteristics affecting tax liability, shifts in tax procedures, and so on. A positive association between individual taxes and incomes would buffer changes in individual disposable incomes, and would therefore offset the other effects of uncertainty in wealth calculations. The overall effect of uncertainty on the perceived wealth effect of debt issue is generally ambiguous.

MISPERCEPTION OF FUTURE TAXES

It is also sometimes argued that the future taxes implicit in the public debt are largely ignored because of complexity in estimating them (Feldstein 1976*a*:335; Buchanan and Wagner 1977:130). This problem, however, seems similar in its effects to uncertainty about future tax procedures as discussed above, which tend to magnify, rather than diminish, the average effective weight assigned to future taxes. In any event, it is unclear why misperceptions or "irrationality" would call particularly for underestimation of future taxes. At this level of analysis, one could just as well argue that government deficits, which are well publicized, make people nervous and induce them to feel poorer.

A more plausible argument is that unusual movements (either up or down) in the public debt—that is, government deficits not arising from the usual pattern associated with the business cycle, government expenditure changes, etc. — would be temporarily misperceived.[10] However, in a preliminary investigation (Barro 1978c), I have been unable to isolate important effects of unusual (or usual) public debt movements on economic activity.

THE VOLUME OF GOVERNMENT EXPENDITURE

The above analysis has treated the amount and composition of government spending as fixed, while considering some consequences of different methods of finance. Therefore, it has been possible to abstract the analysis from evaluations of government expenditure programs. It has, however, sometimes been argued that the existence of the debt-finance option effectively "cheapens" government expenditure, because deficits are politically more popular than taxes.[11] This argument is equivalent to the proposition that a shift, at the margin, from taxes to debt would substantially raise perceived private sector wealth, since a move toward deficit finance would only be politically popular in this circumstance. Therefore, the same theoretical objections may be raised against it.

PUBLIC DEBT AND THE
TIMING OF TAXATION

The set of arguments that includes finite lives, imperfect private capital markets, uncertainty about future taxes, and misperceptions of tax liabilities does not make an impressive *a priori* case for public debt issue to alter perceived private wealth in one direction or the other. In a country like the United States, in which the government's technical advantages at the margin, in the loan process, or in creating liquidity are likely to be minimal, it is reasonable to conclude that substitution of debt issue for taxes will have a wealth effect of second-order magnitude (and of indeterminate direction).

One difficulty with this sort of negative conclusion is that it does not provide a basis for a positive theory of public debt issue. I have attempted to construct such a theory in another paper (Barro 1978*c*) by focusing on the role of public debt issue as a mechanism for smoothing the time path of tax collection. Suppose that taxes entail collection costs or impose distortions on the private economy, and that these costs increase with the fraction of current national income that the government collects in taxes. Although public debt issue does not permit permanent escape from taxation, it does allow rearrangement of the timing of collections. With ''collection costs'' as an increasing function of the ratio of taxes to national income, the optimal method of public finance turns out to involve a pattern of debt issue that rules out any predictable changes in this ratio. This behavior raises a given total of tax revenues in a manner that minimizes the expected overall costs of collection.

Among the empirically important implications of this model, deficits would be used to finance temporary government expenditures, especially the large outlays during wartime, and debt issue would be large during recessions and small or negative during booms. During wartime, debt will avoid large temporary movements in the tax/income ratio; during recessions it will preserve stability of the tax/income ratio over the business cycle in the face of little cyclical fluctuation in government spending. Another result is that the debt/income ratio will tend to decline rather than remain constant during peacetime periods, to average out, *ex ante,* the large positive effects on debt issue of wars and severe contractions; and nominal debt will grow, other things equal, one-to-one with the anticipated rate of growth of nominal national income. The last effect is especially important during the inflation of the last decade in the U.S., when much of the federal deficit for these years (although only about 30 percent of the total for 1975-1976) is associated merely with maintaining the anticipated real value of the outstanding interest-bearing public debt. Finally, the model also implies that certain variables—in particular, the size of the accumulated past debt and the level of government expenditure—would not be important determinants of current debt issue.

My empirical analysis suggests that the principal movements in publicly held, interest-bearing federal debt in the United States since World War I can be explained by three variables: (1) the movement in federal expenditures relative to "normal"—which captures, in particular, the strong response of debt issue to temporary wartime spending; (2) the movement in real GNP relative to trend, which captures the countercyclical response of debt issue; and (3) a one-to-one effect of the anticipated inflation rate on the growth rate of nominal debt. The effects of these three variables on debt issue appear to be reasonably stable over the post–World War I period. For example, the sharp expansion of federal debt for 1975-1976 emerges as a response of somewhat more than the usual size to the sharp contraction of output and to the high value of the anticipated rate of inflation. The overall extent of countercyclical debt movement is, actually, stronger than that called for by the model. However, results for the 1920s and 1930s appear similar in this respect to those for the post–World War II period. The evidence does indicate that the size of the outstanding debt (relative to GNP) and the level of government expenditure (as a fraction of GNP) are irrelevant to current debt issue. Overall, the analysis supports the theory of public debt that neglects direct wealth effects and focuses on the tax-smoothing role of deficits.

THE BURDEN OF THE PUBLIC DEBT

The sense in which the domestically owned national debt constitutes a burden on future generations has occupied substantial attention of economists.[12] This topic is intertwined with the wealth effect of debt issue, as can be illustrated for the case of finite-lived taxpayers that was discussed above. Suppose that the representative current taxpayer is unconcerned with his descendants and, therefore, experiences an increase in wealth when taxes are replaced by debt. As James Buchanan (1958) has argued, the burden on future generations is direct and involves, in particular, the liability for taxes that greets members of future generations as they are born. This first-order argument for debt burden is independent of complications that involve the crowding-out of private investment, the direct role of government expenditure programs, the observation that the resources utilized by government for current expenditures must come out of current output, and so on. The debt burden on future generations is analogous to the one that might arise under a pay-as-you-go social security scheme involving no government purchases of goods and services. Currently old individuals receiving retirement payments would benefit initially at the expense of the currently young taxpayers. These currently young individuals would be able to recoup a portion of their losses, because members of later generations will be born with the liability to pay taxes to finance social security benefits to retirees. Overall, there will be a transfer of wealth from younger generations (including the currently unborn) to older generations.

While this kind of analysis captures the essence of the public debt-burden argument, it is incomplete because it does not discuss the restoration of economic equilibrium after the initial boost to wealth perceptions. Basically, the rise in perceived wealth will increase consumer demand and, therefore, any increase in saving—which increases the supply of private loanable funds—must fall short of the rise in the government's demand for borrowings. The resulting excess of demand over supply will increase interest rates to restore equilibrium in the loanable funds market. The depressing effect of this higher required rate of return on private investment constitutes a crowding-out of public borrowing. Franco Modigliani (1961:730-55) has labeled the associated long-run decline in the economy's capital/labor ratio as the burden of the public debt on future generations (in the sense that each generation, in aggregate, bequeathes a smaller capital stock to its descendants). Although a capital stock reduction would be predicted under the above assumption about wealth perceptions, this effect is not the essence of the debt-burden argument, which has been captured above by the direct intergenerational income transfers that are implied by debt issue or social security.

The arguments for debt burden and for crowding-out of private investment hinge on the assumption that debt issue raises perceived wealth. Neither a burden on future generations nor crowding-out would occur in the case discussed above, where the public intergenerational transfers implied by debt issue or social security are fully offset by compensating adjustments in voluntary private transfers. For example, there may be no net change in income distribution across generations if parents react to debt issue by increasing transfers to their children, or if children react by reducing transfers to their aged parents. With the corresponding absence of a shift in perceived wealth, consumer demand would not be stimulated by the movement from taxes to debt issue. It follows that the supply of private loanable funds would rise one-to-one with the cut in current taxes (increase in current disposable income), so that the extra governmental demand for funds implied by its debt issue would be fully absorbed by the private sector without an increase in the rate of return. Under these circumstances—when public debt issue leaves unchanged the value of perceived wealth—the crowding-out of private investment would not arise.

Imperfect Private Capital Markets

Imperfect private capital markets (or the superior liquidity characteristics of government debt), which may be especially important for underdeveloped countries, also imply that public debt issue may raise perceived wealth. However, the analysis of debt burden and crowding-out for this case is quite different from that described above. Substitution of debt for taxation can work, in part, as an effective governmental intermediation in credit markets. By cutting current taxes, the government can place some funds in the hands of individuals with high (or infinite) borrowing rates who have correspondingly high opportunity rates of return for investment or consumption purposes. These individuals would respond to the tax cut by raising their demands for commodities and—as they exhaust the opportunities with the highest imputed rates of return—by correspondingly reducing the interest they would be willing to pay on borrowed funds. On the other hand—neglecting the government's collection costs for future taxes—individuals or firms with interest rates equal to the government's rate would be initially unaffected by the tax cut. Because of the net increase in private commodity demand, it again follows that the government's increased demand for loanable funds would exceed the increase in private supply. With debt issue, therefore, the interest rate on risk- and transaction cost-free loans will again rise. However, as shown above, the imputed rate of return for the individuals with high borrowing rates must fall. Therefore, the govern-

ment's credit market intermediation implied by its debt issue
leads to a convergence of rates of return across the economy.
The net effect on investment versus consumption is ambiguous, but the diversion of funds from low opportunity rates of
return to high rates is clear. In this event, if the government
actually has a technical advantage in capital market operations, the perceived wealth increase associated with debt
issue is neither an illusion nor an expropriation of future generations, but is rather a movement toward a more efficient
allocation of resources. Although it is appropriate in this case
to view debt issue as raising perceived private wealth, it
would be inappropriate to speak of a public debt burden or of
a crowding-out of private investment.

FISCAL POLICY

The perceived wealth effect of public debt issue (produced in
this case by a finite life effect, by imperfect private capital
markets, or by other reasons for heavy discounting of future
tax liabilities) is also a necessary condition for the efficacy of
fiscal policy—that is, for the use of government deficits
(surpluses) to stimulate (deflate) the economy.[13] Substitution
of debt issue for taxation is assumed to raise perceived
wealth, and thereby to increase aggregate demand. But if
debt issue does not increase perceived wealth, the possibility
of this sort of fiscal policy disappears. Therefore, the argument against a significant wealth effect of public debt issue is
also an argument against the efficacy of fiscal policy.[14]

The weight of empirical evidence on the connection between public debt (or, analogously, the expected benefits less
taxes implied by social security) and aggregate consumer demand suggests a minor impact of uncertain direction.[15] However, the evidence is surely not unanimous, and many estimation problems exist with this type of empirical analysis. Despite these results, which raise doubts about the possibility of

important fiscal policy effects, some large econometric models nevertheless imply that "expansionary" fiscal policy would have a substantial positive impact on economic activity. These models essentially constrain a shift from taxes to debt to have a positive effect on consumer demand—usually by writing consumption as a positive function of current disposable income, without attempting to hold constant the value of anticipated future taxes.[16] This restricted specification unreasonably requires the response of consumer demand to a tax cut to be the same as that induced by a rise in real national income, independently of whether the tax cut is associated either with a deficit that would raise future taxes, or with a decline in the anticipated long-run government expenditures. Some analyses of income determination that do not impose these sorts of restrictions do not seem to show significant fiscal policy effects.[17]

It is thus fair to say that neither economic theories nor empirical analyses provide convincing evidence for the effectiveness of fiscal policy. The area of fiscal policy exhibits a wide gap between, on the one hand, the weight of theory and evidence, and, on the other hand, the general opinion of professional economists and policymakers.

10

JOHN WHALLEY

Tax Developments Outside the United States and Their Implications for Current U.S. Reform Proposals

Comparative tax policies in OECD countries. The United Kingdom, Canada, Australia, and the U.S. Tax reform in Western Europe—value added tax, net worth tax, property tax. The effect of foreign taxes—direct and indirect—on U.S. trade. Overseas taxation of U.S. business operations.

It appears that foreign countries have succeeded for a number of years in administering tax systems with features which are quite different to those which currently operate in the United

States. This suggests that a number of administrative or political constraints, often accepted as data for the purposes of tax reform discussion in the U.S., are not, in fact, operative. Tax reform developments in other countries have in recent years shown similarities to those in the U.S. The process of extensive initial discussion, followed by subsequent scaling down of proposed legislation and a further scaling down upon enactment, seems common to both the U.S. and other countries.

In the case of the value added tax, particular European concerns over administrative issues account for its introduction. The impact of foreign taxation arrangements for trade relations—both merchandise trade and investment activity—between the U.S. and other countries is an unsettled empirical issue. The extent to which foreign tax structures are disadvantageous to the U.S. depends on their selective nature, rather than on the border tax adjustments implied by destination-based taxes abroad. The movement towards a common integrated corporate tax system in the European Economic Community (EEC), with refundable tax credits only between EEC member countries, seems to be disadvantageous to U.S. investment abroad.

AN OUTLINE OF TAX STRUCTURES ABROAD[1]

Outside the U.S., differences in tax structure across both developed economies and less-developed economies are more wide ranging than is commonly believed. There are differences in emphasis between different types of taxation policies, and differences of structure within areas of tax policies.

Tables 1 and 2 summarize the major differences in the structure of taxation between a number of member countries in the Organization for Economic Cooperation and Development (OECD), for which information is available in the OECD Revenue Statistics. In Table 1 the tax collections in twelve countries are broken down into direct taxes, indirect taxes, and into the more detailed components of personal income, corporate, sales, value added tax (VAT), social security, and other taxes. In addition, information is given on the proportion of the gross national product of each economy which flows through the taxation system. Direct taxes[2] include income and corporate taxes; indirect taxes, the broadly based indirect taxes such as retail sales taxes, value added taxes, commodity taxes (Japan), manufacturer's sales tax (Canada), and specific excises on individual items. Social security taxes comprise the combined employer and employee contributions made to social insurance plans of various kinds; others include property, gift, estate, net worth taxes, license fees, and miscellaneous charges.

The United Kingdom tax structure is substantially different in one way or another when compared to each of the other countries appearing in Table 1. The U.S. has a slightly smaller proportion of tax receipts in terms of GNP than Canada, but places much heavier reliance on social security taxes; Canada, in turn, places more reliance on indirect taxes. Canada has a federally operated, broadly based, indirect tax (the manufacturer's sales tax), whereas the U.S. does not. In comparison with Japan, the U.S. collects a substantially larger portion of GNP in taxes. The relatively small size of the public sector in Japan is an important characteristic reflected in the Japanese tax system and, as a fraction of GNP, approximately one-half of tax receipts flow through the public sector. The U.S. places less reliance on the income tax than do the Australasian economies. In both Australia and New Zealand, social security taxes and income taxes were consolidated in the late 1940s, and a large proportion of total tax receipts flow through the income tax.

The U.S. collects a smaller fraction of GNP in taxes than do the major European economies. In the case of particular EEC countries, most notably France, the reliance on the income tax is surprisingly small. France collects approximately 10 percent of total tax receipts through the income tax, while

Table 1
Broad Indications of Comparative Tax Structures

Country	Tax Revenues (All levels $ billions)	Tax Revenues (as % of GDP)	Property	Income	Social Security	Corporate	Sales/VAT	Specific Excise	Other	Direct	Indirect	Other
			Taxes (as % of total)							All Data for 1973 (as % of total)		
Australia	27.9	30.1	9.3	43.6	–	12.3	6.7	18.8	9.4	55.9	38.4	5.8
Belgium	25.8	41.4	2.4	32.0	31.7	7.4	16.5	8.7	1.3	71.3	28.7	–
Canada	56.6	34.0	9.2	33.3	9.5	13.8	12.5	13.6	8.1	57.4	41.4	1.2
France	123.9	36.9	4.0	12.4	40.0	5.4	23.6	9.2	5.5	57.8	37.7	4.6
W. Germany	149.7	35.2	3.1	30.1	34.2	4.4	14.7	10.5	3.1	68.7	29.7	1.6
Italy	55.7	32.3	3.6	15.3	45.9	6.3	14.3	13.5	1.1	67.5	32.5	–
Japan	102.0	20.2	9.6	25.0	25.2	17.0	–	15.8	7.3	67.2	27.7	5.1
Netherlands	38.1	46.9	3.2	27.0	38.4	7.7	14.3	7.7	1.8	73.1	26.4	0.5
New Zealand	4.3	32.2	8.3	51.1	2.8	13.1	8.8	13.7	2.3	67.4	32.6	–
Sweden	31.8	45.9	1.1	46.1	19.3	4.3	11.9	11.4	5.9	69.7	26.1	4.2
U.K.	83.8	36.8	12.4	38.9	18.3	5.2	8.7	14.6	2.0	62.3	37.5	0.2
U.S.	436.6	30.3	13.6	33.0	24.5	10.8	6.7	9.4	2.0	68.3	31.7	–

Source: *OECD Revenue Statistics 1965–1975.*

40 percent of tax receipts are accounted for by social security taxes and 25 percent by the value added tax (the broadly based indirect tax). Although no data on developing and less-developed countries are presented in Table 1, the contrast with the U.S. in terms of tax structure is even more striking. Certain less-developed countries rely almost exclusively on indirect taxes for their source of revenue, and in some cases these indirect taxes are accounted for primarily by export taxes on one or two selected items.

Among the major economies of the world, a diversity of tax structure exists in terms of the relative importance of various kinds of taxation instruments which, in turn, differ substantially in their structure and scope. There does not appear to be a uniform balance between types of taxes, and this suggests the feasibility of a substantially different U.S. tax system from that currently operating. This is illustrated by the discussion of property tax reform in the U.S. Those who argue against extensive reform of the property tax frequently claim that it is not possible for small jurisdictions to find alternative forms of financing. The fact that Scandinavian economies have successfully managed for many years without an extensive property tax, relying heavily on a local income taxation system, suggests this argument is weak.

The range of experience which Table 1 represents is, therefore, important in considering tax reform alternatives. Taxation possibilities are sometimes argued against in the U.S. on administrative or other grounds, when they have been successfully experimented with abroad.

Table 2, illustrating the diversity in the details of tax arrangements by country, outlines some of the principal features of the income tax in each of those nations. As can be seen, rate structures vary substantially. The U.K. has a single marginal rate of income tax covering the majority of taxpayers, with steep progression of marginal rates affecting the top tail of the income distribution (the top 5 percent of income tax payers). A mild progressivity of average and marginal tax rates is present in the Australian-Canadian income

Table 2

Characteristics of Income Taxes by Country

Country	(1) Tax Basis: Individual or Family	(2) 1973 GNP/Occupied Population (in U.S. $)	(3) Initial Marginal Rate (by year)	(4) Top Marginal Rate	(5) Marginal Rate at Income in (2)[a]
Australia	I	$10,588	9.8 (1972/1973)	66.7	30.3
Belgium	F	11,887	20.0 (1974)	60.0	37.5
Canada	I	13,219	4.6 (1973)	61.3	38.9
France	F	11,659	5.0 (1974)	60.0	30.0[b]
W. Germany	F/I	12,919	22.0 (1976)	56.0	23.0
Italy	F	7,184	10.0 (1976)	72.0	20.4
Japan	I	7,824	10.0 (1975)	75.0	15.8
Netherlands	I	12,911	25.0 (1974)	71.0	49.3
U.K.	F	7,011	35.0 (1976)	98.0[c]	35.0
U.S.[d]	F/I	14,349	14.0 (1976)	70.0[e]	27.0

Source: National accounts and government documents for the countries represented.

[a]For those countries which tax the family unit, the marginal rate at 1.5 times the income in (2) has been calculated.

[b]Rate calculated from "Quotient 3" tables (married couple with two children).

[c]This is the top marginal rate on investment income; the top marginal rate on labor income is 83 percent.

[d]In W. Germany and the U.S., individuals have the option of filing separate or joint returns.

[e]This is on investment income; the top rate on labor income is 50 percent.

tax systems. By way of contrast, the French income tax introduces substantial elements of differentiation according to family circumstances. France operates a "quotient rule," whereby tax liabilities are calculated on the basis of tax tables for single individuals, with the total tax liabilities divided by a number which reflects family size (children are counted as one-half). Marriage and additional children in France bring substantial income tax savings, and extensive adoption of similar provisions would substantially change the operation of the system in other countries. Income tax rates in Sweden are not as progressive as is commonly thought; the tax is progressive and federally operated, with marginal tax rates going up to approximately 55 percent, but most local jurisdictions have flat-rate income taxes in the region of 20 to 25 percent.[3]

Besides different rate structures in the income tax, differences occur across countries in the bases for most taxes. This is especially true of the corporate tax. For instance, until 1974 the U.K. taxed corporate profits from stock appreciation on a LIFO basis rather than a FIFO basis. (LIFO and FIFO stand for "last in/first out" and "first in/first out," respectively; under a LIFO system the capital gain accruing on stock of goods in process is taxable; under a FIFO system they are not.) In the year prior to a change in law in 1974, some 60 percent of taxable corporate profits were attributable to capital gains, accruing as LIFO profits (HMSO 1977). The corporate tax in several European countries also contains depreciation provisions significantly more advantageous than in the U.S. The U.K. currently operates a scheme of 100 percent first-year depreciation. Capital expenditures are totally deductible. An even more extensive scheme is operated in Denmark, where it is possible to get a capital expenditure deduction in advance of expenditures by making a declaration of intent to invest.

Relatively few countries operate capital gains taxes outside of North America and the U.K. For instance, there are currently no explicit capital gains taxes in Australia.[4] This tax in the U.K. has recently been revised, with tapering provisions to supposedly accommodate the problem of taxes in inflationary capital gains. Under these provisions, a fixed percent of the value of a capital gain is deductible for each year for which an asset is held, and at the end of a qualifying period no tax is paid upon a realized capital gain.[5]

Canada is notable for its differences in income tax structure compared to the U.S., and in particular for its relatively light tax treatment of capital income for most taxpayers. The Canadian tax has extensive deductibility provisions for increases in holdings of financial assets in qualifying accounts. Under the Canadian Registered Retirement Savings plan, deposits up to the value of $5,500 per year are deductible in any year in which they are made. These are then taxable on withdrawal at any time during the lifetime. In addition, up to $1,000 a year is deductible under the Registered Home Ownership Plan. This remains untaxed when withdrawn, if used for house purchase. There is also a $1,000 interest and dividend exclusion (from Canadian sources), plus a dividend tax credit.

It thus seems fair to conclude that all the major market-type economies have tax structures which differ from the U.S. These are differences in the relative importance of types of taxes, and in details of rate structures and definitions of tax bases. Although the next section attempts to compare U.S. and foreign tax reform experience, these differences make it difficult, since "reform" abroad can be the introduction of arrangements already operating in the U.S. and vice versa.[6]

TAX REFORM MOVEMENTS IN COUNTRIES OUTSIDE THE U.S.

In recent years, the countries whose tax systems are referred to in Tables 1 and 2 have experimented with tax reform of various types. In the majority of cases, tax reform developments have coincided with changes of government, usually the election of a left-of-centre government replacing a right-of-centre regime. There are, however, instances of changes in taxation structure occurring with no change in government, most important those coinciding with economic integration, such as in the EEC. These tax reform attempts seem to have become more frequent in the past five to ten years than during the preceding decade, which reflects increasing concern over both taxation issues and the impact of changes in taxation structure on economic behavior.

In the Australasian countries, the most notable attempt at tax reform occurred with the election of the Whitlam government in Australia in 1972, where an attempt was made to introduce a comprehensive capital gains tax (previously none had existed). Mortgage interest up to an income ceiling became deductible, and changes were made in the deductibility rates for property taxes. The capital gains tax proposal was abandoned as a result of pressure from equity owners. No significant tax reform attempts have been made in New Zealand.

In Canada, tax reform attempts have been more modest than in other countries, reflecting the stability of governmental structure; the Liberals have been in power since the early 1960s. The major tax reform development in Canada in the last decade was the publication of the Carter Commission Report (1969), which became famous for its adherence to the so-called Haig-Simons concept of income enshrined in the principle that "a dollar is a dollar is a dollar." The suggestion is that all income is to be taxed independently of its source and type, whether it be a monetary form or whether it be in some other form.

The major Carter recommendations made in 1969 were that an integrated personal and corporate tax system be introduced; capital gains be taxed on an accrual basis, with five-year revision of the valuation of assets; that inheritances be taxed on receipt; and that the family rather than the individual be the taxable unit. Only a limited amount of change has taken place in the Canadian tax structure in response to these proposals and, in fact, tax changes have been made since which run counter to the Carter Commission proposals. The introduction of capital gains tax, which took place in 1972, was accompanied by the abolition of the federally operated gift and estate taxes, on the grounds that a capital gains tax with deemed realization at death would constitute a double tax at death. While in the opinion of many people this is a fallacious argument, it was nevertheless used to justify the abolition of federal gift and estate taxes, and no subsequent reenactment of those taxes has taken place in Canada. At the same time, there has been extensive development of tax shelter devices, such as the Registered Home Ownership Plan and the Registered Retirement Savings Plan, which have further moved the Canadian taxation structure away from the Carter Commission principles.

In Japan, limited amounts of tax reform have occurred, once again reflecting the durability of the ruling governmental party. A debate continues on whether or not to introduce a capital gains tax, and the amount of tax change which has taken place within the Japanese tax system over the last ten years has been relatively small. The major fiscal modifications have been yearly tax cuts (cuts in rates and increases in deductible allowances) to offset the fiscal drag from the high real growth rate. These yearly tax cuts have proved to be electorally successful.

In the European countries, there have been more extensive tax reform developments than in most countries abroad. Major tax modifications occurred in response to domestic pressures for tax reform and in response to the pressures for tax harmonization with the EEC. The existing Italian tax system, comprising a large number of existing taxes,[7] was reformed in 1973, with a major portion of existing tax structure effectively replaced by three separate taxes—an income, corporate, and a value added tax. While this tax reform does not seem to have coped with the problems of tax administration and evasion in the way in which it was hoped, the impact of the change in tax structure has been very substantial.

In the United Kingdom a sequence of tax reform developments have spanned the last ten years involving, initially, administrative rearrangements in the income tax in the early 1970s, coupled with changes in a combination of taxes to coincide with British entry into the EEC in 1973. The classical (nonintegrated) corporate tax system was replaced by an integrated corporate tax, with a dividend tax credit given to stockholders upon receipt of a dividend. The credit acts as a partial offset to personal income tax liabilities on dividends received.[8] In addition, the existing system of payroll taxes was modified, with the abolition of the selective employment tax which had been introduced earlier in 1966. The existing system of indirect taxation was also changed with the abolition of purchase tax, a multiple rate wholesale tax, replaced by the value added tax whose adoption at that time was a condition of British entry into the EEC.

Following these changes, further extensive changes occurred in the U.K. with the election of the Labour government in 1974. The system of estate duty was changed to a cumulative lifetime capital transfer tax, which taxed all gifts made in life as well as the value of the estate passing at death. In addition, extensive discussion took place on the possible introduction of a wealth tax which, if introduced, would have been the most far-reaching of all the wealth taxes which operate within the European countries. As it happened, the wealth tax was not introduced, due to a combination of administrative delay, parliamentary disagreement, and finally, change of priority by the government.

In other European countries, extensive tax reform was recently proposed in France by Mitterand in the recent national elections. The amount of tax reform discussion in France over the last few years appears to have been quite limited prior to this. Limited change has taken place in West Germany, as is also true in Holland and Belgium. More extensive changes have been discussed in Denmark, partly as a result of the electoral successes of a minority opposition party strongly opposed to the extensive public sector.

These tax reform movements have, to some degree, followed a trend evident in the United States, although in some areas developments have been running in advance of those in the U.S. Discussion is often protracted, enactment is usually slow, and in practice deviates to some extent from the original intent of the reform proposal. In a number of countries, the discussion of the capital gains tax and its possible introduction has continued on and off for some twenty to thirty years. In the case of the corporate tax, however, the alternative systems which involve integrated personal and corporate taxes of either the split rate or the dividend tax credit variety have been extensively experimented with. The number of countries having the classical (nonintegrated) system which operates in the U.S. is now a minority.

IMPLICATIONS FOR THE U.S. FROM TAX EXPERIMENTATION ABROAD

A number of tax reform proposals which have been discussed in the United States in recent years reflect taxation arrangements operating in other countries.

Experience with the Value Added Tax[9]

From time to time in the U.S. there has been active discussion of the possible introduction of a value added tax at the federal level. This has been advocated on a number of different grounds; in some cases as a replacement for existing taxes such as the corporate tax or (on occasions) the property tax, and at other times as a retaliatory trade measure to the taxes which operate abroad in economies of U.S. trading partners. The trade issues of the tax are returned to in the following section, although it will be noted in passing that this advocacy of the value added tax is based on something of a fallacy.

The basic idea of a value added tax is to operate a system of indirect taxation under which it is possible to collect the indirect tax, not at the point of final sale, but in installments as the components of the resale value are assembled while a commodity passes through increasingly higher stages of the production chain. Under a retail sales tax, a car would be taxed at the point of final sale; under a value added tax, the value of steel in the car would be taxed at the point at which it leaves the steel factory, the value added in the chassis of the car would be taxed at the point that it leaves the plant producing the car bodies, the value added in the tires would be taxed at the point at which the tires leave the tire factory, and so on.

If a general value added tax or a general retail sales tax operates (i.e., under both circumstances, a single rate of tax applies to all products and transactions), and the economy is perfectly competitive, the effect of taxing value added is equivalent to a tax at an equal rate on all final products in the economy. A value added tax is therefore often considered to be equivalent to a retail sales tax.

Because of this equivalence in the competitive, broadly based, case, European advocates of the value added tax see it not as a replacement for existing corporate or property taxes, but as a tax which has underlying administrative advantages compared to a retail sales tax. The first of these is the ease of collecting tax revenues if the economy has a small number of large producers of primary products (e.g., a small number of steel producers and coal producers) and a large number of retail outlets. The argument is that it is simpler to collect a large portion of tax receipts from the small number of large producers, rather than delay collection of taxes until retail sale. This argument is particularly important in some of the European countries which have had great difficulty over the years in collecting retail sales taxes. It is important to see this as a European argument which does not apply in the North American context, since in those states in which retail sales taxes operate, no major difficulty is encountered in tax collection.

The second administrative argument in favor of the tax is that the EEC is committed to a form of economic integration under which domestic policies which are perceived as distorting trade between European member states will be eliminated. A fundamental principle underlying tax harmonization in Europe is the abolition of so-called "fiscal frontiers." These are the border posts at the point of entry to a country where taxes on exports must be rebated and taxes on imports assessed. Because of this, the European community is committed to tax harmonization between member states on the basis of the so-called "restricted origin" principle.[10] Under this arrangement, taxes will be administered on an origin basis for internal EEC trade (that is, trade between European member countries), but on a destination basis for extra EEC trade (that is, trade between any EEC country and any country outside the EEC area). The idea is that fiscal frontiers between member states will be eliminated, but border tax adjustments preserved on goods leaving or entering the community. Given this adherence to the restricted origin principle, proponents of the value added tax argue that a retail sales tax is inherently a destination-based tax, and that to operate a retail sales tax on an origin basis is impossible.

These two administrative arguments in favor of the value added tax have been extremely persuasive in the debate on this tax in the European community. They are wholly missing in the U.S. debate, because neither of them applies with any force. This is important to bear in mind in considering the value added tax as a possible tax replacement in the U.S., where retail sales taxes are administered with no great difficulty, and where the origin basis has not been advocated as a desirable form for a nationally based system of indirect taxes. At this point, of course, no federally operated, broadly based, indirect tax operates in the U.S.

A last point of importance with the value added tax concerns its capability to eliminate pyramiding of indirect taxes. A problem with the retail sales tax is that sales to other producers may be taxed, even though they use purchased products for the production of other goods. This can result in a degree of pyramiding of the tax. To all practical purposes, pyramiding within the retail sales tax in North America has been removed by a system of assigning tax numbers to retail outlets, whereby a credit for a tax paid on purchase of an item from a qualifying retail outlet can be claimed if the purchaser is also a retail outlet. It frequently claimed, however, that the value added tax will totally remove pyramiding, which, while true, is not in practice a significant point in favor of the value added tax. A cost of exact removal of pyramiding is that, with the value added tax, it is relatively difficult to produce low rates of tax on particular commodities within the system. It is easy to exempt transactions from the tax coverage, and in this way pyramiding can be directly coped with. It is much more difficult to separately treat commodities in order to produce the effect, under the value added tax system, of a special rate of tax on the final sale of a particular item. It is necessary to apply a separate rate of tax to each of the components of value added as they appear in the production chain. Retail sales taxes thus have more commodity flexibility with respect to tax rates, compared to the value added tax. This is especially important if food (both processed and unprocessed), clothing items, and other goods are to be removed from the system of indirect taxation on redistributive grounds, as is common in North America.

Experience with Net Worth Taxes[11]

From time to time taxes on personal wealth have been advocated for the U.S. Although no legislative impact has been made by these proposals to date, this is a further area where guidance can be obtained from the operation and structure of these taxes abroad.

An important point sometimes neglected in U.S. discussion is that the wealth taxes which presently operate in the European countries are not substantive revenue-raising taxes. West Germany has a top marginal wealth tax rate of .5 per-

cent, based on out-of-date assessments. Holland has a top
marginal rate of 1.0 percent per year. In Sweden, the top
marginal rate is higher, at 2.5 percent per year, but there are
aggregation provisions which place a ceiling on the combined
income tax and wealth tax, such that the combined tax on the
income from wealth does not exceed a certain amount (currently, 85 percent).

Wealth taxes do, however, have one argument in their
favor which suggests that, in spite of this experience in Western Europe, the tax may eventually be taken seriously as a
possible supplement to the existing U.S. income tax. It was
within this context that the tax was actively discussed in the
United Kingdom between 1974 and 1976. In a regime where
there are perfect capital markets it should, of course, make no
difference whether or not taxes are levied on stock valuation
of assets or on the income flow which those assets yield. If an
individual owns stock in a corporation which pays 10 percent
per year, a 50 percent tax on the income which that stock
yields is equivalent to a 5 percent tax on the value of the
stock. The wealth tax, however, becomes attractive once it is
recognized that there are features of the income tax which
yield situations where income flows are exempt from tax.
This is most notable in the case of houses, where the imputed
income from owner-occupied housing goes untaxed, and the
same argument also extends to other durable goods, including
cars, appliances, and other forms of real property. If the income tax is not to be reformed, and if the taxation advantages
to these owned assets are to persist, then a net worth tax can
offer partial offset. The more satisfactory approach, however,
is to modify and change the income tax, and to include these
items as taxable.

Experience with Alternatives to the
Property Taxes Abroad

The property tax in the U.S. has in recent years attracted a
wide amount of attention, because of increasing property tax

liabilities in jurisdictions which have high levels of providing local public services. A number of alternatives to the property tax have from time to time been advocated and rejected. A striking feature in international experience with the financing of local jurisdictions is that certain countries have for many years managed without extensive property taxes. The most notable, as already mentioned, is the case of Scandinavia, where local income taxes operate as a surcharge on the nationally operated income tax, and property is taxed under the net worth tax.

A country where alternatives to the property tax have been extensively discussed recently is the U.K., with the publication of the Layfield Report (1976) on local authority finance. In this report, it has been accepted as feasible to have regionally and municipally operated income taxes as partial replacements for property taxes. Local value added taxes have also been discussed. A particularly complex system of local authority finance exists in Japan, where a number of different local taxes operate. Local income taxes, enterprise taxes, corporate income taxes, sales taxes, and other use taxes simultaneously operate at all levels of government. This suggests that fiscal innovation by local jurisdictions, while administratively complex, is nonetheless possible.

BORDER TAX ISSUES AND U.S. TRADE

An issue of importance to the U.S. in foreign taxation is the effect on the structure and pattern of U.S. trade of taxes operating abroad. It is frequently felt in the U.S. that the major trading partners of that country obtain a trade advantage by operating destination-based, nationally operated, indirect taxes, while the U.S. operates no federally based, broadly based, indirect tax. Under destination-based taxes, imports into these countries (U.S. exports) are liable for a domestic tax when entering the country, whereas the exported items from these countries (U.S. imports) are free of the domestic tax charged. This is true of the value added tax in the European Economic Community, under which exports receive a tax rebate and imports are liable for a tax. It is also true of the commodity tax in Japan, under which the tax is rebated on exports and a tax placed on imports; and of the manufacturer's tax in Canada, under which once again imported goods are liable for a tax, whereas exported goods avoid the tax.

An important point to note is that the view that foreign countries operating destination-based taxes secure a trade advantage is based on something of a fallacy.[12] In long-run equilibrium, a movement from a destination- to an origin-based tax for a general tax[13] will affect only the exchange rate. No effect on real trade flows will result, and no trade advantage is involved. In the long-run equilibrium, the introduction of a tax—or change of basis of a tax—will make no difference at all to real trade flows. The same proposition holds if either a destination- or origin-based general tax is introduced. Under a regime of flexible exchange rates, exchange rates will adjust so that domestic relative prices in the country in which the tax is imposed will be unchanged. A balance will occur in the external sector accounts if there was balance before the introduction of the tax, with the same trade flows in physical terms taking place. Under a regime of fixed exchange rates, domestic price levels will adjust in long-run equilibrium, and once again the same real trade flows will prevail.

This argument suggests that, in long-run equilibrium, the movement from one tax basis to another tax basis (e.g., from an origin to a destination basis) for a general tax is equivalent to a monetary change which has no effect on real values of the international economic system. Real trade flows between trading partners will remain unchanged. Thus, an accusation by the U.S. that trading partners pursue a destination-based tax and obtain a trade advantage, and therefore pressure should be put on them to move to an origin-based tax, is based on a fallacy. This point is an issue in the recent discussion of possible countervailing duties on the import of Japanese color TV sets into the U.S. The claim is that color TV sets being exported to the U.S. by Japanese producers are being sold in the U.S. at prices lower than their sale price in Japan. What this reflects to a large degree is the fact that the commodity tax in Japan, which has a high rate of tax on TV sets (in the region of 25 percent), is not charged on exports to the U.S. The apparent ''dumping'' of color TV sets in the U.S. is thus partly a reflection of the administration of the domestic tax in Japan on a destination basis.

In practice, however, destination-based taxes operated in foreign countries are not general taxes, but selective taxes. Because of this, the issue of trade disadvantage to the U.S. is not that of the destination versus the origin basis, but the selective nature of these taxes. In a number of instances, these foreign taxes can impose a term of trade loss on the U.S. Canada, for instance, is a substantial importer of U.S. manufactured products, and, in turn, exports raw materials and agricultural products to the U.S. The manufacturer's sales tax in Canada is a selective tax on manufactured products, falling heavily on U.S. exports to Canada. Depending on the price elasticities in U.S.-Canadian trade, this tax can change the relative price of imports into Canada in terms of domestically produced goods. In Japan, the commodity tax is a selective tax, but in this case the high tax rates are associated with goods which Japan exports. Among the EEC countries, differential tax rates operate under the value added tax system, and selective effects are also involved. In general, low rates of tax apply to food items, which are also items imported by the EEC from the U.S.

Thus, in practice, the issue of the trade effects of foreign indirect taxes operated abroad becomes obscured by debate on the destination-versus-origin principle. The main issue should be the selective nature of these taxes rather than the border tax issue. Although it is an unsettled empirical matter, it seems clear that in some cases the U.S. gains because U.S. exports are lightly taxed, and in other cases it loses.

DEVELOPMENTS IN THE TAXATION OF U.S. BUSINESS ABROAD

Of the changes in tax treatment of U.S. business abroad, the most notable have been changes which have recently taken place in the European Economic Community. In a number of different countries, in particular the U.K. and West Germany, there has in recent years been a movement away from the classical, nonintegrated system of corporate tax to an integrated corporate and personal tax involving dividend tax credits. Credit systems have been adopted in preference to split-rate corporate tax systems, with a lower corporate tax rate on distributed profits.

An important feature in these developments has been the discussion of crediting methods which are advantageous to domestic stockholders but disadvantageous to foreign stockholders (see Adams and Whalley 1977). If we take as an example a U.S. citizen who has invested in France, the U.S. citizen, upon receipt of his dividends, may receive a credit against French personal income taxes, even though the individual has no liability at all for French personal income taxes. Thus, an issue with the movement from the classical to the so-called ''imputation'' (dividend tax credit) system of corporate tax in the EEC has been the refunding of tax credits. While these credits have, by and large, been made refundable to personal stockholders in companies operating in EEC countries, they have not been refundable where a U.S. parent company invests in an EEC subsidiary company.

In fact, a deliberate act of policy was involved in the adoption of the credit system corporate tax in the U.K. in preference to a split-rate system. It was argued that a credit system would give countries such as the U.K. an advantage in dealing with foreign inward investment, as the nonrefundable nature of credits would force other countries to renegotiate double taxation treaties to the U.K.'s ultimate advantage. This renegotiation of double taxation treaties has, in fact, taken place, and the U.K. and U.S. double taxation treaty has recently gone through a complex sequence of renegotiations. The renegotiation of a double taxation treaty may, however, offset any advantage which the credit system gives to a country over the split-rate system.

A further feature to be borne in mind along with these general developments is that in the EEC within the next ten to fifteen years a harmonized system of corporate taxes will probably develop, with the credit system as the common system. The arrangements are likely to be similar to the arrangements in the indirect tax field under which the restricted origin principle operates. Credits under the imputation system are likely to be refundable across European borders between European member countries, but not refundable between an EEC member country and a non-EEC member country, such as the U.S. This will represent an attempt by the EEC to secure a higher return from the inward investment into the EEC than would have been true in the case of nonintegrated systems of corporate tax.

11

MICHAEL J. BOSKIN

Agenda for Tax Reform

Adverse consequences of increasing tax rates. The income/ expenditure tax debate. Integration of corporate and personal income taxes. Social security revision. The period of account for taxation. Misleading estimates of the effects of some tax reforms—the Treasury and the Tax Expenditure Budget. The need for improved economic analysis of the long-term effects of taxes on the national economy.

The debate over the relative size of the governmental and private sectors of the economy continues to rage unabated. It is clear that the growing size of the public sector, and the large increase in tax rates applying to a growing fraction of the population, have created a variety of perhaps unintended and undesirable outcomes and effects on the private economy. While others in this book may disagree, my own conclusion is that tax rates—especially tax rates on the income from capital—have risen to a point where the combination of inflation and our unindexed tax system seriously retards the process of capital formation. Moreover, current tax rates almost certainly have substantially reduced the labor supply of secondary workers such as the elderly and second earners in a family. The cost to society of these disincentives is very great.

Further, as the relative size of the government sector is expanded, government has attempted to move into areas which are likely to lead to diminishing marginal utility of public sector output. While there are many potentially desirable public and/or private projects, many of those which the government has undertaken have proved to be abysmal failures. Unfortunately, a large number of these retain strong constituencies with effective lobbies which continually pressure Congress to avoid reduction in spending. A book on tax reform is not the place to discuss which expenditure programs are desirable and which are undesirable. At the same time, the serious side effects and unintended adverse incentives created by the growth of the public sector are becoming worse and worse, as the relative size of the public sector continues to expand and marginal tax rates continue to rise. Under the circumstances, it is hard to avoid the conclusion that a substantial case exists for slowing the rate of growth of the public sector relative to the private sector of the economy.

Much more germane to the purpose of this book is the question of how we should go about efficiently and equitably collecting taxes and distributing revenues, given the size of the public sector that we deem desirable. I would like to make the following general suggestions.

First, there is a strong case for gradually switching our base of personal taxation from income to expenditures (consumption). Such a tax, relative to our current tax system, would stimulate badly needed capital formation, remove an enormous inefficiency in the intertemporal allocation of resources across individuals' lifetimes, and increase future productivity, wages, and income.

Second, if a consumption tax is deemed impractical, or is to be implemented only very slowly, there are many important changes that could be made in our current system of income taxation. By far the most important is to index the tax system for inflation. The economic and political harm done by an unindexed tax system, which continually accrues revenues far in excess of real income growth, cannot be overestimated. As Shoven notes, indexing for inflation involves not only appropriately adjusting the bracket rates, but also adjusting the basis of taxation—i.e., the definition of taxable income—to make sure that we are taxing real, rather than nominal, income.

Third, another major income tax revision of extreme importance involves integrating the corporate and personal income taxes. Break points out that this is desirable on a number of efficiency and equity grounds. While it would not be an easy matter to do this partially or gradually from an administrative and implementation point of view, the time is ripe to attempt at least a partial integration of corporate and personal taxes.

Fourth, we should adjust our capital gains taxation to reflect the fact that much of accrued capital gains represents purely inflationary gain. An indexed tax system would accomplish this automatically, of course, and if we switch to an expenditure tax, the need for capital gains taxes would disappear.

Fifth, we must reexamine the basic nature of our social security system, and arrange to separate out the welfare component that provides minimum income support to the elderly from the pure annuity or insurance goal of the system. The former could be financed out of general revenue, and the latter could be financed by some combination of payroll taxes and proof of private insurance for retirement (see Boskin 1977*b*). In brief, separating the transfer and insurance goals, and allowing proof of private insurance for retirement to substitute for social security contributions, would dramatically relieve the immense long-term deficit in social security, and would help to reduce the enormous burden of social security taxes. When combined with income taxes—federal and state—these taxes produce an extremely high marginal tax rate on a very large fraction of the U.S. population.

Sixth, there is much to be said for some form of negative income tax device as a substitute for a wide range of categorical income maintenance programs and subsidies. However, as Kurz notes, there are some immense practical difficulties to be overcome before a reasonable negative income tax proposal is likely to be adopted.

Seventh, we should begin to think of changes in the unit and time period of account for our personal tax system. Whether we keep our individual income tax, or gradually shift to an expenditure tax, the changing demographic pattern of the population, particularly with respect to the formation and dissolution of families, requires us to rethink our basic unit of account for taxation. Currently, it generally pays a husband and wife to file a joint return and split their income; thus they are taxed as if each of them earned half their combined income. Unfortunately, this raises the marginal tax rate on the very first dollar of earnings by the secondary worker in the family to a high rate. Even in families with very modest incomes, the second worker in a family would face an income tax, under income splitting, of 25 percent to 30 percent. This is extremely inefficient, in view of the sensitivity to after-tax wage rates of the labor supply of secondary workers. It is time for us to consider the possibility of separate rate schedules for the second earner in a family, reflecting lower tax rates than those on the first earner in the family.

Another problem with our individual tax system, whether our current individual income tax or an eventual individual consumption or expenditure tax, revolves around the time period of accounting. Currently we have only very limited procedures for income averaging, and for loss carry-forwards and carry-backs. As capital markets improve, annuity markets develop, and we learn more and more about the typical lifetime pattern of earnings at different ages, we should reconsider proposals to expand the time period of account for taxation. While withholding and annual filing are likely to remain with us for a very long time indeed, we should allow for longer term income averaging and longer term loss carry-forwards and carry-backs than in our current tax system. In short, when we think about ability to pay—and subject to practical and administrative considerations—we should think about economic well-being over the lifetime as opposed to over an arbitrarily chosen, very short, accounting period.

THE INADEQUACY OF EXISTING INFORMATION ON THE EFFECTS OF TAXES

Every time a tax reform proposal is formulated, a variety of attempts are made to estimate its economic effects. These include estimates of the effect of the reform on the gross national product, economic growth, unemployment, inflation, and tax burdens by income group. The U.S. Treasury traditionally prepares such estimates. Many private non-governmental sources also produce them. Unfortunately, the available methods of making these estimates are seriously biased. The Treasury model, for example, is simply a cross-tabulation of returns by income and other types of characteristics. That is, there are no behavioral relationships involved in the Treasury model. Therefore, it simply assumes that every firm and every household will continue behaving in exactly the same way before the imposition of the tax reform as they would after the tax change. To take a simple example, suppose we contemplate taxing capital gains in full. The way the Treasury calculates the net impact on tax revenues of such a tax change is as follows: it takes its sample of returns, adds in the extra capital gains which were excluded in the original computation of tax, and then calculates a new tax on that return. In brief, the Treasury would assume that the individuals paying the capital gains tax would go on realizing the same capital gains after the rates had essentially doubled as they did before the tax rate increase! This, of course, is a rather extreme assumption. Suppose that the capital gains rate increased to 100 percent. Who, then, would bother to realize any capital gains at all? Yet the Treasury's method for estimating the revenue gain would assume that people would go on realizing the same amount of capital gains as before the tax increase.

The Treasury is attempting, albeit quite slowly and gradually, to build some behavioral equations into its model. In addition, several private, nongovernmental sources estimate the impact of tax reform proposals. Most of these models are basically designed to serve other purposes. They are almost all Keynesian, short-run, forecasting models which attempt to plot the future course of gross national product and its components over the next several quarters. By their very nature, they are not capable of describing the long-term growth of the U.S. economy. Therefore, they are of very limited applicability in assessing the economic consequences of any tax change which affects capital formation. As an example, if we switch from an income to an expenditure tax, we would gradually increase the capital stock as people saved more and more each year. In the long run, this would lead to a substantial increase in future productivity, income, wages, and tax revenues at constant rates. Unfortunately, the short-run forecasting models are incapable of tracing out such effects.

Therefore, when Congress is presented information about the likely effects of tax policies, the overwhelming bulk of evidence is related to the consequences on revenues this year and next, and on the aggregate performance of the economy over the next several quarters. That is, the deck is stacked against the proposals which temporarily decrease tax revenues but stimulate the long-term growth of the economy. It is perhaps not surprising that politicians, with a notoriously short time horizon of the period between the present and the next election, focus on such information. Unfortunately, however, the future course of economic activity can be substantially affected by such shortsightedness.

A second major device in evaluating tax proposals, which is now published annually and actually projected over the subsequent five years, is the so-called Tax Expenditure Budget. This proceeds from the assumption that any deviation from a certain definition of taxable income is a tax preference which lowers the tax liability of certain individuals and firms, and is analogous to direct government expenditure for those purposes. There are several fallacies in the Tax Expenditure Budget concept. First, before we know what is being taxed at favorable or unfavorable rates, we need to know what a desirable tax base is or should be. The Tax Expenditure Budget starts from the assumption that an income tax, or rather a tax on most market sector income, is the desirable norm. There is much, analytically and empirically, to suggest that an income tax is not a desirable tax base. For example, saving is taxed twice by the income tax, which is inferior on both efficiency and equity grounds to an expenditure tax. Viewed in this light, many items of so-called tax preferences, such as accelerated depreciation, are really negative tax expenditures, because we are not allowing depreciation at the same rate as we would under a consumption tax—that is, expensing of capital equipment. Second, the calculations made of the revenue loss and the size of the subsidy embodied in a particular tax preference in the Tax Expenditure Budget suffer from the same problems as the estimates obtained in the Treasury model—to wit, they assume no economic behavior.

As noted in the introductory chapter, taxes have two major effects. They transfer resources from the private sector of the economy to the government, and they alter the relative prices of goods and services and factors of production. In so doing, they usually do affect economic behavior—for example, the consumption/saving choice, the riskiness of investment, and the work/leisure choice. Hence the estimates embodied in the Tax Expenditure Budget are correct *only if all deviations from the allegedly proper tax base are eliminated simultaneously, and if all supplies of factors of production are totally unresponsive to tax increases.* It is extremely unlikely that this is the case. For example, the Tax Expenditure estimate of the nominally preferential treatment given to capital gains amounts to many billions of dollars. If we tax capital gains as ordinary income, however, in this author's opinion there would be far fewer accrued capital gains, a drastic reduction of realized capital gains, and an increase in leisure and income accruing in other nontax forms. Therefore, the Tax Expenditure Budget estimate of the revenue loss to the Treasury because of the lower capital gains tax rate may be a substantial overestimate. The same is true for each of the items which do substantially affect economic behavior.

TOWARDS IMPROVING THE INFORMATIONAL INPUT TO TAX POLICY

It is clear that there is a very important place to be played by a tax model which takes into account the long-term growth of the economy, capital formation, and labor supply. We need to be interested not just in the effect of a particular tax policy on next year's tax revenues, but on the performance of the economy through time, and on the time pattern of tax revenues. Policies which temporarily increase tax revenues may ultimately decrease them, and vice versa. For example, a large increase in the corporate tax rate might raise more revenue this year, but substantially retard the capital formation process, and hence decrease income and taxes below what they otherwise would have been by a large amount five, ten, or fifteen years down the road. At that time, a new Congress would be faced with the tremendous problem of a much lower tax base than it otherwise would have had, and the necessity of a dramatic increase in tax rates to attempt to raise tax revenues.

In brief, we should attempt to build an analytical and econometric structure which allows us to estimate the future time path of tax revenues over, say, the next ten or twenty years, not just over the next few quarters. Otherwise we will be continuously doomed in any attempt to develop tax policies to stimulate capital formation, because they will continually appear to decrease tax revenues in the short run, with no estimate given of the compensating increase to appear several years down the road as factor supplies expand. Economists have now made enough improvements in their analytical structures, their econometric modeling, and the availability of data, to begin to present reliable information on these matters. This author, for example, together with Professor Martin Feldstein of Harvard University, developed a series of estimates of the likely effect of changes in tax revenues and giving to charity of alternative reforms in the tax treatment of charitable contributions. We estimated a substantial response on the part of charitable donors. The response was large enough that charities would actually lose more than the Treasury would gain, even in the short run, if the deductibility of charitable contributions were eliminated from the individual income or the estate tax (see Boskin and Feldstein 1978; Boskin 1976; Feldstein 1976b). Of course, economists and others may disagree on the precise magnitude of the relevant parameters necessary to analyze each of the tax policy reforms and proposals.

In the chapters above, we saw the importance of certain key parameters. In discussing the switch from an income to a consumption tax, the size of the interest elasticity of saving is crucial. We noted in a discussion of capital gains taxes the importance of a better empirical estimate of the size of the lock-in effect. In the discussion of social security taxes, we noted the importance of estimating the effect of the very high marginal tax rates on the supply of labor. No one would presume that we can yet answer these questions precisely, but much progress has been made in recent years, and our stock of information about these and other magnitudes necessary to

NOTES

2. Peter Mieszkowski: "The Choice of Tax Base: Consumption versus Income Taxation"

1. This section is based on the discussion found in Mieszkowski (1977: Section 3).

2. Issues related to other expensive consumer durables such as furniture, paintings, and other art objects are treated in a later section.

3. Although there are reasons for restricting the use of tax-prepaid assets, there are costs to this restriction. For the availability of both types of loans and assets would enable the household considerable scope for having taxes assessed on the basis of lifetime consumption by appropriate asset manipulation. This could be done as long as the household could anticipate fluctuations in income and consumption.

4. Jerry R. Green: "The Taxation of Capital Gains"

1. It may be possible to revalue securities annually, but this is inapplicable to the vast majority of other capital assets. The recent Treasury Department study, *Blueprint for Basic Tax Reform*(1977), rejected the prospect of accrual taxation because of its costs of administration.

2. The correlation between capital gains and other income is particularly relevant to owners of closely held corporations. A large proportion of capital gains taxes arise in this way.

3. The functional form for the estimating equation has dividends in the denominator of the dependent variable and the log of dividends as a right-hand variable. To the extent that there are errors in the relationship of dividends to wealth, a statistical bias may result. This is not likely to be serious, however, and it is therefore not discussed explicitly below.

4. See Green and Sheshinski (1977) for a quantitative approach to the estimation of these inefficiencies of interest income taxation.

5. See Bradford (1978) or Auerbach (1978) for vigorous arguments supporting the $V = .67$ solution, and Robichek and Myers (1965) or Feldstein, Green, and Sheshinski (1977) for $V = 1$.

6. See Barro's analysis in Chapter 9, or, in a slightly different context, Green and Sheshinski (1977).

7. In the section on dynamic efficiency we considered the valuation of a marginal addition to capital. Here we are concerned with the total valuation of the firm.

5. Paul J. Taubman: "On Income Tax"

1. If this condition did not hold, a consumer could be made better off by altering his consumption pattern.

2. For a brief history and an analysis of this term, see Musgrave (1959).

3. The income tax law currently lets businesses credit against their income taxes 10 percent of the purchase price of certain equipment, which lowers the effective price of the equipment.

4. More formally, consider a two-period model in which income, y, prices, p, and interest rate, r, remain constant. It is also assumed that the person neither receives nor gives financial bequests. Letting c be consumption and t be the constant tax rate, a person's budget constraint is

$$[y_0(1-t) - p_0 c_0] [1 + r(1-t)] = [y_1(1-t) - p_1 c_1]$$

Using this budget constraint, it can be shown that the ratio of after-tax prices in the two periods is

$$p_0 [1 + r(1-t)]/p_1 = [1 + r(1-t)]$$

In a consumption tax system with a tax rate of v, the budget constraint is

$$[y_0 - (1+v) p_0 c_0] (1+r) = [y_1 - (1+v) p_1 c_1]$$

The ratio of after-tax prices in the two periods is

$$(1+v) p_0 (1+r)/(1+v) p_1 = (1+r)$$

5. Saving is positive, both because some people plan to leave bequests and because, in a growing population, there are more young people saving for retirement than retirees dissaving.

6. An optimal tax system could include both income and consumption taxes. For a recent statement, see Feldstein (1978).

7. It is possible to exempt some items or to use differential taxes for luxuries and necessities, but then the system is much more difficult to administer. Moreover, what is, on average, a luxury may be a necessity to some poor people, or vice versa. For example, some poor people buy caviar and some rich people don't.

8. The current income tax code treatment of pension funds contribution in effect converts the income tax to a consumption tax. In other respects, the definition of income is unchanged.

9. His comprehensive income concept differs from the current tax base in that it includes: all realized capital gains; excluded dividends of up to $100 per person, $200 per family; interest on state and local securities; life insurance interest; capital gains on homes; capital gains unrealized prior to death; imputed net rent on homes; health and life insurance premiums paid by employers; and most transfer payments.

10. The increase in tax revenues from both changes would be even higher, since individuals would move into higher tax brackets.

11. Of course, it need not be true that the same revenues would be required as the definition of the tax base changed. For example, one of the ways discussed to tax the interest from state and local bonds is for the Treasury to offer to pay to these governments a subsidy on those bonds that state and local governments voluntarily issue without the tax-free status. This subsidy would increase the federal government's expenditures, though there would be a gain in net revenue. On the other hand, a reduction in tax rates that increased labor supply and savings would, in the long run, increase GNP and the potential tax base. In turn, this might induce an increase in government expenditures.

12. The criteria is not unexpectedness, but unusual necessity. Kidney dialysis is a continuing expensive and life-saving procedure.

13. Drugs are subject to a special limitation, and one-half of medical insurance premiums can be counted as medical expenses.

14. Some recent studies have shown that when people of the same ability are compared, the wage returns to schooling are smaller than the returns on savings accounts. This is consistent with the idea that people also receive nonwage returns from education.

15. Dependents are defined as spouses, children under the age of nineteen, children over nineteen who are still in school, and relatives who receive half their support from the taxpayer. Family members, such as siblings, who jointly support a relative, can share the exemption over time.

16. The 2 percent of family income is designed to eliminate low-income families from the tax roles. This can be accomplished by retaining this provision and eliminating the credit.

17. To the extent that the individual buys tax-free securities, the interest he pays on loans is not deductible.

18. There are limits on how much can be deducted. See Due (1977).

19. Often these costs account for well over half the funds raised.

20. People in the top tax brackets can at times increase their after-tax income by donating appreciated assets. Some generous taxpayers have also been known to set up foundations to maintain their mistresses.

21. See Taussig (1967) and Feldstein (1975) for opposing views.

22. This would not be needed if gains were taxed on an accrual system, as advocated below.

23. See Webster for a definition of boodle.

24. In the economy as a whole, public plus private savings must equal investment plus net exports. Assuming net exports are fixed, and that both saving and investment are related to the interest rate, a policy that increases saving while maintaining full employment will lead to more investment. Similarly, a policy that encourages investment will lead to more saving.

25. Together, these currently reduce tax revenues by about $20 billion.

26. For more details and a longer analysis, see Taubman (1973).

27. The adjustment to price is $(1 - \text{credit rate})/(1 - \text{tax rate})$.

28. There are circumstances in which a taxpayer might want to lengthen the useful life. For example, the investment tax credit is greater for equipment with a five-year than a four-year tax life.

29. They only benefit by the 20 percent reduction in lives.

30. When the investment tax credit was initially enacted in the early 1960s, it was felt that equipment demand was more depressed than building demands, but relative demand for these two categories changes over time.

31. See Taubman (1978) for one possible way to accomplish this for building.

32. Tax revenues currently foregone exceed $2 billion.

33. For a more thorough summary, see Wetzler (1977).

34. Generally, the sale of goods produced by a firm is not treated as a capital gain. Cattle, however, is an exception.

35. Prior to 1977, the inheritor used the value at the time of death as his basis.

36. However, earnings are not eligible for such treatment to the extent that there are untaxed capital gains.

37. To use this provision, taxable income in the current year must exceed the average income by 25 percent plus $3,000.

38. The Michigan Panel of Income Dynamics, the National Longitudinal Survey, and the Retirement History Survey contain data on family income, which approximates gross income, for periods up to ten years; but most available studies with these data sources have concentrated on individual earnings.

39. However, the maximum tax rate on earned income is 50 percent.

40. In this section, we ignore questions of who qualifies as a dependent.

41. Heads of households were placed in an intermediate position, because their extra costs and responsibilities were not adequately covered by personal deductions.

42. Of course, there may be some economies of scale.

43. This figure would be greater, except for the provision adopted in 1969 that the extra tax burden of a single person would be no greater than 20 percent of that of a married couple with the same taxable income.

6. Laurence J. Kotlikoff: ''Social Security, Time to Reform''

1. I would like to thank Michael Boskin, Robert Clower, John and Rita Riley, Harold and Vivien Kotlikoff, and Laurence Weiss for their helpful comments.

2. As discussed below, the system has in the past generated massive transfers from younger to older cohorts. Since younger cohorts enjoy higher lifetime incomes because of general economic growth, these transfers have historically made the system very progressive in terms of the relative welfare of different age cohorts.

3. The idea is to set new levels of exemptions and deductibles appropriate to all taxation of income. Other proposals fall short of entirely eliminating the payroll tax; rather, they seek to use general revenues to finance the disability and health insurance components of OASDHI.

4. Raising the earned income tax credit for low-income families is one easy way to redistribute under the federal income tax.

5. Children may collect through age 21 if they remain in an educational institution.

6. In a life-cycle context, the earnings test does not represent a tax on labor supply between ages 62 and 65, to the extent that the reduction in benefits for early (pre-65) retirement is actuarially fair. The loss in benefits due to working between ages 62 and 65 is made up by permanently higher benefits available at age 65 and beyond. Given the extent of early retirement, it appears that, for many, the reduction of benefits because of early retirement is perceived as less than actuarially fair.

7. I have assumed a constant 12 percent tax rate, and ignored life-cycle growth in earnings. Incorporating either the scheduled growth in taxes or the growth in earnings over the life cycle would lower slightly these projected rates of return.

8. This subsidy to self-employment may bring forth a greater supply of self-employed persons, reducing to some extent the earnings of the self-employed. Thus, the net subsidy to the self-employed may be less than 34 percent of the social security tax.

9. Extending coverage to government workers must, however, be done carefully, or else we will exacerbate rather than reduce redistribution to government workers. While there is no problem for young workers just entering government service, there

is a transition problem of extending coverage to older government workers, since they would receive very high rates of return under the current law. A separate benefit schedule could be used during this transition period to give current government workers a fair, but not excessive, return on their contributions.

10. The 1940 figures are obtained from Census Bureau (1973:31–32). The 1976 figures are unpublished BLS data provided by Lawrence Summers, Harvard University.

11. The data used here are the March *Current Population Survey* (CPS) files for 1968 through 1975.

12. Examination of CPS data indicates that about 30 percent of males and 14 percent of females ages 62 to 65 are gainfully employed during the year. These proportions were applied to population figures obtained in Census Bureau (1978:33).

13. One way to increase understanding would be for social security to send yearly statements to contributors indicating their contributions to date and illustrating the benefit formula.

7. Mordecai Kurz: "Negative Income Taxation"

1. A great deal of the contemporary discussion regarding the need for welfare reform arises from the high tax rates caused by overlapping programs. See, for example, Aaron (1973).

2. In this chapter, we use the term "intact families" to mean families with both a male head and a female head present. Whenever the terms "male head" or "female head" or "wives" are used, they refer to intact families. We use the term "single female head" to mean a female who heads a family without a male present.

3. Perhaps the best documentation of this fact can be found in a sequence of reports entitled "5,000 American Families," published by the Survey Research Center, Institute for Social Research, University of Michigan.

4. L_0 is the maximal number of hours a person can work. It may be taken as twenty-four hours a day, or less than that if "rest" or "sleep" time is regarded as necessary and unavailable for work.

5. For a comprehensive description of this experiment, see Kurz and Spiegelman (1972).

6. It is important to keep in mind that the experimental results apply to the enrolled population, which does not represent a cross-section of the U.S. economy. Important variations in response exist within the experimental population, and these could have significant effects on the prediction of the national consequences of any negative tax program. The figures given in the text should be taken to indicate only the order of magnitude of such effects.

8. John B. Shoven: "Inflation and Income Taxation"

1. It should be noted that this discussion of depreciation applies also to the personal income tax, in that households own depreciable assets in their roles as landlords or owners of small businesses.

2. Note that FIFO would record an $80 profit, whereas real income is most accurately recorded as $60.

9. Robert J. Barro: "Public Debt and Taxes"

1. An interesting note about the pre-1860 period is the experience in 1835 when the national debt was entirely paid off and the government sought desperately for outlets for its surplus. Apparently this problem was solved by the motivation for deficit finance during the sharp economic contraction that began in 1837. For a discussion of this episode, see Dewey (1931:221).

2. See Klein (1975:461-84) on the significance for long-run price level behavior of the shift from the gold standard to a paper money regime.

3. In the case where the interest rate, net of expected inflation, on the public debt exceeds the long-run real growth rate of the economy (which turns out to be a necessary condition for the efficient operation of the private sector), perpetual deficit finance would require a continually rising ratio of public debt to national income. For a discussion of this and related matters, see Barro (1976:343-49). The chain-letter aspect of perpetual deficit finance has been referred to as a Ponzi scheme by Miller and Upton (1974:181) in honor of the "Boston 'money-manager' of the 1920s, who paid people 50 percent interest on funds deposited with him. He did so by using the proceeds of new deposits to pay off old depositors. While it worked, it was a good deal. Those who got in (and out) early made money, but the bubble eventually burst, and those who still had deposits with Ponzi lost everything."

4. A discussion of the Ricardian theorem is contained in Buchanan (1958:43-46, 114-22). See also de Marco (1936:377-98) and Bailey (1971:156-58).

5. The same conclusion applies if the taxpayer borrows to finance his share of the $1 million tax cost, assuming that such loans at 5 percent interest must be secured by life insurance.

6. A rigorous treatment of this private offset effect is contained in Barro (1974:1095-1117). A complication to the analysis arises when some taxpayers have more or less than the average number of descendants. For example, individuals without children may have no ties to future generations and are therefore made better off by debt issue, although such individuals must be matched by other persons with an above-average number of children who are likely to be made worse off by debt issue. A second-order wealth effect from debt issue would arise if these individual effects do not cancel out through aggregation. Another second-order effect is the stimulus of debt issue toward reduced family size, which would be motivated by the corresponding reduction in family liability for the stream of future taxes.

7. Private bail bondsmen are perhaps a response to a differential collection efficiency that favors the private sector. Casual observation of the federal government's student loan program suggests that relative governmental efficiency in the credit markets is actually an amusing idea.

8. See, for example, Bailey (1971:157-58); Buchanan and Wagner (1977:17, 101, 130). The contrary view is taken in Buchanan (1967: 258-60), and in Barro (1974:1113-15).

9. I am assuming that private insurance markets and other institutions are not sufficient to provide full diversification of relative tax risks.

10. The adjustment of the measured government surplus to obtain a "full employment surplus" that takes account of the automatic stabilizer role of the tax system seems to be consistent with this viewpoint. The full employment surplus is discussed in Council of Economic Advisers (1962:78-81).

11. Buchanan and Wagner (1977) present this hypothesis as the major theme of

their book. They attempt to explain much of the rise in the U.S. federal spending/ GNP ratio since World War II as a response to a structural change to a "Keynesian debt policy" that made deficits politically more popular than before. However, this hypothesis seems to conflict with the observation that the federal debt/GNP ratio (Table 1) has actually fallen in the post–World War II period in a manner similar to that after World War I and the Civil War. Detailed empirical analysis of annual public debt movements that I have carried out, as discussed below, indicates that the economic structure that determines the amount of deficit finance has been reasonably stable since at least the 1920s.

12. See, for example, the papers in Ferguson (1964), and the review by Tobin (1965:679-82).

13. I am abstracting here from the impact of changes in the level of government expenditures. That analysis would involve as a central element the economic function of these expenditures, as discussed in Bailey (1971:Chapter 9).

14. It should not be inferred that a positive wealth effect of debt issue is sufficient to build a normative case for fiscal activism. Other considerations involve the adjustment of prices and rates of return, the timing of government policy, and the role of private expectations about government policy formation.

15. The empirical literature includes Kochin (1974:385-94); Tanner (1970:473-85); David and Scadding (1974:225-49); Kormendi (1978); Feldstein (1974:905-26; 1977); Barro (1978b); Barro and MacDonald (1977); and Darby (1978).

16. For example, in the Federal Reserve–MIT–Penn model, the key explanatory variable for consumption corresponds approximately to current personal disposable income (Modigliani 1971:14). A similar current personal disposable income variable is used in the Brookings model, as reported in Suits and Sparks (1965:Chapter 7).

17. The "St. Louis model" reduced-form equations, which use high-employment government expenditures rather than a deficit variable as a fiscal measure, are reported in Andersen and Jordon (1968:11-24). An updated view of this model is contained in Carlson (1978:13-19). Some reduced-form effects on unemployment and output of debt issue and of the "unanticipated" part of this issue are reported in Barro (1977:114; 1978c:Section III).

10. John Whalley: "Tax Developments Outside the United States and Their Implications for Current U.S. Reform Proposals"

1. No single compendium of tax structures by country exists. A useful source for EEC countries is in EEC (1974). Detailed information is available on a country-by-country basis in the Harvard World Tax Series, but the coverage of countries is not complete. For a few countries there are official publications in English, such as the annual *An Outline of Japanese Taxes* (Tax Bureau [Japan] 1977), and some further comparative information is available in Musgrave (1969). Generally speaking, documentation of tax systems is more readily available for developed economies than for the less developed.

2. The use here of the distinction between direct and indirect taxation corresponds to the "modern" use of the term that a direct tax is a tax on income and an indirect tax is a tax on outlay.

3. Large numbers of taxpayers in Sweden are in marginal brackets of approximately 70 percent, and the amount of redistribution which takes place within the tax system where the average and marginal tax rates are in these regions is quite small.

4. An attempt to tax one-half of realized capital gains at income tax rates was made by the Whitlam government on election in 1972. The tax was abandoned before being introduced.

5. This is an inadequate way of coping with the problems of taxing inflationary gains, since it allows real gains to go untaxed after the qualifying period.

6. A good example of this is the absence of any capital gains tax at death in the U.S. This remains, even though the so-called step-up-in-basis was eliminated in the 1976 Tax Reform Act. Among those countries operating capital gains taxes, such as Canada, this feature in the U.S. remains as something of an anomaly.

7. Under the Italian tax system, what would be called the income tax in the U.S. constituted approximately five separate taxes.

8. The adoption of the integrated corporation tax was in anticipation of a harmonized system within the EEC which, at the time, was expected to be either a split rate or imputation type.

9. No single source satisfactorily documents value added tax structures and experience with the tax. Shoup (1969:Chapter 25) contains a clear statement of the objectives of the tax, as does the Neumark Report (1967); Sullivan (1965) is an earlier source describing administrative and other problems with the tax.

10. This terminology is due to Shibata (1967).

11. For more detail, see Sandford, Willis, and Ironside (1975).

12. See the discussion in Shibata (1967), and Krauss and Johnson (1970) on the origin versus the destination basis for domestic taxation.

13. That is, a single rate tax on all goods consumed or produced.

REFERENCES

Aaron, Henry J., ed. 1976. *Inflation and the Income Tax*. Washington, DC: The Brookings Institution.

———. 1973. "Why Is Welfare So Hard to Reform?" *Studies in Social Economics*. Washington, DC: The Brookings Institution.

———, and Boskin, Michael J., eds. 1978. *The Economics of Taxation*. Washington, DC: The Brookings Institution.

Adams, J. D. R., and Whalley, John. 1977. *The International Taxation of Multinational Enterprises*. London: Institute for Fiscal Studies, Associated Business Programmes.

Andersen, L. C., and Jordon, J. L. 1968. "Monetary and Fiscal Actions: A Test of Their Relative Importance in Economic Stabilization." *Review* (Federal Reserve Bank of St. Louis) (November).

Andrews, W. D. 1974. "Consumption-Type or Cash Flow Personal Income Tax." *Harvard Law Review* 87 (April).

Auerbach, A. 1978. "Share Valuation and Corporate Equity Policy." Mimeo. Harvard University. (To be published in *Quarterly Journal of Economics*.)

Bailey, M. J. 1971. *National Income and the Price Level*. 2d ed. New York: McGraw Hill.

Barro, Robert J. 1974. "Are Government Bonds Net Wealth?" *Journal of Political Economy* 82 (November/December).

———. 1978a. "Comment from an Unreconstructed Ricardian." *Journal of Monetary Economics*.

———. 1978b. *The Impact of Social Security on Private Savings—Evidence from the U.S. Time Series*. Washington, DC: American Enterprise Institute.

———. 1978c. "On the Determination of the Public Debt." Working paper. University of Rochester (March).

———. 1976. "Reply to Feldstein and Buchanan." *Journal of Political Economy* (April).

———. 1977. "Unanticipated Money Growth and Unemployment in the United States." *American Economic Review* 67 (March).

———, and MacDonald, G. 1977. "Social Security and Consumer Spending in an International Cross Section." Working paper. University of Rochester.

Benjamin, D. K., and Kochin, L. A. 1978. "The British National Debt." Working paper. University of Washington.

BLS. *See* U.S. Department of Labor.

Boskin, Michael J., ed. 1977a. *The Crisis in Social Security*. San Francisco: Institute for Contemporary Studies.

————. 1973. "The Economics of Labor Supply." In *Income Maintenance and Labor Supply: Econometric Studies,* ed. Glen G. Cain and Harold W. Watts. Chicago: Rand McNally.

————. 1976. "Estate Taxation and Charitable Bequests." *Journal of Public Economics*.

————. 1977b. "Social Security: The Alternatives Before Us." In *The Crisis in Social Security,* ed. Michael J. Boskin. San Francisco: Institute for Contemporary Studies.

————. 1967. "Social Security and Retirement Decision." *Economic Inquiry* (January).

————. 1978. "Taxation, Saving, and the Rate of Interest." *Journal of Political Economy* 86 (April).

————, and Feldstein, Martin. 1978. "The Charitable Deduction and Contributions by Low- and Middle-Income Families: Evidence from the National Survey of Philanthropy." *Review of Economics and Statistics* (August).

————, and Hurd, Michael D. 1977. "The Effect of Social Security on Early Retirement." Working paper 204. National Bureau of Economic Research (September).

Bradford, David. 1978. "The Incidence and Allocation Effects of a Tax on Corporate Distributions." Mimeographed. Princeton University.

Break, George F. 1974. "The Incidence and Economic Effects of Taxation." In *The Economics of Public Finance*. Washington, DC: The Brookings Institution.

————, and Pechman, Joseph A. 1975. *Federal Tax Reform: The Impossible Dream?* Washington, DC: The Brookings Institution.

Buchanan, J.M. 1967. *Public Finance in Democratic Process*. Chapel Hill, NC: University of North Carolina Press.

————. 1958. *Public Principles of Public Debt*. Homewood, IL: Irwin.

————, and Wagner, R. E. 1977. *Democracy in Deficit*. New York: Academic Press.

Cain, Glen G., and Watts, Harold W., eds. 1973. *Income Maintenance and Labor Supply: Econometric Studies*. Chicago: Rand McNally.

Campbell, Colin D., and Campbell, Rosemary G. 1976. "Conflicting Views on the Effect of Old-Age and Survivors Insurance on Retirement." *Economic Inquiry* 14, 3 (September).

Campbell, Rita Ricardo. 1977. *Social Security, Promise and Reality*. Stanford, CA: Hoover Institution Press.

Carlson, K. M. 1978. "Does the St. Louis Equation Now Believe in Fiscal Policy?" *Review* (Federal Reserve Bank of St. Louis) (February).

Carter Commission. 1969. *Report of the Royal Commission on Taxation (Canada)*. Ottawa: The Queen's Printer.

Census Bureau. *See* U.S. Bureau of the Census.

Cogan, J. F. 1978. "Negative Income Taxation and Labor Supply: New Evidence from the New Jersey–Pennsylvania Experiment." Memo No. R-2155-HEW (February). Santa Monica, CA: The Rand Corporation.

Congressional Budget Office. 1978. ''The Administration's Welfare Reform Proposal: An Analysis of the Program for Better Jobs and Income.'' April. Washington, DC: Government Printing Office.

Council of Economic Advisers. 1962, 1978. *Economic Report of the President*. Washington, DC: Government Printing Office.

Cowan, Edward. 1977. ''Background and History: The Crisis in Public Finance and Social Security.'' In *The Crisis in Social Security,* ed. Michael J. Boskin. San Francisco: Institute for Contemporary Studies.

Darby, Michael R. 1978. ''The Effects of Social Security on Income and the Capital Stock.'' Working paper 95. UCLA (March).

David, P. A., and Scadding, J. 1974. ''Private Savings: Ultrarationality, Aggregation, and 'Dennison's Law.' '' *Journal of Political Economy* 82 (March).

de Marco, A. de Viti. 1936. *First Principles of Public Finance.* Trans. E. Marget. London: Jonathan Cape.

Dewey, D. R. 1931. *Financial History of the United States.* 11th ed. New York: Longmans Green.

Diamond, Peter. 1977. ''A Framework for Social Security Analysis.'' *Journal of Public Economics.*

––––––, and Mirrlees, J. A. 1977. ''A Model of Social Insurance with Variable Retirement.'' Working paper 210. Massachusetts Institute of Technology (October).

Due, J. 1977. ''Personal Deductions.'' In *Comprehensive Income Taxation,* ed. Joseph Pechman. Washington, DC: The Brookings Institution.

Economic Report. *See* Council of Economic Advisers.

EEC. 1974. *Inventory of Taxes.* Brussels: European Economic Community.

Feldstein, Martin. 1975. ''Income Tax and Charitable Contributions.'' *National Tax Journal* 28.

––––––. 1976a. ''Perceived Wealth in Bonds and Social Security: A Comment.'' *Journal of Political Economy* 84 (April).

––––––. 1977. ''Social Security and Private Savings: International Evidence in an Extended Life Cycle Model.'' In *The Economics of Public Services,* ed. Martin S. Feldstein and R. Inman. London: Macmillan.

––––––. 1967. ''Social Security and Retirement Decisions.'' *Economic Inquiry* (January).

––––––. 1974. ''Social Security, Induced Retirement, and Aggregate Capital Accumulation.'' *Journal of Political Economy* 82 (September/October).

––––––. 1976b. ''Tax Incentives for Charitable Contributions.'' *National Tax Journal.*

––––––. 1978. ''The Welfare Cost of Capital Income Taxation.'' *Journal of Political Economy* 86 (April).

––––––, and Frisch, Daniel. 1977. ''Corporate Tax Integration: The Estimated Effects on Capital Accumulation and Tax Distribution of Two Integration Proposals.'' Discussion paper 541. Harvard University Institute of Economic Research (March).

———, Green, J., and Sheshinski, E. 1977. "Corporate Financial Policy and Taxation in a Growing Economy." Discussion paper 556. Harvard University Institute of Economic Research (June). (To be published in *Quarterly Journal of Economics*.)

———, and Inman, R., eds. 1977. *The Economics of Public Services*. London: Macmillan.

———, and Slemrod, J. 1978. "Inflation and the Excess Taxation of Corporate Stock Capital Gains." *National Tax Journal* (June).

———, Slemrod, J., and Yitzhaki, S. 1978. "The Effects of Taxation on the Selling of Corporate Stock and the Realization of Capital Gains." Working paper 250. National Bureau of Economic Research (July).

———, and Yitzhaki, S. 1978. "The Effects of the Capital Gains Tax on the Selling and Switching of Common Stock." *Journal of Public Economics* 9 (February).

Ferguson, J. M. 1964. *Public Debt and Future Generations*. Chapel Hill, NC: University of North Carolina Press.

Grabowski, Henry G., and Mueller, Dennis C. 1975. "Life-Cycle Effects on Corporate Returns on Retentions." *Review of Economics and Statistics* 57 (November).

Green, Jerry, and Shesinski, E. 1978. "Approximating the Efficiency Gain of Tax Reform." Discussion paper 516. Harvard University Institute of Economic Research. (To be published in *Journal of Public Economics*.)

Green, Jerry, and Shesinski, E. 1977. "Budget Displacement Effects of Inflationary Finance." *American Economic Review* 67.

Hall, Robert. 1968. "Consumption Taxes versus Income Taxes: Implications for Economic Growth." In *Proceedings of the National Tax Association, 1968*. Columbus, OH: National Tax Association.

Hall, R. E. 1975. "Effects of the Experimental Negative Income Tax on Labor Supply." In *Work Incentives and Income Guarantees*, ed. J. A. Pechman and P. M. Timpane. Studies in Social Experimentation. Washington, DC: The Brookings Institution.

———. 1973. "Wages, Income and Hours of Work in the U.S. Labor Force." In *Income Maintenance and Labor Supply: Econometric Studies*, ed. Glen G. Cain and Harold W. Watts. Chicago: Rand McNally.

HEW. *See* U.S. Department of Health, Education and Welfare.

HMSO. 1977. *National Income and Expenditure 1965–1975*. London: Her Majesty's Stationery Office.

Institute for Fiscal Studies. 1978. *The Structure and Reform of Direct Taxation: Report of the Committee Chaired by Professor J. E. Meade*. London: George Allen and Unwin.

Kaldor, N. 1955. *An Expenditure Tax*. London: Allen and Unwin.

Keeley, M. C.; Robins, P. K.; Spiegelman, R. G.; and West, R. W. 1978. "The Labor Supply Effects and Costs of Alternative Negative Income Tax Programs: Evidence from the Seattle and Denver Income Maintenance Experiments." Research memo 38. Center for the Study of Welfare Policy (May). Menlo Park, CA: SRI International.

Kitagawa, E. M., and Hauser, P. M. 1973. *Differential Mortality in the United States: A Study in Socioeconomic Epidemiology*. Cambridge, MA: Harvard University Press.

Klein, B. 1975. "Our New Monetary Standard: The Measurement and Effects of Price Uncertainty: 1800–1973." *Economic Inquiry* 13 (December).

Kochin, Levis. 1974. "Are Future Taxes Anticipated by Consumers?" *Journal of Money, Credit and Banking* 6 (August).

Kormendi, R. C. 1978. "Are Government Bonds Net Wealth? An Empirical Investigation." Working paper. University of Chicago, Graduate School of Business (February).

Kotlikoff, Laurence J. 1977. "Essays on Capital Formation and Social Security, Bequest Formation, and Long-Run Tax Incidence." Doctoral dissertation, Harvard University.

Krauss, M., and Johnson, H. G. 1970. "Border Taxes, Border Tax Adjustments, Comparative Advantage, and the Balance of Payments." *Canadian Journal of Economics* (November).

Kurz, Mordecai, and Spiegelman, R. G. 1972. "The Design of the Seattle and Denver Income Maintenance Experiments." Research memo 18. Center for the Study of Welfare Policy (May). Menlo Park, CA: SRI International.

Layfield Committee. 1976. *Local Government Finance: Report of the Layfield Committee of Enquiry*. Cmd. 6453. London: Her Majesty's Stationery Office.

Lewellyn, W. 1968. *Executive Compensation in Large Industrial Corporations*. New York: Columbia University Press.

Lillard, L., and Willis, R. 1978. "Dynamic Aspects of Earnings Mobility." *Econometrica*.

McIntyre, M., and Oldman, O. 1977. "Treatment of the Family." In *Comprehensive Income Taxation*, ed. Joseph Pechman. Washington, DC: The Brookings Institution.

Meade Report. *See* Institute for Fiscal Studies.

Mieszkowski, Peter. 1977. "The Cash Flow Version of an Expenditure Tax." Office of Tax Analysis discussion paper 26 (August). Washington, DC: U.S. Treasury Department.

Miller, Merton, and Upton, Charles. 1974. *Macroeconomics: A Neoclassical Introduction*. Homewood, IL: Irwin.

Minarik, J. 1977. "The Yield of a Comprehensive Income Tax." In *Comprehensive Income Taxation*, ed. Joseph Pechman. Washington, DC: The Brookings Institution.

Modigliani, F. 1961. "Long-Run Implications of Alternative Fiscal Policies and the Burden of the National Debt." *Economic Journal* 71 (December).

———. 1971. "Monetary Policy and Consumption: Linkages via Interest Rates and Wealth Effects in the EMP Model." In *Consumer Spending and Monetary Policy: The Linkages*. Conference Series No. 5 (June). Boston: Federal Reserve Bank of Boston.

Munnell, Alicia H. 1974. *The Effect of Social Security on Personal Saving*. Cambridge, MA: Ballinger Publishing Company.

————. 1977. *The Future of Social Security*. Washington, DC: The Brookings Institution.

Musgrave, R. A. 1969. *Fiscal Systems*. New Haven, CT: Yale University Press.

————. 1959. *The Theory of Public Finance*. New York: McGraw-Hill.

————, and Musgrave, Peggy. 1973. *Public Finance in Theory and Practice*. New York: McGraw-Hill.

Myrdal, Gunnar. 1960. *Beyond the Welfare State*. New Haven and London: Yale University Press.

Newmark Committee. 1963. "Report of the Fiscal and Financial Committee." In *The EEC Reports on Tax Harmonization*. Amsterdam: International Bureau of Fiscal Documentation.

Office of Tax Analysis. 1978. *Effective Income Tax Rates Paid by United States Corporations in 1972*. Washington, DC: Office of Tax Analysis, Department of the Treasury.

Okner, B. 1978. "U.S. Taxes and Their Effect on the Distribution of Family Income in 1966 and 1970." In *The Economics of Taxation*, ed. H. Aaron and Michael Boskin. Washington, DC: The Brookings Institution.

Parsons, Donald O., and Munro, Douglas R. 1977. "Intergenerational Transfers in Social Security." In *The Crisis in Social Security*, ed. Michael J. Boskin. San Francisco: Institute for Contemporary Studies.

Pechman, Joseph A., ed. 1977. *Comprehensive Income Taxation*. Washington, DC: The Brookings Institution.

————. 1971. *Federal Tax Policy*. A Brookings Publication. New York: Norton.

————, Aaron, Henry J., and Taussig, Michael K. 1968. *Social Security, Perspectives for Reform*. Washington, DC: The Brookings Institution.

————, and Timpane, P. M., eds. 1975. *Work Incentives and Income Guarantees*. Washington, DC: The Brookings Institution.

Pellechio, Anthony. 1978. "Social Security and Retirement Behavior." Doctoral dissertation, Harvard University.

Ricardo, David. 1951. *The Works and Correspondence of David Ricardo*, ed. P. Sraffa. 4 vols. Cambridge: Cambridge University Press.

Robertson, A. Halworth. 1978. "Financial Status of Social Security Program after the Social Security Amendments of 1977." *Social Security Bulletin* 14 (March).

Robichek, Alexander A., and Myers, Stewart C. 1965. *Optimal Financing Decisions*. Englewood Cliffs, NJ:Prentice Hall.

Robins, P. K., and West, R. W. 1978. "Participation in the Seattle and Denver Income Maintenance Experiments and Its Effect on Labor Supply." Research memo 53. Center for the Study of Welfare Policy (March). Menlo Park, CA: SRI International.

Sandford, C. T., Willis, J. R. M., and Ironside, D. J. 1975. *An Annual Wealth Tax*. London: Heineman Educational Books.

Schiller, B. 1977. "Relative Earnings Mobility in the U.S." *American Economic Review* 68.

Shibata, H. 1967. "The Theory of Economic Unions: A Comparative Analysis of Customs Unions, Free Trade Areas, and Tax Unions." In *Fiscal Harmonization in Common Markets,* ed. C. S. Shoup. Vol. 1: *Theory.* New York: Columbia University Press.

Shoup, C. S., ed. 1967. *Fiscal Harmonization in Common Markets.* New York: Columbia University Press.

———. 1969. *Public Finance.* London: Weidenfeld and Nicholson.

Shoven, John B., and Bulow, Jeremy I. 1976. "Inflation Accounting and Nonfinancial Corporate Profits: Financial Assets and Liabilities." *Brookings Papers on Economic Activity* 1.

Shoven, John B., and Bulow, Jeremy I. 1975. "Inflation Accounting and Nonfinancial Corporate Profits: Physical Assets." *Brookings Papers on Economic Activity* 3.

Stern, P. 1974. *The Rape of the Taxpayer.* New York: Vintage Books.

Suits, D. B., and Sparks, G. R. 1965. "Consumption Regressions with Quarterly Data." In *The Brookings Quarterly Econometric Model of the U.S.,* ed. J. S. Duesenberry et al. Chicago: Rand McNally.

Sullivan, C. K. 1965. *The Tax on Value Added.* New York: Columbia University Press.

Tanner, J. E. 1970. "Empirical Evidence on the Short-Run Real Balance Effect in Canada." *Journal of Money, Credit and Banking* 2 (November).

Taubman, Paul. 1973. "The Investment Tax Credit Once More." *Boston College Industrial and Commercial Law Review* 14 (May).

———. 1978. "Real Estate Depreciation: The President's Proposals Don't Go Far Enough." *Tax Notes* 6.

———, and Shoven, John. 1978. "Saving, Capital Income and Taxation." In *The Economics of Taxation,* ed. H. Aaron and Michael Boskin. Washington, DC: The Brookings Institution.

———, and Wales, T. 1973. "Higher Education, Mental Ability and Screening." *Journal of Political Economy* 81.

Taussig, M. 1967. "Economic Aspects of the Personal Income Tax Treatment of Charitable Contributions." *National Tax Journal* 20.

Tax Bureau (Japan). 1977. *An Outline of Japanese Taxes.* Tokyo: Government of Japan.

Terborgh, G. 1953. *Realistic Depreciation Policy.* Chicago: Machinery and Allied Products Institute.

Tobin, J. 1965. "The Burden of the Public Debt." *Journal of Finance* 20 (December).

U.S. Bureau of the Census. 1949. "Consumer Income." In *Current Population Reports.* Series P-60, No. 5. Washington, DC: Government Printing Office.

———. 1977*a*. "Consumer Income." In *Current Population Reports.* Series P-60, No. 107. Washington, DC: Government Printing Office.

———. 1973. "1970, Employment Status and Work Experience." In *Census of Population,* PC (2) GA. Washington, DC: Government Printing Office.

———. 1978. "Population Estimates and Projections." In *Current Popu-lation Reports*. Series P-25, No. 721 (April). Washington, DC: Government Printing Office.

———. 1977*b*. *Statistical Abstract of the U.S. 1977*. 98th ed. Washington, DC: Government Printing Office.

U.S. Department of Health, Education and Welfare. 1975*a*. "Selected Vital and Health Statistics in Poverty and Nonpoverty Areas." HEW Series 21, No. 26 (November). Washington, DC: Government Print-ing Office.

———. 1975*b*. *Social Security Bulletin: Annual Statistical Supplement 1975*. Washington, DC: Government Printing Office.

U.S. Department of Labor. 1978. *Current Wage Developments*. Vol. 30, No. 4 (April). Washington, DC: Bureau of Labor Statistics.

U.S. Treasury Department. 1977. *Blueprints for Basic Tax Reform*. Washington, DC: Government Printing Office.

Vickery, W. 1939. "Averaging Income for Tax Purposes." *Journal of Political Economy* 47.

Watts, H. W., and Rees, A. 1975. "An Overview of Labor Supply Re-sults." In *Work Incentives and Income Guarantees,* ed. J. A. Pechman and P. M. Timpane. Studies in Social Experimentation. Washington, DC: The Brookings Institution.

Wetzler, J. 1977. "Capital Gains and Losses." In *Comprehensive Income Taxation,* ed. Joseph Pechman. Washington, DC: The Brookings In-stitution.

ABOUT THE AUTHORS

ROBERT J. BARRO is John Munro Professor of Economics at the University of Rochester, and Associate Editor of *Econometrica*. Coauthor with Hirshel Grossman of *Money, Employment, and Inflation* (1976), he has been widely published in economic and public affairs journals. He is Research Associate at the National Bureau of Economic Research.

MICHAEL J. BOSKIN, Professor of Economics at Stanford University and Research Associate at the National Bureau of Economic Research, is a consultant to the U.S. Treasury and the Department of Health, Education and Welfare. An authority on taxation and public finance, he edited the Institute for Contemporary Studies' 1977 publication, *The Crisis in Social Security* (reprinted in 1978). He has written extensively on taxation, social security, econometrics, and labor economics.

GEORGE F. BREAK, Professor of Economics at the University of California–Berkeley, was chairman of the Department of Economics from 1969 to 1973. He is author of *Federal Lending and Economic Stability* (1965) and *Intergovernmental Fiscal Relations in the United States* (1967), both published by the Brookings Institution, and is coauthor with Joseph A. Pechman of *Federal Tax Reform: The Impossible Dream?* (1975). He has also written extensively on taxation and economic matters for government publications and various journals of economics and public finance.

JERRY R. GREEN is Professor of Economics at Harvard University. He is editor of *Economics Letters*, Associate Editor of the *Quarterly Journal of Economics* and *Econometrica*, and is Research Associate at the National Bureau of Economic Research. His international experience includes visiting professorships in Belgium, Israel, and Great Britain, and he has been widely published in economics journals overseas and in the United States.

LAURENCE J. KOTLIKOFF is a post-doctoral fellow in the Department of Economics at UCLA, and a member of the faculty forum of the Shell Oil Corporation. His articles have been pub-

259

lished in the *Journal of Economic History,* the *American Economic Review,* and the *Quarterly Journal of Economics.*

MORDECAI KURZ, Professor of Economics at Stanford University, is Director of the Institute for Mathematical Studies in the Social Sciences, Economics Section. Consultant to Stanford Research Institute and to the World Bank, he is special economic advisor to the Government of Canada and Associate Editor of the *Journal of Economic Theory.* He is coauthor with K. J. Arrow of *Public Investment, the Rate of Return, and Optimal Fiscal Policy* (1970), and has written many journal articles on economic theory, econometrics, and on labor supply and social policy.

PETER MIESZKOWSKI is Professor of Economics, University of Houston, and an authority on public finance, urban economics, and income distribution problems. He has written widely on tax matters, racial discrimination, and land-use regulation.

JOHN B. SHOVEN, Associate Professor of Economics at Stanford University, is experienced in microeconomics and public finance. He is Research Associate at the National Bureau of Economic Research, and has written articles on inflation, taxation, and government policies which were published in economic journals and in magazines designed for the general audience. He is coauthor with Jeremy Bulow of *The Functional Distribution of Real Income* to be published by the Brookings Institution.

PAUL J. TAUBMAN, Professor of Economics at the University of Pennsylvania, is the author of *Sources of Inequality of Earnings* (1975), and coauthor with G. Fromm of *Public Economic Theory and Policy* (1973). He has been widely published in journals of political economy, finance, and social issues.

JOHN WHALLEY is Professor of Economics, University of Western Ontario. He is coauthor with John Adams of *The International Taxation of Multinational Enterprises in Developed Countries* (1977) and, with John Piggott, of the forthcoming *Economic Effects of Tax-Subsidy Policy in the UK: A Large-Scale Computational Approach,* to be published by Macmillan. He has also written extensively on market distortions and international economics, articles published in economic journals and reviews.

INDEX

SELECTED PUBLICATIONS FROM
THE INSTITUTE FOR CONTEMPORARY STUDIES
260 California Street, San Francisco, California 94111
Catalog available upon request

THE CALIFORNIA COASTAL PLAN: A CRITIQUE
> $5.95. 199 pages. Publication date: March 1976.
> ISBN 0–917616–04–9
> Library of Congress No. 76–7715

Contributors: Eugene Bardach, Daniel K. Benjamin, Thomas E. Borcherding, Ross D. Eckert, H. Edward Frech, M. Bruce Johnson, Ronald N. Lafferty, Walter J. Mead, Daniel Orr, Donald M. Pach, Michael R. Peevey.

THE CRISIS IN SOCIAL SECURITY: PROBLEMS AND PROSPECTS
> $5.95. 214 pages. Publication date: April 1977; 2d ed., rev., 1978.
> ISBN 0–917616–16–2, 0–917616–25–1
> Library of Congress No. 77–72542

Contributors: Michael J. Boskin, George F. Break, Rita Ricardo Campbell, Edward Cowan, Martin Feldstein, Milton Friedman, Douglas R. Munro, Donald O. Parsons, Carl V. Patton, Joseph A. Pechman, Sherwin Rosen, W. Kip Viscusi, Richard J. Zeckhauser.

DEFENDING AMERICA: TOWARD A NEW ROLE IN THE POST-DETENTE WORLD
> $13.95 (hardbound only). 255 pages. Publication date: April 1977 by Basic Books (New York).
> ISBN 0–465–01585–9
> Library of Congress No. 76–43479

Contributors: Robert Conquest, Theodore Draper, Gregory Grossman, Walter Z. Laqueur, Edward N. Luttwak, Charles Burton Marshall, Paul H. Nitze, Norman Polmar, Eugene V. Rostow, Leonard Schapiro, James R. Schlesinger, Paul Seabury, W. Scott Thompson, Albert Wohlstetter.

EMERGING COALITIONS IN AMERICAN POLITICS
> $6.95. 530 pages. Publication date: June 1978.
> ISBN 0–917616–22–7
> Library of Congress No. 78–53414

Contributors: Jack Bass, David S. Broder, Jerome M. Clubb, Edward H. Crane III, Walter De Vries, Andrew M. Greeley, Tom Hayden, S. I. Hayakawa, Milton Himmelfarb, Richard Jensen, Paul Kleppner, Everett Carll Ladd, Jr., Seymour Martin Lipset, Robert A. Nisbet, Michael Novak, Gary R. Orren, Nelson W. Polsby, Joseph L. Rauh, Jr., Stanley Rothman, William A. Rusher, William Schneider, Jesse M. Unruh, Ben J. Wattenberg.

FEDERAL TAX REFORM: MYTHS AND REALITIES
$5.95. 270 pages. Publication date: September 1978.
ISBN 0–917616–32–4
Library of Congress No. 78–61661
Contributors: Robert J. Barro, Michael J. Boskin, George F. Break, Jerry R. Green, Laurence J. Kotlikoff, Mordecai Kurz, Peter Mieszkowski, John B. Shoven, Paul J. Taubman, John Whalley.

GOVERNMENT CREDIT ALLOCATION: WHERE DO WE GO FROM HERE?
$4.95. 208 pages. Publication date: November 1975.
ISBN O–917616–02–2
Library of Congress No. 75–32951
Contributors: George Benston, Karl Brunner, Dwight Jaffe, Omotunde Johnson, Edward J. Kane, Thomas Mayer, Allen H. Meltzer.

NEW DIRECTIONS IN PUBLIC HEALTH CARE: AN EVALUATION OF PROPOSALS FOR NATIONAL HEALTH INSURANCE
$5.95. 277 pages. Publication date: May 1976.
ISBN 0–917616–06–5
Library of Congress No. 76–9522
Contributors: Martin S. Feldstein, Thomas D. Hall, Leon R. Kass, Keith B. Leffler, Cotton M. Lindsay, Mark V. Pauly, Charles E. Phelps, Thomas C. Schelling, Arthur Seldon.

NO LAND IS AN ISLAND: INDIVIDUAL RIGHTS AND GOVERN-MENT CONTROL OF LAND USE
$5.95. 221 pages. Publication date: November 1975.
ISBN 0–917616–03–0
Library of Congress No. 75–38415
Contributors: Benjamin F. Bobo, B. Bruce-Briggs, Connie Cheney, A. Lawrence Chickering, Robert B. Ekelund, Jr., W. Philip Gramm, Donald G. Hagman, Robert B. Hawkins, Jr., M. Bruce Johnson, Jan Krasnowiecki, John McClaughry, Donald M. Pach, Bernard H. Siegan, Ann Louise Strong, Morris K. Udall.

NO TIME TO CONFUSE: A CRITIQUE OF THE FORD FOUNDA-
TION'S ENERGY POLICY PROJECT *A TIME TO CHOOSE AMERICA'S
ENERGY FUTURE*
> $4.95. 156 pages. Publication date: February 1975.
> ISBN 0–917616–01–4
> Library of Congress No. 75–10230

Contributors: Morris A. Adelman, Armen A. Alchian, James C. DeHaven,
George W. Hilton, M. Bruce Johnson, Herman Kahn, Walter J. Mead,
Arnold B. Moore, Thomas Gale Moore, William H. Riker.

ONCE IS ENOUGH: THE TAXATION OF CORPORATE EQUITY
INCOME
> $2.00. 32 pages. Publication date: May 1977.
> ISBN 0–917616–23–5
> Library of Congress No. 77–670132

Author: Charles E. McLure, Jr.

OPTIONS FOR U.S. ENERGY POLICY
> $5.95. 317 pages. Publication date: September 1977.
> ISBN 0–917616–20–0
> Library of Congress No. 77–89094

Contributors: Albert Carnesale, Stanley M. Greenfield, Fred S. Hoffman,
Edward J. Mitchell, William R. Moffat, Richard Nehring, Robert
S. Pindyck, Norman C. Rasmussen, Davis J. Rose, Henry S. Rowen,
James L. Sweeney, Arthur W. Wright.

PARENTS, TEACHERS, AND CHILDREN: PROSPECTS FOR CHOICE
IN AMERICAN EDUCATION
> $5.95. 336 pages. Publication date: June 1977.
> ISBN 0–917616–18–9
> Library of Congress No. 77–79164

Contributors: James S. Coleman, John E. Coons, William H. Cornog,
Denis P. Doyle, E. Babette Edwards, Nathan Glazer, Andrew
M. Greeley, R. Kent Greenawalt, Marvin Lazerson, William
C. McCready, Michael Novak, John P. O'Dwyer, Robert Singleton,
Thomas Sowell, Stephen D. Sugarman, Richard E. Wagner.

THE POLITICS OF PLANNING: A REVIEW AND CRITIQUE OF
CENTRALIZED ECONOMIC PLANNING
> $5.95. 352 pages. Publication date: March 1976.
> ISBN 0–917616–05–7
> Library of Congress No. 76–7714

Contributors: B. Bruce-Briggs, James Buchanan, A. Lawrence Chickering, Ralph Harris, Robert B. Hawkins, Jr., George Hilton, Richard Mancke, Richard Muth, Vincent Ostrom, Svetozar Pejovich, Myron Sharpe, John Sheahan, Herbert Stein, Gordon Tullock, Ernest van den Haag, Paul H. Weaver, Murray L. Weidenbaum, Hans Willgerodt, Peter P. Witonski.

PUBLIC EMPLOYEE UNIONS: A STUDY OF THE CRISIS IN PUBLIC SECTOR LABOR RELATIONS
$5.95. 251 pages. Publication date: June 1976; 2d ed., rev., 1977.
ISBN 0–917616–08–1, 0–917616–24–3
Library of Congress No. 76–17444
Contributors: A. Lawrence Chickering, Jack D. Douglas, Raymond D. Horton, Theodore W. Kheel, David Lewin, Seymour Martin Lipset, Harvey C. Mansfield, Jr., George Meany, Robert A. Nisbet, Daniel Orr, A. H. Raskin, Wes Uhlman, Harry H. Wellington, Charles B. Wheeler, Jr., Ralph K. Winter, Jr., Jerry Wurf.

REGULATING BUSINESS: THE SEARCH FOR AN OPTIMUM
$5.95. 300 pages. Publication date: April 1978
ISBN 0–917616–27–8
Library of Congress No. 78–50678
Contributors: Chris Argyris, A. Lawrence Chickering, Penny Hollander Feldman, Richard H. Holton, Donald P. Jacobs, Alfred E. Kahn, Paul W. MacAvoy, Almarin Phillips, V. Kerry Smith, Paul H. Weaver, Richard J. Zeckhauser.

WATER BANKING: HOW TO STOP WASTING AGRICULTURAL WATER
$2.00. 56 pages. Publication date: January 1978.
ISBN 0–917616–26–X
Library of Congress No. 78–50766
Authors: Sotirios Angelides, Eugene Bardach.

INVENTORY 1983